EMERGENCE OF POLITICAL AWAKENING IN KASHMIR

REVIEWS OF THE ORIGINAL EDITION

It is a book that compels you to revisit Kashmir, with unsullied perspective. It unfolds the segment of history, which brings end to the rule of kingdoms in Kashmir and makes it a part of Indian nation-state.

ASHOK KAUL
Professor Emeritus,
Banaras Hindu University

This remarkable book is essential reading for all those seeking to understand the roots of political consciousness in Kashmir.

PROF. AMITABH MATTOO
Jawaharlal Nehru University

This is a pioneering work on the political history of Kashmir, and it seeks to relate the crystallization of mass politics in the State, in the 1930s, to the political and economic transformation during the preceding century which underpinned this event ... his analysis throws a novel light upon the grass-root politics of one of the most sensitive regions of the Indian polity.

PROF. RAVINDER KUMAR
Ex-Director,
Nehru Memorial Museum & Library, New Delhi

When *Emergence of Political Awakening in Kashmir* was first published in 1986 its significance was not grasped by the scholars in the area of Kashmir Studies.

It was the mass upsurge of 1931 – the central theme of this book which generated an immense energy and sedimented consciousness that continues to shape post-independent events and politics.

BHAGWAN JOSH
Ex-Professor, Jawaharlal Nehru University

Emergence of Political Awakening in Kashmir

A Study in Political cum Socio-Economic Background to 1931 Upsurge

UPINDER K. ZUTSHI

MANOHAR
2026

First published 1986
Reprinted 2026

ISBN 978-81-85054-12-4

Published by
Ajay Kumar Jain *for*
Manohar Publishers & Distributors
4753/23 Ansari Road, Daryaganj
New Delhi 110 002

Typeset by
Ajay Arts
New Delhi 110 002

Printed at
Replika Press Pvt. Ltd.

CONTENTS

PREFACE TO THE 2020 REPRINT

Recently, there has again been a spurt in the interest evinced in understanding the enigma that is Kashmir. It happened as a result of the abrogation of Articles 370 and 35A of the Indian Constitution that pertained to the State of Jammu & Kashmir. It has been on the boil since 1990 when the idea of secessionism was induced into the Valley on a mass scale and terrorism took roots there. This was accompanied by the near forced exodus and eviction of the social group of Kashmiri Hindus known generally as Kashmiri Pandits. We find this development to be completely parallel to what happened in the Valley in the year 1931. There was then an upsurge by Muslims against the autocratic ruler who happened to be a Dogra Hindu Rajput from Jammu. The upsurge was triggered by an agitation that was backed by a section of Muslim aristocrats and clerics and launched from the precincts of mosques by some modern educated young Muslim men led by Sheikh Mohammed Abdullah and the resultant death of several demonstrators outside the Central Jail at Srinagar in police firing on 13 July 1931. Consequently, their ire was directed against the Hindu inhabitants who are generally known as Kashmiri Pandits and a sprinkle of some domiciled Punjabi Hindu traders known locally as 'Kheteris'. The agitation was launched ostensibly to protest against alleged desecration of the Holy Quran by a Hindu police official at Jammu but was actually aimed at claiming a share in state services for Muslims. Use of religion was probably necessitated to mobilize masses in their support for there were not sizeable aspirants for Government jobs amongst Muslims at that time. This culture of using religion for what was essentially a secular purpose has come down to our times and was used in 1990 and thereafter by the secessionists to achieve 'Azadi' – freedom from the Indian State. This was accompanied by killing of several individuals considered to be potentially pro-India – workers of the local political outfit All Jammu & Kashmir National Conference and also some Pandits.

There is an interesting comparison between what happened in 1931 and 1990. Both Sheikh Abdullah in 1931 and Yasin Malik of Jammu & Kashmir Liberation Front (JKLF) in 1990 are stated to have been secular yet we find that the constituency they mobilized was that of only Muslims and used religion to do that. In both the situations there were thus natural and inevitable consequences – communal strife in 1931 and exodus of Kashmiri Pandits in 1990. Thus we have no hesitation in characterizing the 1931 agitation and 1990 secessionist movement to have been communal. What we mean by communal is the assumption that all the Muslims irrespective of doctrinal and sectarian, ethnic, strata and class division form one community of the same religious and secular interests which are antagonistic to that of Hindus. We do not deny that the movement started in 1931 and the forces it generated were later channelized into secular direction by Sheikh Abdullah. The effort was unfortunately to be wasted in 1955 when after his removal from power and arrest in 1953 his lieutenant and colleague Mirza Afzal Beg having him as patron started a new political outfit named Plebiscite Front with a green coloured flag. Symbols matter in politics. This either signalled his flip-flop into his earlier communal stance or was simply an act of political opportunism. This had inevitable consequences which Kashmiris are facing till today. Of course, Hindu right-wing forces in Jammu and rest of India also made a contribution towards that end.

What happened in 1931 laid the foundation of the subsequent developments in the State up to the abolition of Dogra autocracy in 1947-8 and beyond. The two families that of the Mirwaiz and Abdullahs who were in the forefront in 1931 still occupy the centre stage in the Valley along with a few new contenders and are expected to remain so for some time to come. This underscores the importance of our study *Emergence of Political Awakening in Kashmir* and its continued relevance for guiding and throwing some light on contemporary politics.

That the book has been found useful and relevant by current scholars writing about Kashmir is evident by the fact that it has been cited by Mridu Rai, the author of *Hindu Rulers, Muslim Subjects: Islam, Rights and the History of Kashmir*, about ten times in her work.

Moreover, pirated copies of my work, though out of print, are still being sold in the market. This shows that there is a demand for the book. That is the reason and justification for this reprint.

The work forms a logical whole. 1931 upsurge was the culmination of a process and not the beginning of modern political processes as believed by some. It forms the crucial political-cum-socioeconomic backdrop to what has been known as the 'Struggle for freedom in Kashmir' from 1931 to 1947 and also subsequent developments until the present times.

In between, after exactly ten years of the publication of this book in 1986, there came out a work with almost the same title *Political Awakening in Kashmir* by one Ravinderjit Kaur. Except for the fact that the author has not been chivalrous enough to admit and acknowledge the existence of my work, it is a welcome addition and has the value of giving a description of political events serially as these unfolded in the State in 1931. However, I find no reason to revise or change my narrative of the story as my treatment of the subject has been of a different nature and genre which the readers will surely find.

We are aware of Sheikh's supposed autobiography *Aatish-i-Chinar* compiled by Muhammad Yusuf Taing in Urdu and published in 1986. Sheikh's account of the genesis of his political resolve does not contradict our characterization of 1931 political agitation launched by him to have been communal. But we strongly believe that the mass character the agitation acquired had the potential of growing into a secular movement later because of the social origin of Sheikh and the inherent contradictions between the different strata that had been mobilized by him. It is no surprise that the All Jammu & Kashmir Muslim Conference established under his leadership in 1932 metamorphosed into All Jammu & Kashmir National Conference in 1939 which came closer to Indian National Congress and collaborated with it. It was inherent in the situation that the trajectory followed by Mohammed Ali Jinnah and him would be different.

I must thank Ajay Jain of Manohar Publishers & Distributors for having graciously offered to bring out this reprint. The original edition was published by his father Ramesh Jain in 1986.

Faridabad
20 June 2020

UPINDER K. ZUTSHI

PREFACE TO THE FIRST EDITION

The present work, as the title suggests, concerns itself with the surfacing of political awakening in the valley of Kashmir, a centrally located territory in what is known in history as the Native State of Jammu and Kashmir—which like other such States operated within the overall British colonial framework—and which is now a unit in the Indian Union. More specifically it attempts an analysis of the character of the 1931 mass upsurge there, its *raison d'etre*, and its consequences. By all accounts, the consequences were felt not only in Kashmir but in the whole of the State.

From 1931 onwards, the State territories experienced a continual spell of agitational politics. That year overt and massive disturbances against the ruler took place at Srinagar and other territories of the State. Following these disturbances, which engulfed a large number of persons from the Muslim religious group, memorials on behalf of the different social groups and 'communities' were presented to the ruler. In these, demands as to the specific needs and interests of these groups, and some that were of a general nature, were raised. A governmental commission—the Glancy Grievances Enquiry Commission—was appointed to go into these and make recommendations. Subsequently many concessions were granted. These included the decision to have only a minimum basic qualification prescribed for eligibility in filling vacancies in the State services, recognizing the proprietary right over land of land-holders in Kashmir and in some other territories where it had been similarly withheld, restitution of ancient mosques that were under the archaeological department of the government to Muslims and, freedom of the press and platform.

Concession of press and platform created room for organized political activity.

With the upsurge began the political career of many who subsequently played an ever increasing role in the politics of the State. The most conspicuous among these was a young State school teacher who was later to earn world-wide fame as Kashmir's leader—Sheikh Mohammed Abdullah.

It is generally to the activities of this one man that the occurrence of the upsurge is attributed, or, to put it in other words, it is supposed to be his charisma that created it. This came to be exercised, according to the two different viewpoints, (a) due to the conspiracy hatched by the British against the State ruler, or (b) a failure on the part of a batch of newly educated Muslim youth, including the Sheikh to enter State service in remunerative positions. And it appears that he himself seems to have shared the idea of complete identity between the cause and himself. For instance, he told this author that he had launched the movement to serve the people (*Khadmat-i-Khalaq*).

However, what these explanations fail to answer is the question of how a young, unknown, politically inexperienced person, with a background in physical sciences which should have left him little time for politicking, and hardly a year's stay at Srinagar after his sojoun at Aligarh, was in a position to establish linkages with the people at large and, what is more, mobilize them in his favour. Moreover, how did he and others associated with him go unscathed in a State which is supposed to have been coercive and repressive—that is until the agitation had gathered momentum? And what is not explained specifically is why and how the agitationists and not the State found support in those sections amongst Muslims who formed a part and parcel of the dominant classes. Presumably it is supposed by them, but wrongly so, that Muslims (who incidentally comprise nearly the entire population of Kashmir and are a predominant section in the State) as a religious group were a 'community' of interests and had always been disaffected and alienated from the ruling dynasty which was different both from the point of view of religion and region. The dynasty was from amongst the Dogra Hindu Rajputs from Jammu and the State had been formed in 1846. Moreover, such a supposition wrongly assesses the nature of the polity there during what is commonly known as the Dogra rule and also the nature of the relationship between the princes and their subjects.

As a matter of fact, no serious effort has yet been made to study systematically the nature of the polity in the State during Dogra rule and the socio-economic processes. Nor can I claim to have done so in this study. However, in order to understand and explain the issues regarding the 1931 upsurge these have been considered. The various aspects have been sifted and brought together here to help understand the causative factors of the upsurge and its aftermath; the upsurge, undoubtedly, both reflected a political awakening amongst wide sections of the populace even as it further contributed to its growth.

The hypothesis that the existence of a wide Western educated class with 'elite' aspirations might have led to the upsurge had to be abandoned for we found none amongst Muslims at that point in time. Similarly, the possibility that it was the result of a newly emerged 'middle class' did not prove to be feasible. We found that there was no single cause. It was the result of an interaction of different forces that were found in conjunction in 1931. The chief amongst them was British colonial imperialism: the State was a vital instrument in furthering their interests in this part of the subcontinent. It is within this framework that the whole cobweb of relationships, contradictions and conflicts developed and resulted in the dawn of political awakening in Kashmir. It is to the exposure of these relationships that the present study mainly addresses itself.

It is hoped that a new and correct understanding of developments prior to 1931, both in political and socio-economic spheres, will emerge and aid in understanding certain enigmatic puzzles of Kashmir politics in the past as well as at present. And above all, it should help dispel the erroneous theoretical position that anything of a mass character can either be the result of a conspiracy or the charisma of an individual which was unwarranted under those circumstances.

ACKNOWLEDGEMENTS

This work was initially produced as a doctoral dissertation at the Centre for Political Studies, Jawaharlal Nehru University. Except for editorial changes it remains by and large the same. By publishing it, it is hoped to reach a wider section of scholars and general readers.

Without the constructive and critical guidance of Prof Imtiaz Ahmad, this work would not have been possible. Also, it is largely due to his persuasion that I ventured into print. To him my unbounded gratitude.

I would also like to record my thanks to the men and institutions, too numerous to name individually, from whom initial material was garnered. However, my specific thanks to Prof Irfan Habib for providing me with invaluable evidence from the British Museum; Ali Mohammed Bhat for allowing me access to his personal file of *Aieena*, and all those whom I interviewed—some of whom find a mention in the bibliography but there are many more.

Had I not been awarded a fellowship at the Jawaharlal Nehru University initially, and helped later by relatives and friends my research programme would not have been possible. To each my sincere gratitude.

I am grateful to Mrs Jasjit Mansing for having undertaken the editorial task which she executed with friendliness and patience, and Ramesh Jain for his cooperation in the publication of the book.

Last but not least, I feel overwhelmed with emotion when I think of those around me whose expectations I was not able to fulfil in the years I was engaged in this work. I feel sad but have no regrets, for I could not have done otherwise.

Chandigarh 1986

U.K. Zutshi

ABBREVIATIONS

Administration Report of Jammu and Kashmir State—ARJKS
British Indian Government—Government
Evidence Recorded in Public by the Srinagar Riots Enquiry Committee, 1931—Evidence SREC.
External—Ext.
Foreign Department Proceedings—FDP
Internal—Int.
Jammu and Kashmir State—State
Jammu and Kashmir State Archives—JKA
National Archives of India—NAI
Nehru Memorial Museum and Library —NMML
Old English Records—OER
Political—Pol.
Political Records—PR
Punjab Government Records—PGR
Research Library—RL
Selections from the Vernacular Newspapers Published in the Punjab—SVNP
Treaty of Amritsar—Treaty
Tyndale Biscoe School Library—TBSL
Written Statements Part I Srinagar Riots Enquiry Committee, July 1931—Written Statements SREC

GLOSSARY

Ahata—Premises
Bhaggat—Minstrel
Chaupan—Shepherd
Darvesh—Mendicant
Dewan—Prime Minister
Dharm—Religion
Dustbardari—To forsake right
Faqir—Mendicant
Gaddi—Throne
Galwan—Horse-keeper
Hakim-i-Alla—Governor
Hanji—Boatman
Hanz—Boatman
Ijarah—Farm (Contract)
Jado Jahdi Azadee—Freedom struggle
Jagir—Revenue assignment
Kamina Kaam—Menial work
Karkhanadar—Manufacturer
Khalsa—Crown land
Miras—Inheritance
Moharir—Clerk
Muqqadam—Village Headman
Nazim—Governor
Nangar—Artisan
Patta—Land permit
Patwari—Village Accountant
Pir Parast—Saint-worshipper
Pohl—Shepherd

Putto—Woollen cloth
Rasum—Customary perquisites
Rawaj—Custom
Rishi—Saint
Sahukar—Moneylender
Sanad—A kind of certificate
Shawl-baf—Shawl-weaver
Tauhin—Desecration
Zamindar—Land-holder
Zar Khareed—Gold-boughten slave
Zila—Territorial unit

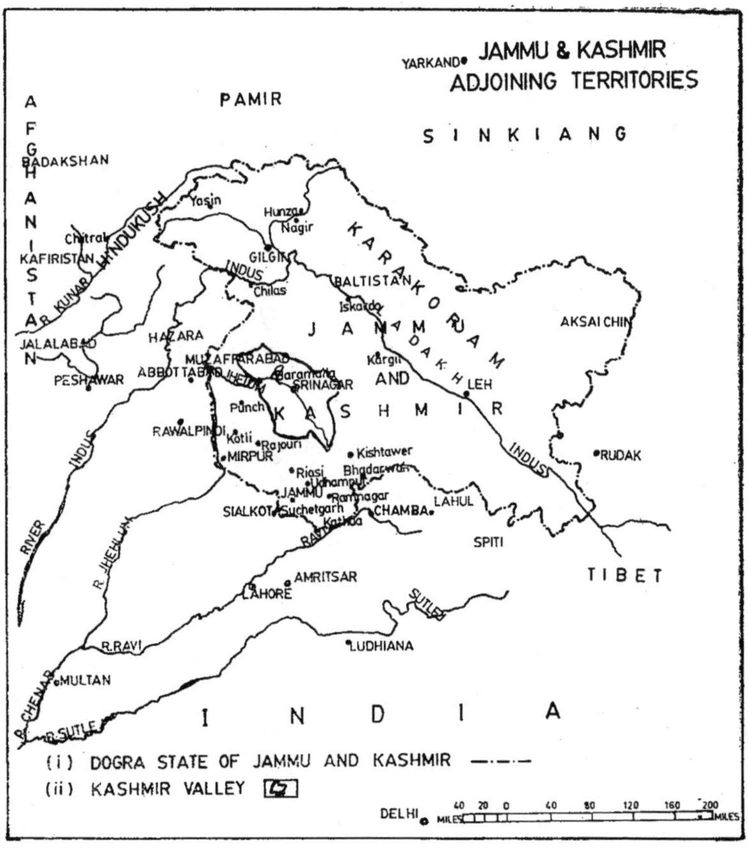

JAMMU & KASHMIR
ADJOINING TERRITORIES
YARKAND
PAMIR
SINKIANG
AFGHANISTAN
BADAKSHAN
Yasin
Hunza
Nagir
Chitral
KAFIRISTAN
HINDUKUSH
R. KUNAR
GILGIT
INDUS
Chilas
BALTISTAN
KARAKORAM
Iskardo
JAMMU AND KASHMIR
LADAKH
AKSAI CHIN
JALALABAD
HAZARA
MUZAFFARABAD
Kargil
PESHAWAR
ABBOTTABAD
JHELUM
Baramulla
SRINAGAR
LEH
Punch
RAWALPINDI
Kotli
Rajouri
MIRPUR
Kishtawer
RUDAK
Riasi
Bhadarwah
Udhampur
JAMMU
Ramnagar
LAHUL
SIALKOT
Suchetgarh
CHAMBA
Kathua
SPITI
RAVI
RIVER INDUS
R. JHEHLUM
AMRITSAR
LAHORE
TIBET
SUTLEJ
LUDHIANA
R. RAVI
MULTAN
R. CHENAB
R. SUTLEJ
INDIA
(i) DOGRA STATE OF JAMMU AND KASHMIR
(ii) KASHMIR VALLEY
DELHI
MILES 40 20 0 40 80 120 160 200 MILES

1

INTRODUCTION

One of the initial problems for any student of the political history of Kashmir—called Kasheer by its native inhabitants—is to identify when exactly political awakening occurred in the area. Unfortunately this is not an easy task and historians of Kashmir have not concerned themselves with this problem. They have made only off-hand and tangential remarks on this subject in their writings though a good number of them have dealt with political awakening in Kashmir. The consensus seems to be that the rise of political awakening in Kashmir can be traced to the beginning of 1931 when a series of events culminated in the mammoth demonstration, held on 13 July outside the central jail precinct, in Srinagar. The demonstration resulted in several dead and wounded and triggered off a public reaction of unprecedented magnitude.[1] For example, Prithivi

1. For a first-hand account of these events, see Prem Nath Bazaz, *Inside Kashmir* (Srinagar, 1941), pp. 116ff.

Bazaz, a noted commentator on the contemporary history of Kashmir, was a witness to these events. He was an active participant in the public activities both before and after 1931 and, in fact, rose to be one of the leading political figures of modern Kashmir. The account cited above bears a clear imprint of the fact that his observations were made in the vein of a person who was engaged consciously in

Nath Kaul Bamzai,[2] a historian of acknowledged standing, Prem Nath Bazaz,[3] Muhammad Yusuf Saraf,[4] and Rasheed Taseer[5] in their writings about the struggle for freedom in Kashmir have all hinted at the critical significance of 1931 as the starting point of a major political upheaval and awakening in Kashmir.[6]

However, none of the historians have provided any indication of the reason or reasons why they regard 1931 as an important landmark in the study of political awakening in Kashmir. This can only be inferred from the general tenor and logic of their arguments. Bamzai seems to suggest that the importance of the year 1931 lies in the fact that: 'It was on that day [13 July] that open demonstrations against the despotic rule of the Maharaja [the autocratic political authority of the Jammu and Kashmir State] took place.'[7] Admitting that demonstrations had been staged even earlier by the shawl-weavers and also by the peasantry, Bamzai clarifies his reasoning thus: 'But never before had the entire Muslim population [that formed, as is the case now, the bulk of the population] risen as one man against the authorities.'[8] What is sought to be emphasized in this statement is the fact that the participants in the demonstration that took place on 13 July 1931 did not belong

not only the writing but also the making of history. What concerned him most at the time of writing this account, and this needs to be kept in view throughout while consulting it, was the twin goal of democratization and secularization of politics in Kashmir.

2. Prithivi Nath Kaul Bamzai, *A History of Kashmir, Political, Social, Cultural: From the Earliest Times to the Present Day* (New Delhi, 1973), revised edn., pp. 713ff.

3. Prem Nath Bazaz, *The History of Struggle for Freedom in Kashmir, Cultural and Political: From the Earliest Times to the Present Day* (New Delhi, 1954), pp. 151ff.

4. Muhammad Yusuf Saraf, *Kashmiri Fights for Freedom* (Lahore, 1977), Vol. 1, pp. 357ff.

5. Rasheed Taseer, *Tahrik Huriyat Kashmir: 1931 ta 1939* (Urdu) (Srinagar, 1968), Vol. 1, pp. 84ff.

6. Bamzai and Saraf are the only ones who have made definite use of the expression 'political awakening'.

7. Bamzai (1973), p. 715.

8. Ibid., pp. 715-16.

to any one particular class or strata and that the mass outburst following it was of an unprecedented magnitude.

Saraf draws attention to some of the events that had taken place in Kashmir since 1877[9] and then goes on to make the assertion that the wave of political awakening began in Kashmir in 1931.[10] Leaving aside the obvious contradiction, which may be dismissed as a mistake arising from lack of proper articulation, his work offers no insight as to the basis of his assertion. The general tenor of his argument suggests that his reasoning hinges on the fact that the wave of political awakening in early 1931, by which he implies probably the spread of an 'agitational mood', was directed at the sharing of power. He writes: 'The wave of political awakening which had thus begun to blow was construed as a danger by the State Hindus because of their obstinate unwillingness to share power with the majority [Muslims].'[11]

Sardar M. Ibrahim Khan uses the expression 'political consciousness' to convey what has been here referred to as political awakening. He asserts that political consciousness came to the people of Kashmir 'at the beginning of the present century',[12] but subsequently narrows down his statement and traces the start of 'political consciousness in the real sense' to the work of a number of young men educated at Aligarh who came together as members of a group they founded.[13] This would also seem to make political consciousness in Kashmir a post-1930 phenomenon since it was in 1930 that the young men returned from Aligarh.

Thus it is evident that 13 July 1931 has been accorded the position of a landmark in the works of history produced on the struggle for freedom in Kashmir.[14] To those analytical

9. Saraf (1977), pp. 333-39.

10. Ibid., p. 360.

11. Ibid.

12. Sardar M. Ibrahim Khan, *The Kashmir Saga* (Lahore, 1965), p. 16.

13. Ibid., p., 19.

14. This is noticed in yet another work on Native Indian States: See Barbara N. Ramusack, *The Princes of India in the Twilight of Empire: Dissolution of a Patron-Client System, 1914-1939* (Columbus, 1978), p. 171.

writers who view the struggle for freedom in the perspective of the process of democratization, it is of special significance for in their estimate it marks the starting point of that process.[15] Thus Bamzai writes: 'It is from that date that the people took upon themselves the task of securing for themselves the right of democratic self-rule.'[16]

The events of 13 July 1931 do not command historical importance only; they have contemporary interest too. Attention continues to be drawn to this date because of the political importance given to it: 13 July is observed every year as Martyrs' Day and is a state holiday. However, many questions remain unanswered. For example, can political awakening be said to have emerged in Kashmir in 1931, and what made such a development possible then? What caused it to be manifested from a sectional platform and be imbued with a communal ideology? Why was it marked by 'communal discord', a phenomenon that is often claimed to be contrary to the traditions of Kashmir?

It can be said categorically that the year 1931 did mark the emergence of mass political awakening. However, to then attribute this specifically to the demonstration of 13 July 1931, unique though this might have been, is not a tenable proposition. It remains to be seen whether the participants in this demonstration, or at least their leaders were in any way consciously motivated by the idea of re-shaping the power structure governing them.[17]

One fact is incontrovertible: the 13 July demonstration, unlike those said to have taken place earlier, was not a spontaneous

15. Bamzai (1973), p. 716; Bazaz (1954), p. 154.

Such apparently has also been the belief of all 'Representative Governments' that have ruled the Indian state of Jammu and Kashmir up to this time. The first such government, headed by Sheikh Mohammed Abdullah, observed 13 July as 'Martyrs Day' and declared it a government holiday. This was obviously done to commemorate the happenings on that day in the year 1931. Every subsequent government has continued the practice

16. Bamzai (1973). p. 716.

17. For an attempt to theorize on the theme of political awakening, see John Plamenatz, 'Public Opinion and Political Consciousness' in F.F. Ridley, ed., *Studies in Politics* (Oxford, 1975), pp. 220-29.

occurrence. It was not resorted to simply as a means to obtain redressal of either immediate or long-felt economic or other grievances. Rather this demonstration was a culmination of the mobilization carried out in Srinagar which had the overtones of political agitation.[18] The agitation continued until it was brought to an end by a formal agreement,[19] 'Temporary Truce' signed on 26 August 1931 between the Maharaja's government and the representatives of the agitating public – the 'Muslims'—who were 'elected' to present the grievances of the Muslims before the Maharaja.[20]

The objective of this agitation despite what its manifest contour may suggest,[21] was to wrest by mounting public pressure what the leaders of the agitation had earlier failed to secure by petition from the ruling authorities: a change in the Maharaja's policy of recruitment to the State administrative services so as to enable the 'Muslims' in whose name the plea was made, to have a due share in proportion to their population.[22]

Whether the demand for reservation in the services was intended solely to secure the narrow self-interest of the petitioners in obtaining suitable employment (a view that has acquired much currency), or whether it arose to secure a change in the

18. The first public meeting, that was called for by a beat of drum, was organized at Jama Masjid, Srinagar, on 8 June 1931. His Highness' Government, Jammu and Kashmir, *Written Statements Part I Srinagar Riots Enquiry Committee, July 1931* (Jammu, 1931), p. 1 (hereafter *Written Statements SREC*).

19. Bazaz (1941), p. 143.

20. The representatives were so chosen in a public meeting in the precinct of the Shah-i-Hamdan mosque on 21 June 1931 and were as follows: Mirwaiz Maulvi Mohammed Yusuf Shah, Mirwaiz Maulvi Ahmadullah Hamdani, Sad-ud-Din Shawl, Syed Hasan Shah Jalali, Shahab-ud-Din, Ghulam Ahmad Ashai, and Sheikh Mohammed Abdullah. Besides them three representatives of Jammu Muslims were also signatories to the agreement. They were Yakub Ali, Ghulam Abass, and Gauhar Rahman.

21. The agitation was launched apparently to protest against what was alleged to have been an act of the desecration of the Holy Quran—'*Tauhin Qoran*'—by a Hindu police official.

22. Cf. Bazaz (1954), pp. 148-49; Bamzai (1973), p. 711. See also the statement of Maulvi Mohammed Abdullah Vakil in *Written Statements, SREC*, Pt. I, op. cit.

existing power structure, or both, is not certain. Nonetheless, the fact remains that the demand, if met, would have meant a shift in the existing state power structure. Demands to this effect had also been raised earlier. They had been raised first by some young, modern, educated Pandits, who had agitated in the British Indian press demanding 'Kashmir for Kashmiris'.[23] In 1924, some leading Muslim aristocrats had petitioned the Viceroy for proportional reservation for Muslims in the state services.[24] The agitation launched in 1931 marked an advance in the sense that now mass support was sought to be demonstrated to back up such a demand. The Maharaja appeared to be unperturbed and conveyed this to the agitators through a proclamation issued to his 'Beloved-People' on 9 July.[25] The message was rejected by the leading agitators who intensified the agitation by delivering frenzied speeches.[26] They thus worked consciously to create a situation of confrontation between the people and the authorities. The result was the specific demonstration of 13 July and its aftermath.

The agitation was marked by the use of mass communication, ideological indoctrination, civil disobedience and the election of formal representatives. It virtually pronounced a death sentence on the absolute prerogative of autocratic political authority. The process of the alienation of the masses from the

23. See Bamzai (1973), p. 703; Bazaz (1954), p. 145; and Khan (1965), p. 16.

24. See Bamzai (1973), pp. 703-4; Bazaz (1954), pp. 137-38; Taseer (1968), p. 71; and Saraf (1977), pp. 335-36.

25. The proclamation, besides attending to the contour of the agitation and the consequent communal strife, stated:

'In regard to recruitment for the State services prior consideration is and shall always be given to the public interest and the obligation of maintaining the efficiency of the administration at the highest possible level can never be overlooked. There is also no desire to follow a blind rule of percentages for the various communities irrespective of considerations of qualification and merit. Subject to these conditions the policy governing recruitment will be such that no class or community should gain undue predominance in any branch of the public service and that adequate representation is secured to duly qualified Hereditary State Subjects.' G.S. Raghavan, *The Warning of Kashmir* (Allahabad, 1931), pp. 78-83.

26. See Taseer (1968), pp. 98-101.

existing political authority was set afoot. This was expressed in their own idiom as evident in the following slogan which gained currency:

اسہ لگژھ آسن شاہ سلطان
بے گنوناہ مارہ گیہ آسہ مسلمان
اکۍ لدکھ قلس - اکۍ جیلخان
اسہ لگژھ آسن پنن سلطان

(We want Shah-i-Sultan.
We, the innocent Musilms, are doomed.
Some are locked in the fort, some are behind bars.
We want our own Sultan.)

Why the mass political awakening occurred then, why it was imbued with communal ideology and why it was marked by communal discord, can only be known if those forces, and their development, which made the agitation and the events of 13 July possible are identified. Only a systematic and well documented inquiry into this subject can produce the answer. The present study is an attempt in this direction.

Popular opinion, insofar as it goes beyond recapitulating the agitation simply as a series of incidental happenings,[28] holds two alternate views. One is that the 1931 agitation was engineered by the British Indian Government (hereafter referred to

27. Quoted in Raghavan (1931), p. 98.

28. Many of the commoners, who lived during those days and were contacted, recapitulated the start of the events, or the

واقعہ

as they called these in their idiom, with the episode of the desecration of the Holy Quran.

as the Government) in an attempt to subdue the ruling prince, Maharaja Hari Singh. The reasons given for British motivation are two-fold. Firstly, that the Maharaja was a patriot among Native Indian Princes and had expressed himself freely at the Round Table Conference in London (1930-31). Secondly, that the British took exception to Hari Singh's haughty temperanent which he is supposed to have displayed in his dealings with them. Diametrically opposed to this is the view that projects the agitation as the handiwork of a spirited educated Muslim young man, Sheikh Mohammed Abdullah, who is believed to have made Muslims aware of their plight and aroused their ire against the Maharaja's rule. Thus, what is conveyed in substance in this: that the agitation had an instantaneous cause; and this is believed to have been either a machination of the British Indian Government or the result of the charisma and stance of one individual—Sheikh Mohammed Abdullah.

Similar views are also reflected in the historical works which cover the events of 1931. Bhagwan Singh, for whom these were a 'communal trouble of the worst type in the State', and H.L. Saxena, who has characterized these as a Muslim 'rebellion', both describe them as clearly a handiwork of the Political Department of the British Government of India.[29] They have worked out an identical theme though Saxena has attempted a more elaborate and schematic treatment of the subject. According to him, these events were the result of a conspiracy engineered by the British and were brought about by 'using' an ever 'UNLUCKY' and thus disgruntled Sheikh Mohammed Abdullah who

> was a very impressive speaker and had the great capacity to arouse religious frenzy and passions among Muslims by reciting passages from the Holy Qoran in a most sonorous voice, which enthralled his co-religionists to their very depths.[30]

29. Lt. Col. Bhagwan Singh, *Political Conspiracies of Kashmir* (Rohtak, 1973), p. 21; H.L. Saxena, *The Tragedy of Kashmir* (New Delhi, 1975), pp. 4, 10, 109 and 113.

30. Saxena (1975), pp. 104-8.

The Maharaja's patriotic fervour and bold speeches, at the First Round Table Conference convened at London to sort out the future constitutional arrangements for India, were unpalatable to the British Government. He 'demanded an equality of status for his Motherland [India] in the British Commonwealth of Nations' and supported the idea of evolving a 'Federation' for India which would be joined by the Native Indian States as well. This was the 'proverbial last straw on camel's back'.[31] The Maharaja had resisted their influence in his territories ever since his Coronation Ceremony in February 1926. The most outstanding source of discomfiture for the British was the Maharaja's persistent efforts to regain full control and authority over Gilgit—the strategic frontier outpost in India's north—where the Government had sought to establish its control since the creation of the State in 1846 and had finally established what was known as the Gilgit Agency in 1889. Thus, the Government, in order to teach the 'unruly' Maharaja 'a lesson', and also gain full possession of the strategic area of Gilgit, had already set in motion its age-old policy of 'divide and rule'. This was sought to be achieved by creating a mechanism and a process of setting Muslims against the Maharaja, in particular by fabricating Muslim demands with regard to State services.[32] Perhaps the stage had been unwittingly set by the Maharaja who was well-meaning and had instituted several beneficial reforms for the people at large. These included the Agriculturists' Relief Regulation and the launching of the Cooperative Movement which hit the moneylenders, or Sahukars, who were almost all Hindus—the Maharaja's co-religionists. One amongst them is said to have 'shrewdly remarked at the time that the new Maharaja was giving too many facilities to his Muslim subjects, and he would soon rue his actions'.[33]

Quite contrary to the above view is that which considers the chain of events of 1931 to have been essentially a spontaneous development. However, even this view admits, more often than not, some involvement of the British Indian Government. There

31. Ibid., pp. 109-13.
32. Ibid., pp. 2-4, 97-99.
33. Ibid., pp. 86-94.

are varying degrees of emphasis on this and different opinions on the ways in which this is conceived to have been operationalized. Nor are all those who hold the view that it was a spontaneous development unanimous as to what forces were mainly responsible for its occurrence. They do not even agree as to why it acquired a momentous shape which earned it the characterization of 'upsurge', 'elemental upsurge', and 'revolt' Prem Nath Bazaz, the most widely read author on the contemporary history of Kashmir, was the first to attribute the emergence of the agitation to a group of Muslim young men who, having completed their respective courses by 1930, found that they were unable to enter into State service directly in high and remunerative positions. Sheikh Mohammed Abdullah, who is stated to have played a prominent role in the agitation, was one of them. These young men are said to have acted as an organized group—the 'reading room party'.[34] This view has been maintained with little or no alteration by him in his later writings and is also held by others such as Prithivi Nath Kaul Bamzai, Rasheed Taseer and Muhammed Yusuf.[35]

The works of Bazaz and Bamzai merit particular attention because of the definite perspective which underlies their accounts. They have presented the outbreak of the agitation as a specific historical development brought about in the wake of the 'DAWN OF MODERNISM'. This dawn of modernism, including modern education, is seen by these authors to have been ushered in as a result of the initiative and intervention of the British Indian Government in pursuit of its own imperial interests.[36]

The accounts provided by Bazaz and Bamzai are more or less similar in substance. Bamzai is more explicit—his work

34. Bazaz (1941), pp. 97ff.

35. See Bazaz (1954), p. 147; Prem Nath Bazaz, *Democracy Through Intimidation and Terror: The Untold Story of Kashmir Politics* (New Delhi, 1978), p. 9; Bamzai (1973), p. 711; Taseer (1968), pp. 76-77; Saraf (1977), p. 355. This view has also been echoed by authors writing on 'Kashmir Problem'. See Josef Korbel, *Danger in Kashmir* (Princeton, 1954), pp. 16-17; Lord Birdwood, *Two Nations and Kashmir* (London, 1956), p. 34; Jyoti Bhusan Das Gupta, *Jammu and Kashmir* (The Hague, 1968), pp. 54-55.

36. Bazaz (1954) and Bamzai (1973).

having been undertaken at a later stage and he had the advantage of access to archival sources—and provides more facts particularly with respect to the new ideological influences in Kashmir. He says that the Muslim young men, during their stay in British India, had come in contact with Muslim leaders and propagators of Pan Islamism. Frustrated at their failure to enter State service on their terms they felt that 'unless they had the backing of the masses, they had no future in the land of their birth'. They carried on 'a whispering but ineffective campaign against what they termed a Hindu State'. In this, they are stated to have had the 'tacit support of the British Indian Government as well as the British minister [in the Maharaja's government]'.[37]

Bamzai also gives reasons for the support extended by the Government to these young men and their objectives. The Maharaja's attitude towards the British had 'convinced the British that Maharaja Hari Singh was not a prince to toe their line'.[38] In brief, the Government intended 'to further their interests in Gilgit and to bring the State under their effective control'.[39]

The Maharaja is stated to have had exhibited his 'haughty and independent nature when on his accession to the *gaddi* he had withdrawn many facilities and easements [*sic*] which the [British] Resident used to enjoy at Srinagar'. Speaking on behalf of the Princes at the Round Table Conference held at London, he said:

> As Indians and loyal to the land whence we derive our birth and infant nature, we stand as solidly as the rest of our countrymen for our land's enjoyment of a position of honour and equality in the British Commonwealth of Nations.[40]

37. Bamzai (1973), p. 711
38. Ibid., p. 712.
39. The Maharaja is stated to have secured respite 'for himself only when he gave up the demand of restoration of Gilgit to him, withdrew his administrative machinery from there, and handed over the Gilgit Wazarat to the Government on a "60-Year lease" in 1935'. Ibid., p. 713.
40. Ibid., p. 712.

The bone of contention between the British and Maharaja Hari Singh was really his frontier policy. After his accession to the throne in 1925, he pressed on the Government to abolish its Agency at Gilgit. The Government, for whom Gilgit had always been a tender spot, 'desired [now] a fuller and unhindered control of this frontier'. This was because of its strategic importance; both in terms of stopping the flow of communist ideas and their counter moves in Soviet Central Asian territories. It is stated that as early as 1919, the Government had directed the State government to keep a vigil over any Bolshevik literature which might find its way into its territories via the Central Asian Road. The Maharaja's persistence on the restoration of Gilgit caused the Government to write to him about an alternative arrangement. That proposal was withdrawn and shelved after the internal disorder broke out.[41]

Bamzai is vague in his description of the way and the time when the young men took recourse to mass agitation. However, a comparison of his account with the description given by Bazaz lends clarity to the facts provided by the former. In the beginning of 1931, a fierce and violent campaign was started by the Muslim press at Lahore and other cites of the Punjab against the Maharaja. Leaflets and journals containing stories of deliberate suppression of Muslims in the State were distributed in thousands among the people, instigating them to rise against the Maharaja. The State government was alleged by the authors of the propaganda literature to be entirly Hindu and determined to keep the Muslim majority in perpetual serfdom. The Anglo-Indian press joined the chorus of denunciation of the Maharaja and his government. This propaganda, however, did not result in any civil commotion in Kashmir because there was no such directive from the Mirwaiz, Ahmad Ullah, the chief preacher of Srinagar, whose staunch followers the people were. He died in 'early March' [*sic*] that year and was succeeded by Yusuf Shah. The new Mirwaiz was an enthusiastic young man and, having himself witnessed the freedom struggle of the masses while a student of the Theological College at Deoband, was in full sympathy with the aims and objectives of the Reading Room Party. Thereafter, Sheikh Mohammed Abdullah,

41. Ibid.

as an active member of this group, is stated to have launched the agitation and used the mosque as his pulpit.[42]

Regarding the content of the speeches, which may be regarded as containing the ideology propagated by the leaders of the agitation, Bamzai's description is again vague, perhaps deliberately so. He states that the Sheikh exposed the hardships and the depressed condition of the people.[43] However, it is clear from Bazaz, and more so from his earlier work,[44] that the mass agitation was launched using the emotive slogan of 'Islam in danger' subsequent to the occurrence of certain incidents at Jammu. Bazaz too brings to the fore the general condition of the masses and believes that a situation the like of which arose in 1931 could have arisen as early as 1925 had there been a few educated 'patriotic' young men to lead the masses:[45]

> Dressed in rags which could hardly hide his body and barefooted, a Muslim peasant presented the appearance rather of a starving beggar than of one who filled the coffers of the State. He worked laboriously in the fields during the six months of the summer to pay the State its revenues and taxes, the officials their *rasum* and the moneylender his interest. Most of them were landless labourers working as serfs of the absentee landlords. They hardly earned, as their share of the produce, enough for more than three months. For the rest they had to earn by other means. During the six months they were unemployed and had to go outside the boundaries of the State to work as labourers in big towns and cities of British India. Their lot, as such, was no good, and many of them died every year, unknown, unwept and unsung outside their homes.[46]

Bazaz does not describe or even indicate what specifically led to such a situation. It is Bamzai who gives some indication

42. Ibid., pp. 713-14.
43. Ibid., pp. 714-15.
44. Bazaz (1941), p. 121.
45. Bazaz (1954), p. 145.
46. Ibid., p. 144.

of what led to general distress among the masses towards 1931. He says:

> The increase in population and the consequent pressure on land made the lot of the peasant pitiable indeed. The onsetting of trade depression all over the world reduced the workmen and petty shopkeepers to low straits. The shawl embroiderers and the papier machie artists were thrown out of job. Distress and frustration were writ large on every face.[47]

The account provided by Rasheed Taseer,[43] insofar as it has a bearing on the subject under consideration, fails to add anything to those given by Bazaz and Bamzai. Though a later work, it lags far behind these. There is no clear prespective projected in it. Yet it requires attention because it is in Urdu and hence has the potential of creating more influence locally.

A curious picture is sought to be presented by Taseer. The occurence of the agitation is related to the activities of the Reading Room Party but not as being the result of a conscious effort. It is presented as a spontaneous outburst of Muslims against certain alleged indiscreet acts of Hindu officials. Otherwise, it presents Muslims as loyal to their Maharaja. The acts alluded to are said to have been the result of British diplomacy. Taseer says the British were at this stage eager to create a dangerous situation for the Maharaja who, they thought, was the first person from amongst 'the faithful subjects' to throw a challenge to Britain's government. Thus, propaganda was launched amongst Hindus that the Maharaja had no regard for the 'Hindu Dharm' and was dancing to the tune of the Muslims. This was designed to fulfil two objectives. First, that it was expected that this would lead to harsh treatment of the Muslims by the Hindus in their capacity as rulers. Second, in consequence the Muslims would rise against the Hindus and this would automatically place the Maharaja in a helpless situation so far as the British were concerned. The efforts of the British are said by the author to have been buttressed by communal

47. Bamzai (1973), pp. 706-7
48. Taseer (1968).

Hindus. In particular, efforts are said to have been made by one of the ministers in the Maharaja's government, Thakur Kartar Singh, to launch propaganda against the Muslims. The Rajput Sabha, through which he operated, labelled the demands of the Muslims as 'communal' and as such started opposing them. It was also alleged that the 'movement' had been started to dethrone the Maharaja and establish 'Muslim Raj'. These sentiments are stated to have been echoed by other 'sabhas' too, meaning probably other associations of Hindu membership. Thus, Taseer argues that the Maharaja's co-religionists were on the one hand recommending that he reject the demands of the Muslims and, on the other, were conspiring to create a favourable situation for the British to operate by raising the cry of 'Hindu raj in danger' and creating communal tension.[49]

Taseer's attempt to deny the agitation its proper character not only militates against well-established facts but is also not in accord with his own contentions. Unlike Bazaz and Bamzai, he does not state that the Reading Room group was established by its founders to seek fulfilment of their self-interest. Instead he projects them as men who had set for themselves social and political goals. Exposed to the political climate prevailing at Aligarh, they are stated to have returned home on 12 April 1930 with a 'semi-perfect political vision' about the future of their land. Historic importance is attached to the day of their arrival at Srinagar. The establishment of the Reading Room group is considered to have been a daring move. Its founders are stated to have undertaken alongside paper-reading (considered by the authorities to be an offence), activities with regard to secret political discussion, and efforts, both on an individual and collective plane, to rid the people of the State of economic backwardness. They are clearly said to have started deliberations to secure and safeguard the rights of the people of the State, in particular the Muslims.[50]

It may be a fact that Thakur Kartar Singh and other Hindus opposed the demands of the Muslims to the extent that these affected their interests. However, Taseer's contention that these

49. Ibid. pp: 76ff.
50. Ibid., pp. 76-78.

elements were conspiring with the British against the Maharaja seems to be untenable, for it is not quite certain what the Dogra Rajputs, including Thakur Kartar Singh, would have achieved by seeing the Maharaja's position weakened in any way. Of all the people in the State it is they who would have liked to see rule of the Maharaja flourish—who himself was a Dogra Hindu Rajput—as they themselves were the principal beneficiaries of his rule.

Muhammad Yusuf Saraf claims to have reflected in particular on the phenomenon of the political awakening in Kashmir,[51] but he also fails to bring into focus any definite picture. Nor does he help in improving our understanding of the main problem. His work, though he claims it to be an impartial account of the struggle for freedom in Kashmir,[52] is clearly an exercise in furthering the well-known theory of treating the Hindus and Muslims of the Indian subcontinent as naturally forming two nations. Nonetheless, there are two important things which need to be observed in his work for our purpose. One is the absence of any reference to the alleged role of the British in the events of 1931. The other is the account that he gives of the contents of the memorandum submitted by some of the leading Muslim aristocrats to the Viceroy in 1924.[53] He provides neither the memorandum nor sites his source. However, this document is now available in India.

Munshi Naseer-ud-Din,[54] in a work which has remained unnoticed, presents the agitation as a spontaneous development without any pretensions of viewing it in an historical setting or perspective. The account, insofar as it has a bearing on the subject under consideration, suffers from the defect of sequential inaccuracies. However, it is significant for two reasons. One is

51. This is apparent from the fact that one of the chapters in his work (Saraf 1977) is entitled 'Political Awakening'.

52. Despite his confession that 'it is not wholly possible for a historian to remain detached', he tries his best to impress upon the reader that his view is not that of a 'partisan' and asserts, that 'TRUTH must, inevitably, prevail in the end'. Ibid., pp. xvii-xviii.

53. Ibid., pp. 335-38.

54. Munshi Naseer-ud-Din, *Tarikh Jangi Azadiye Kashmir* (Urdu) (Srinagar, 1971).

that it does not subscribe to the view that the Reading Room Party was formed primarily by those who had been exposed to the new political climate during their student careers in universities in British India. Second, it reflects on the socio-economic conditions of the people in 1931.

Naseer-ud-Din regards the agitation to have been an extension of the movement he started to put up a strong front against the injustices found then in Kashmir.[55] Although he does not give any clear date, its beginning can be placed somewhere in early 1930. He is emphatic in saying that it was started before Sheikh Mohammed Abdullah became associated with it and assumed the role of a leader. His express claim is that the movement was 'God's creation'.[56] He attempts to trace the genesis of his individual resolve and subsequent actions to an idealistic origin, and to establish that the determinants and the objectives of the movement as visualized by him were a result simply of his spontaneous perception of the oppressions. However, the facts provided do not justify otherwise this claim. There exist glaring inconsistencies in it. Furthermore, he fails in his attempt to idealize the origin of the movement and to recognize the influences which acted on him and shaped his perceptions.

Naseer-ud-Din's account makes it apparent that he himself and the movement were inspired by a definite outlook, which had as its underlying assumption the view that all Muslims formed a 'community' whose interests were identical in all respects. The whole 'community' is supposed to have undergone similar experiences and faced oppressions alike. Yet, the evidence given by him does not suggest this. He is either not conscious of the fact that his outlook was the result of an external influence or refuses deliberately to acknowledge it. He does not make any mention of such an influence while recounting the genesis of his resolve. Yet, it is clear from his later account that he consciously subscribed to a doctrinal identity—he was an Ahmadiya.[57] This also explains why he, of all the people, found his first 'like-minded friend' in his cousin Bashir Ahmad, whose

55. Ibid., pp. 68ff.
56. Ibid., pp. 5-6.
57. Ibid., p. 150.

father, Maulvi Mohammed Abdullah Vakil, happened to be the preacher of the newly formed Ahmadiya sect at Srinagar.

Naseer-ud-Din claims that he and Bashir Ahmad established the Reading Room.[58] He, however, thinks it was an utter failure. He admits that it was visited by well educated persons but asserts that they turned it into a centre for playing chess and other games. While it became clear that there was no positive and encouraging response from the educated people, it was decided to approach the people directly.[59] The need was felt for such a person who could act as a 'leader' and arouse the ignorant and illiterate masses. Thus, the mantle fell on Sheikh Mohammed Abdullah whom he and his associates groomed, he claims, to take up such a role.[60]

Naseer-ud-Din does not say anything directly about the alleged role of the British in the events of 1931. However, he admits that the British agencies lent their support to those involved in the fight for freedom both before the start of the movement and for its duration.[61] To explain the sudden flaring up of the movement he suggests that diverse elements were brought together because they had lived in the same milieu and hence shared similar experiences.[62]

It shall be demonstrated in this study, in contradistinction to what has generally been unhelped, how little the educated young men including Sheikh Mohammed Abdullah had to do with the occurrence of the agitation of 1931 or its success. The Sheikh did play a limited role but nothing similar to what has been hitherto projected. It will be shown that forces long active appeared in conjunction in 1931. The major force in this interplay was undoubtedly British imperialism which, for reasons of its own, was responsible for making 'Jammu and Kashmir State' in 1846. This development and the implications arising from it form the central concern of this work.

58. Ibid., pp. 71-72.
59. Ibid., pp. 77-78, 82.
60. Ibid., pp. 82-84.
61. Ibid., p. 46.
62. Ibid., p. 13.

2

THE MAKING OF JAMMU AND KASHMIR STATE

Jammu and Kashmir State[1] (hereafter referred to as the State) came into existence in 1846, after the first Anglo-Sikh war of 1845-46, with Maharaja Gulab Singh as its first ruler. Until then, there was no such distinct political entity. The territories of the State had constituted a part of the Sikh Kingdom and been ruled by different dynasties at different times.

The State was not a personal creation of Gulab Singh but was rather the outcome of an agreement between him and the representatives of the British East India Company. The prospect for such an eventuality was first envisaged in the treaty that laid down the terms for the conclusion of the first Anglo-Sikh war.[2] Within a week of this, a treaty was signed between Gulab

1. It is often wrongly referred to as Kashmir. This seems to be a legacy of the British Raj in India. The British referred to it so and spelt it first as 'Cashmere' and then occasionally as 'Kashmere'. Later, however, 'Kashmir' became the standard form.

2. Article 12 of the treaty, which reads as under, envisaged so! 'In consideration of the services rendered by Rajah Golab Sing, of Jummoo, to the Lahore State, towards procuring the restoration of the relations of amity between the Lahore and British Governments the Maharajah hereby agrees to recognise the Independent Sovereignty of

Singh, who until the conclusion of the war was a feudatory of the Sikhs,[3] and the representatives of the Company. The treaty (commonly referred to as the Treaty of Amritsar[4] and hereafter referred to as the Treaty) was enunciated on 16 March 1846.[5] But before this, on 15 March, Gulab Singh had been bestowed with the title of Maharaja,[6] the emblem of sovereignty. The Treaty stipulated the creation of a new state by transferring the territories between the rivers Ravi and Indus, 'for ever, in independent possession,' to Gulab Singh and his natural male descendents.[7] In consideration thereof, Gulab Singh agreed to pay the British Government seventy-five lakhs of rupees (Nanakshahi).[8]

The Treaty was neither a 'Sale Deed'—a label that has been generally attached to it[9]—nor an act of generosity on the part

Rajah Golab Sing, in such territories and districts in the hills as may be made over to the said Rajah Golab Sing, by separate Agreement between himself and the British Government, with the dependencies thereof, which may have been in the Rajah's possession since the time of the late Maharajah Khurruck Sing, and the British Government, in consideration of the good conduct of Rajah Golab Sing, also agrees to recognise his independence in such territories, and to admit him to the privileges of a separate Treaty with the British Government.'

For the full text of the treaty, see C.U. Aitchison, ed., *A Collection of Treaties, Engagements and Sanads: Relating to India and Neighbouring Countries* (Nendeln, 1973), Kraus rep., Vol. 1, pp. 50-54.

3. Towards the end of the war, Gulab Singh was made the wazir and in that capacity played the crucial, and decisive, role of the chief spokesman of the Sikhs in the negotiation of the terms of peace with the British. However, he was removed from that position soon and the conclusive part of the settlement and the drafting of the treaty was carried out without his participation. For the most comprehensive and well-documented biographical sketch of Gulab Singh, see Bawa Satinder Singh, *The Jammu Fox: A Biography of Maharaja Gulab Singh of Kashmir, 1792-1857* (London, 1974).

4. This is so because the treaty was enunciated at Amritsar.

5. For the text, see Aitchison (1973), Vol. 12, pp. 21-22.

6. Joseph Davey Cunningham, *A History of the Sikhs: From the Origin of the Nation to the Battles of the Sutlej*, H.L.O. Garrett, ed. (Delhi, 1966), rep., pp. 288-89.

7. Article 1.

8. Article 3.

9. It was labelled so during what is historically known as the 'Quit

of the British Government in India to favour Gulab Singh. In fact, many British people felt that Kashmir had been lost to them

Kashmir Movement', and also formed the substance of the popular slogan raised then.

بعنامہ امرتسر توڑ دو کشمیر چھوڑ دو

(scrap the sale deed of Amritsar, leave Kashmir). The movement was launched in 1946 by the All Jammu & Kashmir National Conference and formed an almost conclusive stage in its struggle for the establishment of representative government in the territories of the State. Cf. Rasheed Taseer, *Tahriq Huriyat Kashmir* (Urdu) (Srinagar, 1968), Vol. 1. p. 50.

There was nothing new in the assumption underlying the characterization of the Treaty as a Sale Deed. The view that the arrangement made by the Company in 1846 with regard to the territories of the State entailed a sale was an old one, and was probably pronounced first by those who were nostalgic about Kashmir. The most piognant statement of such a view and a candid expression as to the reasons for making an exclamation with regard to the supposed deal is found in the words of W. Wakefield, who visited Kashmir in 1875, and like many others before and after him, wrote an account thereof. 'We wantonly threw away', he wrote, the chance of 'doing what seems impossible in India otherwise—colonizing a portion of our Eastern possessions'. He continues: 'But it was not to be. The huckstering spirit that so often pervades our national policy, and which caused the great Napoleon to apply to us the term of a nation of shopkeepers, was dominant in this case; for, relinquishing all the advantages that accrued to us from its possession, this supreme government sold this fair province to the Rajah Gulab Singh, for the paltry and insignificant sum of seventy-five lacs of rupees, £750,000 in our money.' W. Wakefield, *The Happy Valley* (London, 1879), p. 85. See also Colonel Fred. Markham, *Shooting in the Himalyas* (London, 1854), p. 335; and Dugsal, *Letters from India and Kashmir, Written 1870* (London, 1874), pp. 162-63.

The view that the Treaty entailed sale was subsequently pronounced by others also. Iqbal, the poet, who lamented the establishment of the rule of a Dogra dynasty over Kashmir, bemoaned:

دہقان و کشت و جوے و خیاباں فروختند
قومے فروختند و چہ ارزاں فروختند

(Their fields, their crops, their streams,

after providence had placed it in their charge.[10] Rather, the arrangement with Gulab Singh was the outcome of the exigency of the situation arising out of the protracted but still indecisive war of the British with the Sikhs. Gulab's importance lay in the position and power that he enjoyed as the leading feudatory of the Sikh sovereign.

Gulab Singh received, by the Treaty, legal title over the territories but not their possession—that the Company itself did not have.[11] Only the part that he had held earlier as a feudatory of the Sikh sovereign was under his actual control. The rest had to be consolidated by Gulab Singh himself. In the process, exchange of certain territories was made with the mediation of

Even the peasants in the vale,
They sold, they sold all, alas!
How cheap was the sale!)

See G.M.D. Sufi, *Kashir: Being a History of Kashmir, from the Earliest Times to Our Own* (New Delhi, 1974), Vol. 2, p. 768; Taseer (1968), p. 50; and Bawa Satinder Singh (1974), p. 103.

The third Dogra ruler, Maharaja Partap Singh, also used this as a plea, some time after the introduction of land settlement in Kashmir, for the proprietary right over all the lands there having been reserved for the 'ruling chief'.

10. See, for example, what one of the many British visitors who thronged into Kashmir during summer had to say: '. . .the action of the English in parting with Kashmir has been a good deal criticised both at the time and since, for it was asked: what had the Raja of Jummu [Gulab Singh] done for us that his territory should be thus largely increased?' Margaret Cotter Morison, *A Lonely Summer in Kashmir* (London, 1904), p. 59.

11. The territories transferred to Gulab Singh by the British Government did not constitute a part of its occupied territories; these formed a part of the territories which had been ceded to it, only a week back, in lieu of a part—rupees one crore—of the indemnity that the Lahore Court had expressed its inability to pay. Their possession was still in the hands of the agents of the Sikh sovereign. (See and cf. Article 1 of the Treaty and Article 4 of the treaty between the Lahore Court and the British Government referred to in f.n. 2.)

Of the territories secured thus, the British Government retained the trans-Beas region that lay contiguous with its newly acquired possessions of Jullunder Doab and was considered to be militarily advantageous. The rest was transferred to Gulab Singh. *Foreign Department Proceedings* (hereafter *FDP*), Governor-General's Despatch to Secret Committee, 4 March 1846, no. 7, National Archives of India

the British Government.[12] That was not all. The British Government's aid and assistance was also sought to redeem Kashmir from the Sikh Nazim, Sheikh Imam-ud-Din, who was resisting its occupation by Gulab Singh's deputy. The Sheikh's resistance had made the adjoining 'Hill Chiefs' restive and led them too to intransigence against Gulab Singh. The British Government's intervention put an end to this and led to the Sheikh's exit from Srinagar on 23 October after he had been both admonished and offered certain inducements.[13] Gulab

(New Delhi) (hereafter NAI). Cf. Khushwant Singh, *A History of Sikhs* (Princeton, 1966), Vol. 2, pp. 56-57.

12. Chamba, situated on both sides of Ravi, was transferred by the Treaty to Gulab Singh. But its Chief, who had been tributary to the Sikh Durbar, objected to occupying that position under Gulab Singh. Besides he claimed Bhadrawah, which, he said, had been granted to him by Ranjit Singh. However, it was at that time held by Gulab Singh and also formed a part of the territories transferred to him by the Treaty. This difficulty was removed by an arrangement by which Gulab Singh retained Bhadrawah and acquired Lakhanpur, which formed a part of the territories acquired by the British Government by the treaty of Lahore and lay in the possession of Gulab Singh, and Chandgraon. The Raja of Chamba then transferred his allegiance to the British Government. Aitchison (1973), Vol. 12, p. 6.

Hazara was exchanged for the territories of Kathua, Suchetgarh and part of Manawar with the Lahore Durbar when it became apparent that Gulab Singh would not be able to control the tribes there. Ibid., pp. 4, 5.

In addition to the aforesaid exchange of territories, the transfer of the territories of Sujanpur, part of Pathankot and certain lands between the rivers Chaki and Beas to the British Government took place. This was for the charges on account of the maintenance of some Hill Chiefs who settled in British territory. Ibid., p. 5.

13. For a detailed, systematic and analytical account of this episode, see Virendra Kumar, *India Under Lord Hardinge* (New Delhi, 1978), pp. 295-300. Also see Bawa Satinder Singh (1974), pp. 126-29; Diwan Kirpa Ram, *Gulabnama*, Sukhdev Singh Charak, trans. (New Delhi, 1977), pp. 339-42; Hassan, *Tarikh Kashmir*, Maulvi Mohammed Ibrahim, trans. (Urdu) (Srinagar, 1957), pp. 553-55; Ghulam Nabi Shah, *Wajiz-ul-Tawarikh* (Persian Mss.) Research Library (Srinagar), fo. 60B; Jagmohan Mahajan, *Circumstances Leading to the Annexation of the Punjab, 1846-49: A Historical Revision* (Allahabad, 1949), pp. 46-58; N.M. Khilnani, *British Power in the Punjab 1839-1858* (Bombay, 1972), pp. 46-56; and F.M. Hassnain, *British Policy Towards Kashmir, 1846-1921: Kashmir in Anglo-Russian Politics* (New Delhi, 1974), pp. 20-21.

Singh entered Srinagar as the first Dogra Maharaja of the State on 9 November 1846.[14]

Contrary to general belief,[15] the State was not an independent one, for independence, unlike sovereignty, cannot be divided. The various articles in the Treaty are sufficiently indicative of the fact that certain limitations were put upon the State in its external affairs;[16] the last one in particular makes it evident that Gulab Singh accepted the 'supremacy of the British Government'.[17] Nor was it a feudatory, a status to which it was reduced later in 1860. Juridically, it was a sovereign state that had

The Sheikh's attempt at resistance has been highlighted by Hassnain as a 'rebellion' (p. 18) in which Kashmiris are shown to have participated (pp. 19-20). And Taseer has magnified it as an attempt by Kashmiris in the way of '*Jado Jahdi Azadee*'—freedom struggle. (Taseer, 1968, p. 48). But a comparative study of the above cited sources and a few others does not warrant it to have been either. It seems to have been nothing more than an attempt by the Sheikh to get concessions for the security of his wealth and property and in this he succeeded.

14. *FDP*, Secret Branch, 26 December 1846, nos. 1240-41 and K.W. Lawrence to Curie, 9 November 1846, NAI.

15. Researchers too have upheld that. See M.L. Kapur, *Kashmir Sold and Snatched* (Jammu, 1968), p. 19: S.C. Bajpai, *The Northern Frontier of India: Central and Western Sector* (Calcutta, 1970), p. 63; and Mohan Krishan Teng, in S.N. Gadru, ed., *Kashmir Papers* (Srinagar, (1973), p. 16. They have noted, and rightly so, the expression 'Independent possession' in the first article of the Treaty. We would suggest that note should be taken also of the expressions 'independent sovereignty' and 'independence' in the prelude to the Treaty. See f.n. 2. However, other articles in the Treaty, that clearly restricted the independence of the State, cannot be overlooked.

16. Article 4 forbade him to change the limit of the territories of the State 'without the concurrence of the British Government'. Article 5 made it obligatory on him to 'refer to the arbitration of the British Government any disputes or questions' that may arise between him and any neighbouring state. By Article 7 he was forbidden from employing any British or European or American subject 'without the consent of the British Government'.

17. In token of this Gulab Singh engaged himself to 'present annually to the British Government one horse, twelve perfect shawl goats of approved breed (six male and six female), and three pairs of Cashmere shawls'. Article 10.

accepted for itself a tributary status and certain restrictions in the exercise of its external sovereignty. Otherwise, it was left autonomous. This is what K.M. Panikkar rightly conveys when he uses the expression 'totally independent in its internal affairs'.[18]

Nevertheless, there was the fact of British Paramountcy which cannot be ignored. It had been in operation and on the increase since 1818. There were no set limits to the magnitude of its exercise over the various Native Indian States. By taking note of this phenomenon it becomes clear that right from its creation the State was brought under British Paramountcy,[19]

18. K.M. Panikkar, *The Founding of the Kashmir State: A Biography of Maharaja Gulab Singh, 1792-1858* (London, 1953), p. 126. It was first published under the title *Gulab Singh* in 1930.

19. That the British Government came to have paramountcy over the State right from its inception is maintained by Dilip Kumar Ghose also. He disputes, what he says was emphasised by K.M. Panikar, the 'independent status' of the Maharaja and argues that whatever meaning might be attributed to the phrase 'independent possession' in the first article of the Treaty Gulab Singh's independence was certainly qualified by the assertion of British supremacy in the last article. His arguments, in so far as these dispute the 'independent status' of the State, are alright but his assumption of Panikkar's emphasis is incorrect. Panikkar did not emphasise the independence of the State—not atleast in the work cited by Ghose. What he emphasised there was that the State was left by the Trealy 'totally independent in its internal affairs', see Panikkar (1953), p. 126. And this was in accordance with the intentions of Lord Hardinge, to which Ghose gives more credence as against the explicit terms of the Treaty. These, he asserts, were not meant to be interpreted literally by its authors—at least not Hardinge. Nevertheless, the terms which Hardinge intended to stipulate with Gulab Singh were to be '*so drawn as to bind us [the British Government] to the least possible interference in his affairs* consistently with the maintenance of our paramount position over the Raja and his country' (emphasis added). But Ghose ignores and holds back the first half of his stated intentions. Probably it was thought prudent to do so in order to support his thesis that the State was created 'in the interest of frontier defence' and as such the 'British Indian Government should have an adequate control over its affairs'. Even from the standpoint of such a thesis, with which we do not agree at all, one could ask the obvious question as to why no such provision was included in the Treaty, a fact which is recognized by Ghose himself but not questioned. See Dillip Kumar Ghose, *Kashmir in Transition*,

though the degree of its operation over the State was comparatively limited. Unlike in the other Indian States, and this is important, the Resident in the State was not appointed and no subsidiary force was to be maintained. This was not a case of negligence but perfectly in accordance with what the Governor-General of British India, Lord Hardinge, intended.[20] It was not because he wished to favour Gulab Singh. The hard realities of the situation constrained him to take this decision.

The British certainly expected the State, along with what remained of the Sikh Kingdom, to act as a bulwark against the Afghans and prevent them from making their power felt, or from extending their influence, this side of the Indus.[21] This was a role which Lord Hardinge felt had been played well by the Sikh Kingdom under Ranjit Singh. It had saved the British the necessity and anxiety of defending the traditional doorway to India used by all the earlier invaders who, unlike the British, had come by land.[22] This was obviously not so much because

1885-1893 (Calcutta, 1975), pp. 2-3. For text of Hardinge's letter, see *FDP.* Governor-General's Despatch to Secret Committee, 4 March 1846, no. 7, NAI.

20. Twelve days before the Treaty was signed, he wrote in a secret despatch to the Secretary of State, on 4 march 1846: 'The conditions which may be stipulated with Raja Golab Sing. . .will be so drawn as to bind us to the least possible interference in his affairs consistently with the maintenance of our paramount position over the Raja & his Country.' Ibid.

21. In his despatch of 19 March 1846 to the Secret Committee, Hardinge wrote: '. . .both [Sikhs and Dogra Rajputs] will have a common interest in resisting attempts on the part of any Mahomedan power to establish an independent State on this side [of] the Indus or even to occupy Peshawar.' *FDP*, Governor-General's Despatch to Secret Committee, 19 March 1846, no. 8, NAI.

22. In a private letter to Hobhouse dated 2 September 1846, Hardinge wrote: 'This entrance has always been the highroad taken by every invader. A Hindoo Government, acting as our advance-guard had for thirty years barred this entrance against all intruders—their very existence depends on it. A Hindoo Government under Runjeet Singh fulfilled all these conditions without any expense or anxiety to us.' Bikramjit Hasrat, ed., *The Punjab Papers: Selections from the Private Papers of Lord Auckland, Lord Ellenborough, Viscount Hardinge, and the Marquis of Dalhousie, 1830-1849 on the Sikhs* (hereafter *The Punjab Papers*) (Hoshiarpur, 1970), pp. 110-11.

of any real threat from the Afghans as it was to prevent any turbulence and revolt within their own possessions.[23] Shah Zaman's—the king of Kabul—repeated incursions and their impact on the remnants of erstwhile muslim powers had perhaps first led the British Government to this realization.[24]

But the purpose which led the British to create the State was essentially different.[25] The British bestowed the emblem of sovereignty on Gulab Singh primarily to weaken the Sikhs by driving a permanent wedge between them and the Dogra Rajputs of the 'hills'[26]—a policy that had been toyed with by the British decision-makers earlier.[27] This had now become an urgent necessity because the Sikh republican army, though

23. See Asghar H. Bilgrami, *Afghanistan aad British India, 1793-1907: A Study in Foreign Relations* (New Delhi, 1972), pp. 96-97.

24. Ibid., pp. 16-17.

25. Dilip Ghose's contention, and the way he has substantiated it, is liable to make one draw an inference to the contrary. His contention is that the State was 'created in the interest of frontier defence'. To support this he puts the cart before the horse in the corresponding footnote by changing the order of the contents as exist in the source from which he quotes. He states: 'The State was made over to Gulab Singh in the hope that he would resist any attempt by a "Muhammadan power to establish an independent State on this side of the Indus" and also act as a "counterpoise against the power of the Sikh Prince".' Ghose (1975), p. 2.

In fact it runs like this: '. . .a Rajpoot principality of the Hill Districts has been constructed, extending from the Ravee to the Indus and including the province of Cashmere. . . .'

As it was of the utmost importance to weaken the Sikh Nation before its Govt. should be re-established I considered the appropriation of this part of the ceded territory to be the most expedient measure I could devise for that purpose by which a Rajpoot Dynasty will act as a counterpoise against the power of a Sikh Prince, the son of the late Runjeet Singh, and both will have a common interest in resisting attempts on the part of any Mahomedan power to establish an independent State on this side [of] the Indus or even to occupy Peshawar.' *FDP*, Governor-General's Despatch to Secret Committee, 19 March 1846, no. 8, NAI.

26. Khushwant Singh (1966), pp. 56-57; and Sarjit Singh Bal, *British Policy Towards the Punjab* (Calcutta, 1971), p. 80.

27. Bikrama Jit Hasrat, *Anglo-Sikh Relations, 1799-1849: A Reappraisal of the Rise and Fall of the Sikhs* (Hoshiarpur, 1968), pp. 247-48.

defeated in the war, had proved itself too strong to be completely beaten, and the British found it difficult to annex Punjab immediately.[28]

Gulab Singh was the only man who could be both a suitable person and a willing ally in the implementation of this plan. First, many of the territories in the hills were already under his management. Second, as a dependent of the Sikhs he was expected to take part in the hostilities against the British, but he had kept himself aloof.[29] This was because of his antipathy towards his masters. And this Hardinge knew well.[30] Gulab

After Ranjit Singh's death in 1939, there started among the aspirants for power a keen struggle for supremacy. With this ensued a period of factional intrigues and political instability. This resulted in the army acquiring a republican character and becoming the real sovereign in the kingdom. In such a state of affairs, the British felt concerned to see the power of the Sikhs weakened. Militarily they were not prepared to deal with the situation. This was because of their recent involvement in Afghanistan where they had suffered a loss of men and material.

They naturally then looked to the organic weakness so reminiscent of the feudal states and which they had exploited to extend their colonial possessions in India. In the struggle for power the three Dogra brothers—Gulab Singh, Dhyan Singh, and Suchet Singh—and Hira Singh—Dhyan Singh's son—were also engaged. All the four had been bestowed with the title of Raja by Ranjit Singh and given fiefs which lay in the 'hills' in and around Jammu. The British waited in vain for these Dogra Rajputs to secede and thus 'break-up' the Sikh kingdom. They became hopeful when Dhyan Singh, Suchet Singh and Hira Singh became a prey to the political murders which became rampant at Lahore. It was expected that Gulab Singh, who now tried to lay his hands upon their possessions also, would soon establish a separate Dogra Rajput kingdom in the hills. He too wished so, and this was known to the British. But to their dismay he was not able to realize his goal.

28, Khushwant Singh (1966), p. 55.

29. Hasrat (1968), p. 276.

30. In a private letter to Ellenborough dated 7 June 1846 he writes: 'Early in 1845, Jawahir Singh [Sikh Wazir] persuaded the army to march against Jummoo. Golab Singh despairing of being able to defend himself, threw himself into the hands of the Panchayats and was brought prisoner to Lahore. He was there treated with great severity; and

Singh's ambition was to establish a separate kingdom over the territories he held, where he would be the sovereign. Long before the outbreak of the Anglo-Sikh war (1845-46), he had approached the British and sought their support to achieve this goal. In return he had promised them whole-hearted cooperation and support in crushing the Sikhs.[31]

The British had not responded then. But now their political and military interests demanded that Gulab Singh be appeased and that his wishes be fulfilled. This was necessary also to ensure that he would withhold support to the Sikhs in future. Besides, to be able to act as a 'counterpoise against the power of the Sikh prince', the role Lord Hardinge wanted the new State to play, Gulab Singh's power and prestige needed to be enhanced.[32] All this must have cautioned the British against imposing too many restrictions on his powers.

The reluctance on the part of the British Government to annex Kashmir to its dominions in early 1846 cannot be attributed either to its ignorance of the place or to disinterest. The Government had, in fact, shown a lot of interest in it earlier, as we shall see in some detail shortly. Furthermore, the decision not to annex it was not at all received well by British interests.[33] The Queen's Proclamation of 1858 guaranteeing the continued existence of the Native States in India made them almost cynical about Kashmir.[34] If, despite all this, the British still put

subsequently, when the army offered him the Vaziership he repeatedly declined the offer. When the invasion took place, he remained at Jummoo and took no part against us, but tendered his allegiance on condition of being confirmed in the possession of his own territories. . . .He had no cause of gratitude or attachment to the Lahore Darbar, by whose orders and intrigues his own family had been nearly exterminated, his possessions taken, and his son slain. During the whole campaign he had purposely kept himself aloof. . . .' *The Punjab Papers*, op. cit., p. 94.

31. Hasrat (1968), pp. 254-55.

32. 'They [Goverument] had their own interest, also, to attend to; which in policy required that the Sikh State should be weakened and that the Hills should be separated from the plains.' Hardinge to Ellenborough, 19 March 1846, *The Punjab Papers*, op. cit., p. 95.

33. Hasrat (1968), pp. 288-89.

34. Ghose (1975), p. 5. Also see G.J. Alder, *British India's Northern Frontier, 1865-95: A Study in Imperial Policy* (London, 1963), p. 101.

Kashmir under Dogra rule, the decision can only be attributed to the prevailing circumstances.

Punjab had not been annexed yet. Therefore, Lord Hardinge found it politically unwise and militarily impossible to hold Kashmir.[35] At the same time, he also found it necessary to snatch it from the Sikhs to weaken them.[36] There was no local ruling family with which any arrangement could be made. In fact, there had existed none after its annexation to the expanding Mughal Empire in 1586. Later, the Sikh Nazim, Sheikh Imam-ud-Din, aspired to be confirmed in the possession of Kashmir and sought British assurance and support. Even if, hypothetically speaking, the British Government broke its agreement with Gulab Singh it still could not consider such a proposition. It was the established policy of the British Government then not to have a Muslim political power on this side of the Indus.[37] Evidently, it was the immediate need of the British imperial interests in 1846 and not Gulab Singh's 'perfidy' towards his masters, as F.M. Hassnain believes,[38] which dictated that Kashmir be juxtaposed with its adjoining territories to form the new state.

The State was, right from its emergence, included within the pale of British Paramountcy—a relationship whose limits were undefined and depended solely on the configuration of relative forces at a given time. Further, the Government would expect that it, created as it was as an instrument to secure and safeguard British imperial interests as these stood in early 1846, should be capable of performing the role that was assigned to it in their scheme. Such an intent naturally demanded that certain

35. In a letter to a near relative, he wrote: 'The distance from Kashmir to the Sutlej is 300 miles of very difficult mountainous country, quite impracticable for six months. To keep a British force 300 miles from any possibility of suport would have been an undertaking that merited a strait-waistcoat and not a peerage.' Charles Viscount Hardinge, *Viscount Hardinge* (Oxford, 1891), p. 133.

36. Ibid.

37. See Currie to Broadfoot, 19 January 1845, Hardinge to Ellenborough, 18 August 1845, Hardinge to Lady Hardinge, 1 March 1846, Hardinge to Hobhouse, 2 September 1846, *The Punjab Papers*, op. cit., pp. 81, 90, 103 and 110.

38. Hassnain (1974), p. 17.

prerequisites be fulfilled by the ruling power of the State: (a) loyalty towards the British; (b) external strength; and (c) internal stability.

In the event of a weakness in any of these they were bound to exercise their paramount power based upon the reality of their military and political strength and not on any treaty or agreement. The means they would employ and to what extent would depend upon the exigency of the situation and the demands of the time.

As against this, the ruling power of the State—the 'Maharaja'—was bound, like any other ruling power, to jealously guard his possessions from any interference, and to try to preserve what little the Treaty guaranteed him. Any move that bore a suspicion of being aimed at reducing his power, or which resulted in reducing it, would be resented by him and, if possible, thwarted. At the same time, any development which could be used by the ruler to enhance his power would be welcomed by him, and, if the circumstances were favourable, would possibly be utilized.

Gulab Singh began well as a loyal subordinate ally of the British and declared himself, of course without being ironical, to be their 'Zar Khareed'[39]—'gold boughten slave'. From a low rank in Ranjit Singh's army, he had risen to the position of a fief-holder at Jammu and earned the title of Raja from the Sikh ruler. From thereon he had been instrumental in extending the Sikh Kingdom to include Ladakh after having subdued the principalities around Jammu. These along with the fiefs bestowed upon his brothers, Dhyan Singh and Suchet Singh, and nephew Hira Singh who had equally risen in the Sikh court and then had fallen prey to the political murders that ensued after Ranjit Singh's death, had accrued to his management.[40] The Sikh republican army had proved to be too strong to permit any secessionist tendency in him and had even become a threat to the continuation of these possessions under him.[41] The British

39. Cunningham, op. cit.. f.n. 1, p. 289.

40. Lala Sohan Lal Suri, *Umdat-ut-Tawarikh*, V.S. Suri, trans. (Chandigarh, 1972), Daftar 4, Pts. 1-3, p. 322.

41. Hasrat (1968), pp. 248-49; also see f.n. 30 above.

not only confirmed him in these possessions but added more, which included Kashmir and Gilgit; and, what is more significant, bestowed upon him the title of Maharaja—the sovereign status. He was also given help in establishing himself as a *de facto* sovereign of the State.

Externally, the State was to be strong enough to be able to thwart, in cooperation with the Sikhs, any attempt on behalf of the Afghans to extend their influence on this side of the Indus. On its north and across the Indus also were some Muslim principalities but these were too small to be a source of any immediate anxiety. These could pose a problem in the eventuality of a great power approaching their frontiers and using them for its own ends. However, there was no immediate threat of this and the State was viewed as a balancing force against the Sikhs.

Gulab Singh, therefore, was required to be strong enough to play the role thrust upon him.[42] But Hardinge never had a high opinion of his strength.[43] His doubts were subsequently confirmed when he found Gulab Singh unable to consolidate his territories.[44] That he was conscious of Gulab Singh's weakness and the necessity to add to his strength is clear from what he wrote to his wife on 2 March 1846:

> Unfortunately, it is necessary to improve his condition because he did not participate in war against us and his

42. Ghose (1975), p. 2.

43, In a private letter to Ellenborough dated 23 January 1845, he writes: '. . .if the [Sikh] troops can be prevailed upon to move in hostilities against Golab Singh, I see no probability of the latter being able to do more than defend himself in his hills. . . . He has not the popularity; he may bribe the Sikh Sardars, but the troops detest him, and the petty hill rajas whom he has despoiled equally detest him. I believe he has recently sent money and jewels on to our bank of the river.' *The Punjab Papers*, op. cit., p. 82. Cf. Hasrat (1968), p. 248. The events that followed shortly thereafter proved that his apprehensions were more than justified.

44. In a despatch to Hobhouse dated 21 January 1847, he writes: '. . . Golab Singh is neither militarily nor mentally so great as he was supposed to be. . . .He could be expelled by the Mussalman in one compaign. He has no real strength; he has been outwitted by a fool, and he is greatly ashamed of himself; . . . .' *The Punjab Papers*, op. cit., p. 117.

> territory touches ours. We can protect him without inconvenience and give him a slice of the Sikh territory which balances his strength in the same degree against theirs.[45]

It was surely to meet this purpose that Article 9 of the Treaty affirmed : 'The British Government will give its aid to Maharajah Gulab Singh in protecting his territories from external enemies.'

Stability was implied by consolidation and was an essential requirement both for the viability of the State and its ability to play the role designed for it. Stability could be ensured only if the ruling power was in a position to govern 'effectively' and sustain its position of strength. After the establishment of Dogra rule, the continuation and stability of the State were likely to depend upon the ruler's capacity to 'dominate' and to win the allegiance of the majority of his subjects. This in turn would depend upon his ability to cultivate a system of legitimization for himself. Needless to say, in order to ensure stability and legitimacy, the particular characteristics of the territories and the people would naturally be of crucial importance.

The territories which had been knitted together and placed under the State included the frontier regions of Ladakh, Iskardo (Baltistan) and Gilgit in the north, Kashmir in the middle, Muzafarrabad, Poonch, Rajouri, Kotli-Mirpur, Bhimber and Hazara in the west, the Dugardesh of Jammu and other principalities in the south, and the tracts lying contiguously with the newly acquired British possessions in the Punjab, what is now Himachal Pradesh, in the south-east. The people who inhabited these territories shared two things in common : the feudal state of their respective societies and the rule of the Dogra Maharaja. Otherwise, they were quite distinct from one another in their history, race, religion, and language.[46]

Since the ruler who was to govern them was a Dogra Rajput from Jammu, the ability of the Maharaja to ensure stability thus depended on how well he could integrate these diverse

45. Ibid., p. 104.

46. See Sir Federic Drew, *The Jammu and Kashmir Territories : A Geographical Account* (London, 1875).

elements and enforce obedience from them. This had obvious limitations due to the state of these societies. Apart from other things, the problem of reconciling this huge population to the certainty of what was going to be for them an unpalatable rule was bound to prove an everlasting burden on the ruler. His success would depend either on force or on legitimation of his authority through some mediating agency. This would imply his winning over the dominant social class in society to which the people looked for leadership.

3

PARAMOUNT POWER AND THE STATE

The British Indian Government met its immediate imperial interest by creating the State in early 1846. This did not rule out other interests the East India Company might have had, or might develop in future, on account of trade or other imperatives in the territories placed under it. It is reasonable to presume that the pursuit of such interests, as and when the overall needs of the Paramount Power permitted, would determine the policy and the consequent interaction of the Government with the State's ruling power—the Maharaja. Therefore, it is necessary to first enquire if the Company had any such interests in the State territories and see what these were before the development of this interaction and its outcome can be traced.

Before 1846

The activities of the Company which can be said to manifest its interest in these territories are ascribable to a much earlier period. As early as 1783,[1] George Forster, who was in the

1. George Forster, *A Journey from Bengal to England, through the Northern Part of India, Kashmire, Afghanistan, and Persia* (London, 1808), Vol. 2, p. 1.

'civil service' of the East India Company, had found his way into Kashmir. From the short but keen account[2] that he gave about trade, taxation, etc., in Kashmir, it appears that he was not a vain traveller but an 'explorer'. This is equally apparent in the case of William Moorcroft—a native of Lancashire and a superintendent of military stud belonging to the East India Company in Bengal—who along with George Trebeck travelled, rather sojourned, between the years 1820 and 1823 in the territories that were later put under the State.[3] His extended stay and hectic activities in Ladakh and later on in Kashmir, and the account given by him show the interest evinced by the East India Company in shawl wool trade and shawl manufacture in these places.[4] It will not be out of place here to mention that long before, in 1774, Warren Hastings had directed George Bogle, and sent him on an exploratory and political mission to Tibet,[5] to find out the commercial and political relations then existing between Tibet and Kashmir.[6]

By 1841 the British Government had already developed an established interest in the consumption of shawl wool. Therefore, when the flow of shawl wool to Rampur[7] stopped in that year as a result of the invasion of western Tibet by Zorawar Singh, the British Government felt the pinch. This was one of the reasons for the British request to the Sikh ruler at Lahore

2. See, for example, ibid., pp. 2, 22, 26, 27, 32 and 33.

3. Horace Hayman Wilson, ed., *Travels in the Himalayan Provinces of Hindustan and the Panjab, in Ladakh and Kashmir, in Peshawar, Kabul, Kunduz, and Bokhara by Mr. William Moorcroft and Mr. George Trebeck, from 1819 to 1825* (Reprint New Delhi, 1971), Vols. 1 & 2. Cf. S.C. Bajpai, *The Northern Frontier of India: Central and Western Sector* (Calcutta, 1970), pp. 49-50.

4. See Wilson, op. cit., Vol. 1, pp. 346-50, 451-52, 454 and Vol. 2, pp. 164-95.

5. Clements R. Markham, *Narratives of the Mission of George Bogle to Tibet and of the Journey of Thomas Manning to Lhasa* (London, 1876) p. v.

6. Ibid., p. 8. Cf. Prithivi Nath Kaul Bamzai, *A History of Kashmir, Political, Social, Cultural : From the Earliest Times to the Present Day* (New Delhi, 1973), revd. edn., pp. 646-47.

7. Situated on the bank of the river Sutlej, it was the capital of the British-protected state of Bushahr.

to withdraw Zorawar Singh from Tibet.[8] As it happened, Zorawar Singh was killed in a fight with his adversaries and his forces were routed. Next year another force was sent by Raja Gulab Singh, who was at that time the Sikh feudatory at Jammu and whose servant Zorawar Singh had been, to retrieve the position. His forces met with success and subsequently a treaty of peace was singed between the two parties. The treaty included a provision that was clearly aimed at preventing the disruption that had been caused for some years in the flow of shawl wool to other territories.[9] This provision in the treaty was clearly contrary to the British interest. To presume that they would be keen to do away with the thus resultant situation is only fair. As will be shown below, efforts were actually made by the British Government to do that after the creation of the State.

> Moorcroft drew pointed attention to Ladakh's
> ...centrical situation, by which it becomes the great thoroughfare for an active commercial intercourse between Tibet, Turkistan, China, and even Russia on the one hand, and Kashmir, the Panjab and the plains of Hindustan on the other.[10]

Thus from the perspective of any future trade with the Central Asian territories, and this was already receiving attention at their hands,[11] Ladakh was bound to assume an importance, as it subsequently did, for the British.

8. For a more elaborate account of Zorawar Singh's invasion of western Tibet and British Government's concern about it and its consequent reaction, see Bajpai (1970), pp. 40-45; Bawa Satinder Singh, *The Jammu Fox: A Biography of Maharaja Gulab Singh of Kashmir, 1792-1857* (London, 1974), pp. 32-36. Also see Alastair Lamb, *Britain and Chinese Central Asia: The Road to Lhasa, 1767 to 1905* (London, 1960), pp. 65-69.

9. 'That in conformity with ancient usage, tea, pushum and shawl wool shall be transmitted by the Ladak road.' Article 2 of the treaty as reproduced in Bajpai (1970), Appendix 3.

10. See Wilson, op. cit., Vol. 1, p. 346.

11. Devendra Kaushik, *Central Asia in Modern Times: A History from the Early 19th Century*, N. Khalfin, ed. (Moscow, 1970), pp. 34-37, 49-50.

G.T. Vigne, 'an agent of the East India Company,'[12] came to Kashmir in 1835 and also later in 1837. In his comprehensive account,[13] he confirmed the information given by Moorcroft 'as singularly correct'[14] and added much more to it. He gave a detailed description about Kashmir,[15] and of almost everything that could be needed by the Company at that time as well as some useful information about Gilgit and other surrounding principalities. He also made a forecast of the 'results of the planting of the British flag on the ramparts of the Huri Purbut'[16]—a fortified hill at Srinagar. According to him, the occupation of Kashmir would be 'looked upon as the accomplishment of the one thing needful for the consolidation of the British power in Northern India . . . .'[17] He saw the advantages of utilising Kashmir because of its geographical features both as a 'fortress and a magazine' in defending the British possessions from any invading power in India's northwest.[18]

Kashmir's utility as a prospective summer resort was also visualized. Its occupation was expected to effect the 'desertion of Simla as a Sanitorium'.[19]

Further it was anticipated that with the help of British 'skill and capital', and the natural conditions seen to be present there, Kashmir could become the 'focus of Asiatic civilization : a miniature England in the heart of Asia'.[20]

An elaborate account of the revenues of Kashmir and

12. Baron Charles Hugel, *Travels in Kashmir and the Punjab*, Major T.B. Jervis, ed. (Reprint Delhi, 1972), p. 98.

13. G.T. Vigne, *Travels in Kashmir, Ladak, Iskardo and the Countries Adjoining the Mountain Course of the Indus, and the Himalaya North of the Panjab* (London, 1842), Vols. 1 and 2.

14. Ibid., Vol. 1, p. 111.

15. Cf. 'After reading Vigne's account we can say with a fair amount of accuracy that what he did not mention about Kashmir was not worth knowing at his time by a European.' R.K. Parimu, *A History of Muslim Rule in Kashmir, 1320-1819* (Delhi, 1969), p. 25.

16. Vigne (1842), Vol. 2, p. 66.

17. Ibid.

18. Ibid., p. 67.

19. Ibid., p. 66.

20. Ibid., p. 68.

Jammu was prepared by the British Government as early as 1837.[21]

The activities of the British were not limited to exploration only. There is sufficient evidence available to suggest that they had already begun to cultivate influence in Kashmir; their confidants were the well-known family of Naqashbands.[22] The

21. *Foreign Department Proceedings*, Secret Branch, 18 November 1843, nos. 13-17, 18, 19, National Archives of India (New Delhi).

22. Baron Charles Hugel, who travelled in Kashmir during the years 1835-36, wrote: 'In the evening [of the first day of his arrival at Srinagar (18 November 1835)] I received a message of welcome by Samed Shah, the deputy of Mohammed Shah Nakshbandi, a person of great consequence in Kashmir, who is said to feed two hundred poor men daily. He requested premission to visit me. In return, I sent him the letter of introduction which Captain Wade had given me to him. Hugel, op. cit., p. 105.

'Every European who had travelled in Kashmir had largely shared in his [Mohammed Shah Nakshbandi] attentions, and they were particularly useful to Moorcroft during his long sojourn in the valley. He seems naturally to hope now, that the [British East India] Company may repay this hospitality to him in some way or other; and it is his present object to go from Lahor to Ludiana, where Captain Wade resides, and get some acknowledgement, from the official resident, of his services to English travellers.' Ibid., pp. 147-48. Captain Wade referred to is obviously none other than Captain C.M. Wade who happened to be then the British Political Agent at Ludhiana.

The observations made by Hugel are largely confirmed by the evidence available from the official records of the British: 'Khwajah Mohomed Shah Nakshbundee a great spiritual adviser and "Pir" among the population of Kashmere, and part of Turkestan was first brought prominently forward to our notice by Baron Hugel and Mr. Vignes, bringing him with them from Kashmere to Lahore, and to Loodiana. His family is the first for respectability in Kashmere and his attentions to every European traveller to the Valley, need no comment. I have myself among others experienced their value. Your predecessor in office always maintained a correspondence with Mahomed Shah, on whose visit to Lahore, he wrote in his favour to Maharaja Runjeet Singh, and orders were in consequence sent to the Governor of Kashmere, Colonel Main Singh, to treat him with attention, which the latter did during the life time of Runjeet Singh.' *FDP*, Secret Branch, 1 March 1841, no. 34, Political Agent Peshawar to Governor General's Agent Loodiana, 18 July 1840, NAI.

'The Nakshbundees of Cashmere are, I believe Government is already aware, a family of great respectability, residing in Cashmere, but

family had its origin from the ruling class of Tashkent,[23] and enjoyed an elite status—both in temporal[24] and spiritual spheres[25]—in Kashmir. It owed its rehabilitation there, after it had been uprooted and had established itself in Ladakh, to the

whose character is held in great esteem, far beyond the limits of that country. They have also been very obliging, and in some instances of real service, to European travellers in Cashmere . . . ." Ibid., Agent to Governor General for the affairs of Punjab and N.W. Frontier to Officiating Secretary to Government of India, 25 August 1840, NAI.

23. The family claimed descent from the royal house of Tashkent and its settlement in Kashmir was of a recent date. The first to settle there was Abd-ur-Rahim. He was the son of Mohammed Yusuf—the hereditary ruler of Tashkent, and came to Kashmir during Afghan rule (1756-1819). Wilson, op. cit, Vol. 1, pp. 241-42.

24. Abd-ur-Rahim's son 'Shah Nyas, . . . obtained from the Afghan governors of Kashmir very extensive and valuable grants of land, the revenues of which were chiefly appropriated by him to acts of charity and benevolence'. Ibid., p. 242.

For a time, on the conquest of Kashmir by Ranjit Singh, his jagirs were confiscated. But soon, at Moorcroft's 'intercession' he received a grant of 'a pension of five thousand six hundred rupees'. Ibid., Vol. 2, p. 98.

Shah Niaz's son, Mohammed Shah was 'a person of great consequence in Kashmir' in 1835, and was said to 'feed two hundred poor men daily'. Hugel, op. cit., p. 105. When he accompained Hugel to Lahore in early 1836, and was recommended there to Ranjit Singh, a *jagir* was assigned to him. The number of villages granted in the jagir was five. Ibid., pp. 353-54.

A near contemporary native historian mentions the grant of village Brain in *jagir* to Shah Niaz for the services rendered by him. Hassan, *Tarikh Kashmir* (Political Section), Maulvi Mohammed Ibrahim, trans. (Urdu) (Srinagar, 1957), p. 523.

According to the historian Mohammed-ud-Din Fauq, Shah Niaz received five villages, namely Brain, Kalaroach, Wailo, Safanagri, Babapora, in *Jagir* from Ranjit Singh on the recommendation of Moorcroft. Mohammed-ud-Din Fauq, *Mukamal Tarikh Kashmir* (Urdu) (Lahore, 1912), Vol. 3, p. 92. But, in view of the statements by Moorcroft, Hugel and Hassan, he seems to be wrong.

25. This was obviously because of their claim to be Syeds and on accounts of 'learning and piety'. Hugel, op. cit., p. 147; Wilson, op. cit., Vol. 1, p. 242.

goodwll of an agent of the British East India Company—Moorcroft.[26]

1846-1858

From the machinations prior to 1846 and the fact that the agreement with Gulab Singh was decried by various British interests, it seems difficult to conceive that the Government would forsake the State territories and its interests in them for ever and completely. It seems in fact to have implicitly reserved the right of disposal of the State territories accordingly to its liking in the event of Gulab Singh or his successors failing to have natural male descendents.[27] Even if such an opportunity did not come its way, the Government could still, should the *raison d'etre* of the State disappear due to a turn of favourable circumstances, invoke any of the justifications that it had used in the case of other states to tamper with the status of the State or work for its outright annexation. The capacity to act in such a manner lay in its military and political strength and could not be curbed by any treaty or engagement whatsoever.[28] A contingency like that may well have arisen in the case of Gulab Singh's early death as was expected at one point of time. For the British circles in India continued to be imbued with a considerable amount of passion to possess the valley of Kashmir; and the men who mattered were alive to the fact that this was not entirely

26. After his jagirs were confiscated, as stated above, Shah Niaz had left Kashmir and established himself in Ladakh which was not included yet in Ranjit Singh's dominions. (Ibid., p. 242) It is obviously after Moorcroft's intercession and grant of pension to Shah Niaz that the family was reestablished in Kashmir.

27. Cf. the use of the explicit words to 'Maharaja Gulab Singh and heirs male of his body' in article 1 of the Treaty with the Doctrine of Lapse. The latter had been established as early as 1834. See William Lee-Warner, *The Life of the Marquis of Dalhousie* (London, 1904), Vol. 2, p. 148; Sri Nandan Prasad, *Paramountcy Under Dalhousie* (Delhi, 1964), p. 29; R.C. Majumdar, ed., *The History and Culture of the India People: British Paramountcy and Indian Renaissance* (Bombay, 1963), Vol. 9, Part 1, p. 975.

28. For a logical and coherent treatment of the operation of British Paramountcy in its various facets, from its inception to 1848, see Prasad (1964), pp. 1-33. Also see Majumdar (1963), pp. 10-50.

impossible.[29] Gulab Singh, however, was to live long enough not only to install his son Ranbir Singh as the Maharaja in early 1856[30] but also to see the British in the throes of mutiny and revolt of 1857-58. The Government was, thus, in no hurry to force the pace of events unless, of course, the State deviated from what was expected of it, and ceased to serve the Government's purpose.

Gulab Singh continued on his part to remain apparently loyal to the Government in both words[31] and deed. He cooperated with it during their 'second war' against what remained of the Lahore kingdom in 1849.[32] During 1852, he sent his forces to help the Government in its action against the frontier tributary of Khagan.[33] Again, during the revolt of 1857, his son and successor not only remained loyal to the British but also supported them in the suppression of the revolt.[34]

29. See and cf. the following excerpts from the respective correspondence of Lord Dalhousie, the Governor-General of British India (1848-56), and Henry Lawrence, Member Punjab Administration Board:

Lord Dalhousie, in a letter to his friend, wrote on 21 October 1851: 'I hear privately that all the people about the C-in-C are very eager for war in the event of Gulab Singh's death. This being so, I shall take care to tie him up hand and foot, when I go, as I did his predecessor. Gulab has diabetes, and I fear, if the medical reports are correct, that he will not last many months.' J.G.A. Baird, ed., *Private Letters of the Marquess of Dalhousie* (Reprint Shannon, 1972), p. 179.

Lawrence wrote on 28 September 1849 to Dalhousie: 'Like most natives he [Gulab Singh] is a watcher of events, but a clever and far-seeing one . . . If we allow him to be our humble friend and ally he will be so; but there are so many Europeans panting for the possession of this valley [Kashmir], that it will not be an easy task to keep the peace.' J.L. Morison, *Lawrence of Lucknow, 1806-1857* (London, 1934), p. 236.

30. Personally he took over the position of the *Hakim-i-Alla* of the Kashmir Province and continued to hold it till his death.

31. See, for example, letter dated 6 January 1851 in Baird (1972), p. 150.

32. See Bawa Satinder Singh (1974), p. 151.

33. See letter dated 4 December 1852 in Baird (1972), p. 234.

34. Bawa Satinder Singh (1974), pp. 161-62. Also see Prithivi Nath Kaul Bamzai (1973), p. 664; G.M.D. Sufi, *Kashir: Being a History of Kashmir from the Earliest Times to Our Own* (New Delhi, 1974), Vol. 2, p. 794; and F.M. Hassnain, *British Policy Towards Kashmir, 1846-1921: Kashmir in Anglo-Russian Politics* (New Delhi, 1974), pp. 38-39.

After the Dogra-Sikh schism had been effected, and Gulab Singh was busy in the consolidation of his territories, the situation at Lahore changed materially, much in favour of the Government, as a result of the signing of yet another treaty[35] on 22 December 1846, with what had remained of Ranjit's kingdom. The terms of the treaty were such as to make Lord Hardinge[36] consider that it was 'in reality, annexation brought about by the supplication of the Sikhs'.[37] This was followed in 1847 by yet another significant development, the way to which was perhaps paved by the Treaty of Bhyrowal. That was the exchange by Gulab Singh of the frontier territory of Hazara with the Lahore State for territories in the interior and those contiguous with Jammu.[38] With this the State territories ceased to be coterminous with those of the Afghans obviating the need for the State to play the role expected of it earlier *vis-a-vis* the Afghans.[39] Not much later, on 29 March 1849, the Punjab was annexed to the British Dominions, thereby removing the *raison d'etre* of the State. Not without reason, we find the euphoria of an imminent war with Gulab Singh taking hold of the minds of the British.[40]

The Government did not remain indifferent towards the principalities lying towards the north and across the Indus. As early as August 1847, Vans Agnew was deputed to Gilgit on a mission.[41] From the diaries which he sent to Henry M. Lawrence, Resident at Lahore and the Agent to Governor

35. It was signed at Bhyrowal. For its text, see C.U. Aitchison, ed., *A Collection of Treaties*, Vol., 1. pp. 56-58.

36. Governor-General of British India.

37. *Broughton Papers*, Hardinge to Hobhouse, 5 April 1847, as cited in Hasrat, (1968), p. 297.

38. As noted earlier in ch. 2 the territories transferred to Gulab Singh by virtue of the Treaty originally included Hazara also.

39. Cf. Sarjit Singh Bal, *British Policy Towards the Panjab 1844-49*, p. 80, f.n. 69.

40. See Bawa Satinder Singh (1974), pp. 156-61.

41. *FDP*, Secret Branch, 27 November 1847, nos. 60-69. The weekly diaries sent by Agnew to the Resident at Lahore and Agent to Governor-General for North-West Frontier are also available in published form. See *Punjab Government Records, the Political Diaries of the Resident at Lahore and his Assistants, 1846-49* (Lahore, 1915), Vol. 6, pp. 275-302.

General for the North West Frontier, it is evident that he had been deputed to cultivate the tribal chiefs, in particular the Chiefs of Hunza and Nagar.[42] This was done at a time when there was absolutely no problem on their account. Hence, the action can be attributed only to the aggressive compulsions or designs of the imperial power and not to any defence considerations.

No sooner was Gulab Singh made the Maharaja and had showed delay in the consolidation of the territories transferred to him than he received advice, sugar-coated with flattery, that implied an anxiety on the part of the Government to ensure the internal stability of the State.[43] But before he could ensure the stability, Gulab, as has been seen, had to encounter hostility in the consolidation of his territories. This prompted the Government's intervention as a result of which alone could Gulab achieve the consolidation of his territories.

The Government's intervention led to the enforcement of its agreement with Gulab Singh and the consolidation of his territories but also exposed his weakness[44] and thus provided the Government with a lever. By this time the Government's position had considerably improved; the circumstances had changed since the creation of the State had been seen as the best option. Not unexpectedly, therefore, we find emanating from the Government something more than general advice. Henry M. Lawrence, who had been deputed to help Gulab Singh and later accompanied him to Srinagar after the exit of Sheikh Imam-ud-Din from Kashmir, gave him 'advice' with regard to the making of certain arrangements necessary for the 'stability' of his dominions. The advice was first offered verbally to Gulab Singh's Dewan, Jowalla Sahai, and to Gulab Singh personally

42. See the communication with the Chiefs of the principalities of Hunza and Nagar. Ibid.

43. Henry Lawrence wrote 'that the Maharaja being now a great sovereign should cheerfully forget small matters and employ all his energies in acquiring possession of his extensive territory, & in them, by forbearance, consideration & mercy [establish] his reputation and [perpetuate] his name'. *FDP*, Secret Department, Enclosures to Secret letters from India, Vol. 104, enc. 10, letter 27, Henry Lawrence to Currie, 31 March 1846 as quoted in Bawa Satinder Singh (1974), p. 125.

44. Cf. ibid., p. 135.

and then enshrined in a letter to him. Not only was Gulab Singh desired to make arrangements towards that end, but the two conditions that the British thought 'absolutely necessary' for the purpose were also outlined for him. These were:

> First, that all grades be treated with consideration and kindness so that they may remain faithful from selfish motives. Secondly that a sufficient army be maintained and kept in an efficient and loyal state. These two points effected, the Government of a country is easily carried on, for no enemy can arise from within and provision is made against invasion.[45]

Although Henry Lawrence gave prudent 'advice' to Gulab Singh and expected to have it followed yet conscious efforts were made to preserve Gulab Singh's authority rather than undermine it.[46] The demands of the two objectives were reconciled by the Agent by suggesting to the Secretary to the Government of India, F. Currie, that he 'depute a respectable native agent who can keep government informed without being an incubus on the local authorities and detracting from their credit without himself having any authority'.[47] Mirza Ahmed was accordingly

45. *FDP*, Secret Branch, 26 December 1846, nos. 1243-47, Lawrence to Gulab, 6 November 1846, NAI.

46. Lawrence on his way to Srinagar made a diversion in the way to Islamabad (Anantnag) 'as much with the view of letting the Maharaja enter his capital without British bayonets as for any sightseeing purposes . . .'. *FDP*, Secret Branch, 26 December 1846, nos. 1240-41 & K.W., Lawrence to Currie, 9 November 1846, NAI.

To Lt. Nicholson, who was left behind by Lawrence in Kashmir for a few days on his departure, a 'request' was made to pay his 'special attention' to the following :

'Maharaja Golab Singh is an independent sovereign of his country and should be treated with all respect, consideration . . . . Your duty will be in an unobtrusive manner, to see to the fulfilment of the terms of the treaty and arrangements lately consented to by the Maharaja. You will receive no petition from the inhabitants of Cashmere, or other quarters, but if you perceive or hear of any acts of tyranny you will report them to me.' *FDP*, Seeret Branch, 26 December 1846, nos, 1243-47, Lawrence to Nicolson, 15 November 1846, NAI.

47. *FDP*, Secret Branch, 26 December 1846, no. 1242, Lawrence to Currie, 12 November 1846, NAI.

appointed the 'vakil'.[48] The spectre of Paramount Power, thus, began to haunt the Dogra rulers right from the beginning.

Gulab Singh on his part was not averse to accepting 'advice'. He wrote to Henry Lawrence before he left Kashmir on 16 November and intimated him about the measures he would take to comply with it.[49]

In furtherance of such methods of control, rather than as an 'innovation',[50] Henry Lawrence deputed one of his assistants, R.G. Taylor, to Kashmir in 1847, after receiving information about Gulab Singh's 'oppression' of the people. This 'oppression', it seems was the result of the institution of *quo warranto* by Gulab Singh, in pursuance of consolidation, to the holders and claimants of various land grants. Taylor stayed in Kashmir for quite some time, listened to the various complaints and also looked into the different measures taken by Gulab Singh.

Gulab Singh did not exhibit any reluctance to surveillance by the Government. On the contrary, he was keen to exhibit his readiness to carry out the advice.[51] Henry Lawrence's pronouncement on the response of Gulab Singh not only shows his satisfaction over the execution of the 'advice' that was necessary for 'stability', but is pregnant with the idea that Gulab could now be pressed for things other than this. Lawrence remarked in his letter to H.M. Elliot, Secretary to the Government of India:

> . . . [it] shows both an anxiety on His Highness' part to meet the wishes of the British government and a confident belief that he has done so in his late measures for the amelioration of the condition of all classes in Cashmere.[52]

48. The Baron Erich Von Schonberg, *Travels in India and Kashmir* (London, 1853), Vol. 2, pp. 125-26.

49. *FDP*, Secret Branch, 26 December 1846, nos. 1243-47, Gulab to Lawrence, 13 November 1846, NAI.

50. It is surprising that some researchers too have presented it to have been an innovation. See M.L. Kapur, *Kashmir Sold and Snatched* (Jammu, 1968), p. 20; Mohan Krishan Teng, et. al., *Kashmir Constitutional History and Documents* (New Delhi, 1977), p. 17. Kapur has stated it definitely while Teng et. al. have been a little circumspect.

51. *FDP*, Sercret Branch, 30 October 1847, nos. 116-17, Taylor to Lawrence, 8 September 1847 and Lawrence to Elliot, 30 September 1847, NAI

52. Ibid., Lawrence to Elliot, 30 September 1847.

Probably this was a signal that it was worthwhile now to press for demands other than those which were needed simply for the stability of the State and its ability to fulfil the Treaty obligations. In the light of the furtherance of their other interests can an explanation be found for the warnings issued to Gulab Singh a little later by Henry Lawrence[53] and Lord Hardinge.[54] These were tantamount to a threat to appoint a Resident in his territories in case he did not comply with their 'just' demands. The proposal of this emanated from Lawrence[55] and the basis for it was the report recently given by Vans Agnew which was critical of the Maharaja's administration. Both Lawrence and Hardinge remaind unconvinced about the alleged oppression reported by Vans Agnew and considered it undesirable to appoint a permanent representative.[56] The threat seems to have been only a pressure tactic employed by the Paramount Power to bring Gulab Singh round to, as Lawrence concluded in his remonstrance, 'eschewing the practices of a trader'.[57] This implied a desire to make Gulab Singh give up monopoly of trade in his territories. This and the 'reforms' that he was advised to introduce were obviously necessary for the development of British trade with, and across, his territories. The threats had a wider implication also. They were intended to impress on Gulab Singh that the autonomous status of the State—what was said to be 'independence'—could not be taken as an immutable reality by him but depended on his readiness to comply with the 'just' demands of the Paramount Power.

A further factor that prompted the Government to act at the earliest was the attractiveness of Kashmir as a summer resort

53. *FDP*, Secret Branch, 28 January 1848, nos. 41-42, Lawrence to Gulab, 29 November 1847, NAI.

54. *FDP*, Secret Branch, 28 January 1848, no. 43-A, Governor-General to Maharaja, 7 January 1848, NAI.

55. *FDP*, Secret Branch, 28 January 1848, no. 35 & K.W., Lawrence to Elliot, 29 November 1847, NAI.

56. Ibid. See also *FDP*, Secret Branch, 28 January 1848, no. 43, Governor-General's Minute, 1 January 1848, and ibid., no. 44, Foreign Department Despatch to Officiating Resident at Lahore, 7 January 1848, NAI.

57. *FDP*, Secret Branch, 28 January 1848, nos. 41-42, Lawrence to Gulab, 29 November 1847, NAI.

for its officers. Moved by a desire to forestall the rise of any 'inconvenience',[58] it asked its officiating Resident at Lahore as early as December 1847, to 'prohibit all officers, civil and military, from proceeding into Cashmere or other parts of Golab Singh's territory without the previous sanction of the Govt. of India'.[59]

The first batch of British visitors who had entered Kashmir were those few Europeans who had been there as 'travellers' earlier, i.e., before Gulab Singh took possession of the region. They started a trend which increased over time. John Martin Honigberger, who visited Kashmir perhaps somewhere in 1849, found 'several English visitors' there at that time.[60] They, he wrote, were treated by the Maharaja with the 'greatest hospitality'[61] yet they did not restrain themselves despite the restrictions placed on their conduct and behaviour by the Government. Many of them had 'frequently taken with them very large quantities of saffron, and other products of the country, much beyond what they could really use during their sojourn'.[62] In 1850, the government in Punjab with the concurrence of the Government formulated and issued a set of 'Rules for the guidance of Officers, and other Travellers, visiting Cashmere and the Dominions, generally, of Maharaja Golab Singh'.[63] A study of these rules makes it clear that they were meant to regulate the conduct of the British visitors to Kashmir. However, these rules did not deter three British officers in 1851 from indulging in acts which were considered to be inimical by the Punjab Government. One of these involved violence with a Dogra

58. *FDP*, Secret Branch, 27 November 1847, nos. 60-69, Foreign Department Despatch to Resident at Lahore, 16 November 1847, NAI. John Lawrence, who was at that time officiating Resident at Lahore, strongly buttressed the idea of forestalling the rise of any 'inconvenience' in his reply to the query made in the above-mentioned despatch. *FDP*, Secret Branch, 31 December 1847, nos. 144-46, Lawrence to Elliot, 1 December 1847, NAI.

59. Ibid., Foreign Department Despatch to John Lawrence, 31 December 1847.

60. John Martin Honigberger, *Thrty-Five Years in the East* (Calcutta, 1905), p. 182.

61. Ibid.

62. Ibid., p. 183.

63. *FDP*, Secret Branch, 31 May 1850, nos. 63-64, NAI.

soldier.[64] Under the circumstancss, the Punjab government decided to depute one of its officers to Kashmir during summer. He was to act as'refree' in any misunderstanding that might arise between the authorities there and the British visitors and also take cognizance of any oppression or irregularities that might be charged against the British officers. Gulab Singh was accordingly informed by the Punjab government. His assent was received by them in February 1852.[65]

1858—1885

As an aftermath of the suppression of the Indian revolt of 1857-58 and the assumption of the Government directly by the British Crown, there occurred a general shift in the policy of the Government towards the Native States in India. The Queen's proclamation,[66] issued on 1 November 1858, assured the Princes that their 'rights, dignity and honour' would be respected and that 'all treaties and engagements' entered into by the East India Company with them would be 'scrupulously maintained'. It meant, in effect, the repudiation of the earlier policy of annexation by the Government. From 1858 onwards, it thus became an axiom of British policy to see that the Native States continued to exist.

Charles Canning, the Governer-General of British India during those critical days and the first representative of the Crown, the Viceroy, implemented a 'general scheme of strengthening an Indian aristocracy which would buttress British rule'.[67]

64. *FDP*, Political (hereafter Pol.), 13 January 1852, no. 149, NAI. For details with regard to these incidents and the proceedings thereof, see *FDP*, Pol., 14 December 1852, Proceedings Vol., nos. 70-81, NAI.

65. *FDP*, Pol., 14 December 1852, nos., 82-83, Melvill to Elliot, 27 February 1852, NAI. It has been asserted by one researcher that this arrangement was accepted by Gulab after making 'some protests' against it. But there is no evidence to suggest that it was so. See Kapur (1968), p. 25.

66. Proclamation by the Queen in Council to the Princes, Chiefs, and People of India, as reproduced in Ramesh Dutt, *The Economic History of India* (New Delhi, 1970), Vol. 2, pp. 169-72; see also Gopal, *British Policy in India, 1858-1905* (Madras, 1975), p. 3.

67. Ibid., p. 7.

He adopted towards Princes a policy of 'punishing resistance and rewarding obedience'.[68] This policy of conciliating the Princes was furthered by ensuring to them the continuity of their states by discarding the Doctrine of Lapse. By issuing the Sanads of Adoption to them, a transformation had been quietly effected. There were to be no categories of states; all were now the 'feudatories', with the Crown of Britain having 'suzerainty' over them. Loyalty to the Crown was the condition on which the right of adoption was conceded.[69]

Maharaja Ranbir Singh, who had remained loyal to the British and had actively supported them in the suppression of the revolt, was honoured.[70] Further, a *sanad* to the aforesaid purpose was sanctioned to him on 9 March 1860.[71] This, in view of the fact that the Treaty affirmed succession to only natural male decendents of Maharaja Gulab Singh, was significant and thus ensured the continued existence of the State. Concomitant with this was the obligation for the State to entertain all the requirements of the British imperial system into which it had now been absorbed directly. This was an engagement that was clearly not envisaged by the British Government in India at the time of the creation of the State. The State, it has been seen earlier, was created simply to work as a counterpoise against the Sikhs. This measure had become inevitable on account of the Government's inability in 1846

68. Ibid., p. 8. 'He held two durbars, in Agra and in Lahore, to which the loyal Princes were summoned, confirmed in rank and titles and in some cases given an additional decoration.' Ibid.

69. K.M. Panikkar, 'The Indian States Under the British Crown', in Majumdar, ed., (1963), Vol. 9, Pt. 1, p. 961.

70. His services were appreciated by the Governor-General. And the Queen sent him presents and commended his loyalty and sincerity. (*Persian Records*, Jammu and Kashmir Government, 1857, File No. 165, as cited in Hassnain (1974), pp. 38-39). He was even offered a Khilat amounting to rupees one lac and a *jagir* in Oudh. But he refused to accept saying that he had done his duty out of loyalty and goodwill. Prem Nath Bazaz, *Inside Kashmir* (Srinagar, 1941), p. 39.

71. *Persian Records*, Jammu and Kashmir Government, 1860, File No. 165, as cited in Hassnain (1974), p. 39. It is interesting that Sir Charles Wood, then Secretary of State for India, was not happy about firmly closing the door to annexations, especially of pleasant hill stations. See Gopal (1975), p. 9.

to crush the Sikh Power completely and annex their kingdom. The State was expected, along with the Sikhs, to work as a bulwark against the Afghans. Nowhere have we come across any evidence to suggest that the State had been contemplated as an immutable fact by its creators. It was created in response to a specific situation which did not last long. The Sikh kingdom was annexed in March 1849. After Gulab Singh exchanged the frontier territory of Hazara in 1847 the question of his working as a bulwark against the Afghans was also removed. Therefore, the attempts of Dilip Kumar Ghose and G.J. Alder to justify the later acts of the Government on that basis appear to be misleading and unhistorical.[72] They seek justification for the Government's attempts to extend its control over the State and its territories not in something that developed later but in what they believe was envisaged at the time of its creation: frontier defence. The underlying assumption, that the State was created as a permanent feature, is untenable. The continuation of the State, it has to be made clear, can be attributed to the renewal of the British policy towards Native States since 1858. Henceforth, it was clearly expected to shoulder the imperial responsibility in its quarter and its ruling authority had to have the necessary will and capacity to do so. The view that emphasises defence to have been the motivating force behind the British projections into the north in India is erroneous. For, the British thrust in this quarter towards the mid-nineteenth century and later was surely aggressive, as has been noted earlier and shall be shown subsequently; it is with such a policy and the capability of the State to help implement it that the future of the State was inextricably linked.

The interest of the Government in the shawl wool trade of western Tibet prior to the creation of the State has been referred to earlier. The Government did not lose sight of this interest after the creation of the State. Efforts were made to utilize the newly created situation for the furtherance of the trade. For

72. Dilip Kumar Ghose, *Kashmir in Transition 1885-1893* (Calcutta, 1975); G.J. Alder, *British India's Northern Frontier, 1865-95: A Study in Imperial Policy* (London, 1963).

instance, when the first Boundary Commission was appointed by the Government in July 1846 to determine the eastern boundaries of the State territories—for this there was a provision in the Treaty itself[73]—the Commissioners were instructed to secure Spiti[74] and compensate Gulab Singh elsewhere. The purpose was to have direct access from Rampur to the shawl wool producing districts of Chang Thang in western Tibet. An attempt was also made to contact the Tibetan authorities and to seek from them an alteration in the provisions of the treaty of 1842 referred to earlier.[75] The alteration asked for clearly aimed at removing the impediments in the way of the British diverting shawl-wool to their own territories.

The trading interest of the Government was not confined to Tibet alone. The Boundary Commission of 1846 and the one appointed in July 1847 were both instructed to explore the prospects of trade also with Central Asia.[76] The trading interest prompted the Punjab government in 1849 to authoritatively tell Gulab Singh that his officers could not be permitted to interrupt the 'establishment of trade between Thibet and British Provinces'. He was so told because one of his officials in Ladakh, Bustee Ram, was reported to have confiscated the goods of Yarkand traders.[77]

In the early 1860s the British Provincial Government in the Punjab, while taking stock of trade with the territories across the Himalayas, saw a few obstacles in its way. The primary one was thought to be the prohibitive duties imposed by the State on goods passing through its territories.[78] Consequently, the Maharaja was persuaded to reduce the import and transit

73. Article 2.

74. *FDP*, Secret Branch, 26 December 1846, no. 1335, Lawrence to Agnew, 31 July 1846, NAI. See also Alexander Cunningham, *Ladak: Physical, Historical, and Statistical* (London, 1854), p. 13.

75. *FDP*, Secret Branch, 26 December 1846, no. 1336, Hardinge to Vazir of Lhasa, 4 August 1846, NAI.

76. Ibid., 26 December 1846, no. 1335, Lawrence to Agnew, 31 July 1846; Ibid., 28 August 1847, nos. 139-83, Foreign Department Communique to Cunnigham, 27 July 1847.

77. *FDP*, Pol., Letters from Court, 4 June 1851, Company to Government of India, 1851, no. 19, NAI.

78. Alder (1963), pp. 22-23.

duties within his territories in 1863. Thus, the mode of collecting custom duties was simplified and a transit duty of only 5 per cent was imposed on goods conveyed via Srinagar in 1864.[79]

These concessions were obviously not enough to satisfy the Punjab government officials, who were keen to have a British Agent appointed at Leh. It was found 'absolutely necessary to improve and open out Cashmere'. This they also wanted to do on account of what they presented as the Russian threat from across the Karakoram and Pamir ranges to India's northern frontiers.[80] The political development at this time in Chinese Turkistan, resulting in the establishment of an independent kingdom with Yakub Beg as its ruler, and the consequent prospects of increased trade gave a fillip to their eagerness. Pressure was brought to bear upon Lord Lawrence, the Governor-General and Viceroy, to sanction the appointment of a British Agent at Leh.[81]

Lord Lawrence agreed to the proposal reluctantly—that too as a temporary measure and only for one season. Accordingly, Dr. Henry Cayley was appointed to the post in 1867. He was not only to act as a Commercial Agent, but was also asked 'to collect and to sift political information regarding the progress of events in Chinese Turkistan'.[82] When informed, the Maharaja protested against this appointment and represented that both Montgomery and Lawrence, who had visited Ladakh to study the issue of having a British officer there, had agreed that it would amount to interference in the internal affairs of the State. While acknowledging the State as a gift from the British Government and Lawrence as its founder, he emphasised that he considered his 'action and deeds' as 'agreements and Treaties'. He reminded Lawrence that he had been

79. Bajpai (1970), p. 66.

80. *FDP*, Pol. A, May 1863, nos. 77-78, Note on his tour in Thibet, Chinese Tartary and the mountainous country lying east and north-east of Kashmir by C.H. Strutt, 29 March 1863, NAI. Also see ibid., November 1868, nos. 1-6, Extract from the report on the trade with Central Asia by T. Douglas Forsyth.

81. Alder (1963), pp. 25-26.

82. *FDP*, Pol. A, March 1868, nos. 6-9, NAI.

loyal to the British cause, and pleaded that 'occurrences in Tibet and Turkistan and information regarding trade with India can be gathered by staying in Spiti, on the frontier between the British territory and Ladakh'.[83] But nothing came out of this representation and he had to swallow 'the easier pill' as the Governor-General had said a medical man would be as compared to a purely political officer.[84]

On the basis of what Cayley felt dnring his stay at Leh and the request he made to his government for the continuation of the Agency, it was decided to continue the British Agency at Leh. Accordingly, the Maharaja was informed in October 1867 that the Government would continue deputing an officer to Ladakh as long as it deemed fit owing to the obstructions created by the Maharaja's servants to trade there. The Maharaja did not acquiesce for long and deputed his Dewan, Kirpa Ram, to make a representation to the Lieutenant-Governor of the Punjab. The Dewan pleaded that the Commercial Agent at Leh had been appointed first only for the year 1867 and had to make enquiries into the state of trade with Turkistan and to see that the scale of duty that was fixed in 1864 was observed. Since the scale that was fixed in 1864 had been implemented, there was no justification for the continuation of the Agency. He also pointed out that its continuation was not only a violation of the customs and usages followed so far but also damaged the prestige of the Maharaja's authority. It had created an impression on the minds of his subjects that the Maharaja was incapable of effectively carrying out the administration of his country. The Dewan gave an assurance that the desire of the British Government to open the Chang-Chenmo route and the encouragement of trade with Turkistan would be fulfilled.[85]

The Lieutenant-Governor justified the decision of his

83. *Kashmir Government Records*, File No. 371, Ranbir Singh to Lt. Governor Punjab, 26 Bisakh 1924, as quoted in Hassnain (1974), p. 50.

84. *Argyll Papers*, 1867-81, 147, p. 5, India to Punjab, 22 Jan. 1867, as cited in Alder (1963), p. 28.

85. *FDP*, Pol. A, January 1869, nos. 352-58, Memorandum on the verbal representation by Dewan Kirpa Ram, 2 July 1868, NAI.

government on the basis that the appointment of a Commercial Agent was in accordance with the practice prevalent among the civilized nations of Europe. He, however, suggested that a proclamation could be circulated among the people to dispel the notion that had arisen in their minds.[86] Accordingly, a proclamation to that effect was made:

> The Maharaja is in the same position in regard to his dominions as the late Maharajah Gulab Singh. . . . Dr. Cayley, or any other officer in his position, has no power or right to interfere with the internal administration of the country, or to listen to the complaints of jageerdars or other subjects of the Maharaja. . .the Maharaja is a faithful feudatory of the British Government with which the most friendly relations exist, and possessed of full sovereign powers in his own territory.[87]

The Maharaja was still not satisfied and deputed Dewan Jwala Sahai and Dewan Kirpa Ram to approach the Viceroy. They pleaded that the appointment should not be renewed and in return were prepared to concede on behalf of the Maharaja withdrawal of all duties hitherto levied on merchandise conveyed by traders to and from British India via Ladakh. Furthermore, permission for the deputation of the officer stationed in Kashmir during summer months to Leh for one month every year was promised. As a matter of political expediency the Viceroy wanted to oblige the Maharaja,[88] but

86. Ibid., Memorandum of reply to representation by Dewan Kirpa Ram, 6 July 1868.

87. Ibid., Proclamation by T.H. Thornton, 8 July 1868.

88. The Viceroy, John Lawrence observed: '. . . the presence of a British Official is, in itself, irksome and inconvenient to the Maharaja, and however discreet may be the conduct of the occupant of that situation, his mere deputation gives rise to surmises which cannot but cramp the action and lessen the self-respect of the Ruler himself, while, by some of his subjects, it is regarded as a pledge, and even a menace, of further and more direct interference in the affairs of a kingdom which we have agreed generally to consider and to treat as independent . . . the case of Cashmere is peculiar, and our policy in regard to kingdoms on the frontier is now, and ought to be, especially one of avowed conciliation

he could not resist the strong official pressure in India and at home and gave his sanction to the deputation of a Commercial Agent at Leh.

The British desire to foster their trading interests with Turkistan led them to force a commercial treaty on the Maharaja again in 1870. The treaty provided for a survey of all routes and the nomination of a route which would be 'a free highway in perpetuity and at all times for all travellers and traders'. Two Commissioners, one each from the State and the Government, were to be appointed to supervise the route, settle disputes and exercise jurisdiction within a defined limit on each side of the route. Arrangements were to be made for the independent agents to provide transport, and the establishment of supply depots and rest houses was to be decided. The Maharaja agreed to levy no transit duties on the free highway or on goods passing unopened through Kashmir. The Government in return undertook to refund all important duties on goods transmitted in bond through India to State territories and eastern Turkistan.[89] The Viceroy, Lord Mayo, assured the Maharaja, during the negotiations between the Government and the Maharaja about the contents of the proposed treaty, that the 'British Government will at all times be guided by the most scrupulous respect for your honour, and by a sincere desire to exalt your dignity in the eyes of your subjects, and to maintain the integrity of your authority within your own territories'.[90]

and scrupulous forbearance. The position of the territory, the zeal and fidelity displayed by its Rulers to the British cause, at various important epochs, . . . and the earnest desire of the Government of India to have, in the space between British India and Central Asia, at least one friendly State, and one Ruler, thoroughly well disposed to British ascendency and influence, . . . [it is] both wise and politic to run the risk of some possible impediments to commerce and some misconstruction of political motives, in order to secure, in the Ruler of Cashmere, a cordial supporter instead of a luckewarm friend.' *FDP*, Pol. A, November 1868, no. 82, Seton Karr to Thornton, 9 November 1868, NAI.

89. Ibid., July 1870, nos. 90-115, Treaty between the British Government and the Maharaja, his heirs and successors.

90. Ibid., Viceroy to Maharaja, 8 February 1870.

Impelled by the same urge as that of the British on the Indian side of the Karakoram and Pamir ranges, another European Imperialist power—Czarist Russia began its expansion towards the Central Asian territories after the Crimean War of 1854-56. After the revolt of 1857-58 had been suppressed and re-consolidation effected by the Government, renewed and effective efforts were initiated to boost trade with Central Asian territories. Strong pressure was mounted, and fears were expressed by the Punjab officials to the Government.

Lawrence, it has been noted, was averse to sanctioning any measure that would appear to be an interference in the internal affairs of the State. Likewise, he did not do anything to curb the trans-frontier activities of the Maharaja.[91] One plausible explanation for this could be that Lawrence was firmly opposed to the exploration of the 'dangerous areas beyond the red line' by British officials.[92] Under the circumstances, the State was employed to do this difficult job.[93]

Lord Mayo did not approve of the cultivation of any sort of relations by the Maharaja with Russia. Hence, it was only natural that he should not have liked the State territories coming close to those occupied or likely to be occupied by the Russians. This is implied in the warning he gave to the Maharaja in 1870 to the effect that he should 'commit no aggressions on his neighbours and make no attempt to extend his authority beyond the limits which had been conferred on his father'.[94] These neighbours were obviously none other than the tribal Muslim principalities across the Indus on the north.

91. Alder (1963), p. 105

92. Ibid., p. 32.

93. It was about this time that a number of agents were deputed by the Maharaja to the Central Asian territories to gather information about them. It was with this purpose that a school for learning the Russian language was opened at Srinagar. Hassnain (1974), pp. 48-49. In 1868 secret agents were sent by him to contact the Russians at Tashkent. This was done to obtain information for the British Government in India. *FDP*, Secret Branch, August 1877, nos. 127-32, K.W., NAI; ibid., April 1873, no. 82, NAI.

94. *Secret Letters and Enclosures from India and Madras*, Vol. 13, p. 917, Mayo to Durand, 21 September 1870, enclosed with 76, India, 12 October 1872, as cited in Alder (1963), p. 107.

This was later reversed by Lord Lytton and logically led to the complete reduction of the State. Northbrook, his predecessor, had however already taken steps to pave the way for this.

Northbrook, who fell in line with the official opinion to extend effective control over the Maharaja, was convinced of the need to appoint a Resident in his territories. He concurred with the opinion of C.U. Aitchison, the Foreign Secretary, in that

> the appointment . . . is one of great and increasing importance. If properly filled the advantage to Government both in respect to the control of the political doings of Cashmere and the information to be obtained from Central Asia will be very great.[95]

Consequently, a communication was sent to the Maharaja in September 1873 in which he was informed about the intention of the Government to appoint a British Resident at his Court—a proposal with which his father had only been threatened by Henry Lawrencc and Lord Hardinge. He was assured that the proposed appointment was to be made 'for reasons relating to the external relations of British India, and the Viceroy has no intention of interfering more than heretofore in the internal affairs of Cashmere'.[96]

The communication, being the first of its kind, gave a jolt to the Maharaja, as it was bound to.[97] To be in a position to convey properly what he thought about the matter, the Maharaja sought an opportunity to express himself verbally to the Lt. Governor of Punjab, R.H. Davies and, through him, to the Governor-General.[98] Davies eventually held two successive interviews with the Maharaja at Jammu. During the course of the second interview the Maharaja also handed over to him a written statement. Davies was not able to persuade the Maharaja to agree to accept a Resident.[99]

95. *FDP*, Secret Branch, March 1875, nos. 19-29, K.W. 1, NAI.
96. Ibid., Lt. Governor Punjab to Maharaja, 26 September 1873.
97. Ibid., Wynne to Thornton, 14 October 1873.
98. Ibid., Maharaja to Lt. Governor Punjab, 14 October 1873.
99. Ibid., Lt. Governor to Northbrook, 7 December 1873.

The Maharaja regarded the proposal as a 'diminution of the dignity of his State' and anticipated that it would lead ultimately to interference in his internal affairs. In answer to a suggestion made to him to also appoint a representative with the Government of India, he stated he had no pretensions to deal with the Government on equal terms. He pleaded that only the kind of control that had been exercised before should continue. Any change was 'most unexpected' by him in view of the 'services' that he had rendered and was always ready to render. As proof of his sincere intentions, he was even prepared 'to allow one of his sons to be detained in British territory as a hostage'. He considered the appointment of a Resident as an innovation that was not contemplated either by the Treaty or *Sanads* or the practice that had been followed since the creation of the State. However, to meet the requirement of the Government he offered two concessions. One was permission to the British Joint Commissioner at Leh to stay there round the year and the other was that the officer at Srinagar could now stay for eight instead of only six months as earlier.[100]

This was accepted by the Governor-General as he considered these concessions adequate to fulfil the present requirement.[101] However, Lord Lytton, who arrived in India in 1876 as the new Governor-General and Viceroy of India, was sent by the Conservative Government at home as a deliberate choice to meet fresh imperial objectives. The objective set out for him was to see that the Afghan policy and the frontier administration 'be viewed as an imperial concern' and measures be adopted to 'co-ordinate the entire trans-frontier policy of the Government of India from Ladakh and Kashmir to the Persian Gulf in accordance with the exigencies of imperial objectives. . . .' This entailed the extension of the British sphere of influence fully over Afghanistan by establishing the British Residency there. One related problem was the uncertainty about the political future of the tribal territories lying between the rivers Kunar and Indus. Their significance had increased in view of

100. Ibid., Lt. Governor to Northbrook, 7 December 1873 and Maharaja's Memorandum.

101. Ibid., Northbrook to Davies, 25 March 1874.

the discoveries made about the passes in the Pamir range and the perception of a practical possibility of Russian presence along the banks of the River Oxus. Lytton desired the extension of control over these territories as a counter move. He thought of two possibilities to secure it: to bring these either under the aegis of the Afghans or of the State. His preference was for the first alternative, but the basis on which he wanted to pursue that alternative failed. So he had to follow the second alternative.[102]

The Maharaja was to be asked to extend his frontiers, in reversal of the earlier policy. But before this step was taken, it was decided to tighten control over his affairs. This was to be done by the appointment of a regular Agent at Gilgit, or elsewhere in the State, and the stationing of British troops whenever found necessary. To put the proposals personally to the Maharaja, Lytton met him at Madhopore on 17 and 18 November 1876.

After briefing the Maharaja, Lytton conveyed to him the urgency felt by the British Government to see the states of Chitral and Yassin brought under the control of their 'friend and ally'. As was expected, the Maharaja did not say no. However, it is significant to note that he wanted to have a 'written authority to commence negotiations, in order that it may not be in the power of evil-disposed persons hereafter to accuse him of entering into relations with foreign states for his own ends'.[103]

As to the question of appointing a British Agent at Gilgit for the further security of the frontier and the transmission of regular reliable information, the Maharaja showed his readiness to agree to the proposal if and when the circumstances demanded such an appointment. For the present, however, he offered to construct a telegraph line to Gilgit so that the same requirements could be met through direct communication. This, the Maharaja thought, would obviate the British

102. Suhash Chakravarty, *From Khyber to Oxus: A Study in Imperial Expansion* (New Delhi, 1976), pp. 124ff.

103. *FDP*, Secret Branch, July 1877, nos. 34-60 B, Memorandum of a conversation held at Madhopore on 17 and 18 November 1876 between the Viceroy and the Maharaja, NAI.

need to station an agent at Gilgit. When Lytton still insisted on the appointment of such an officer, he pleaded that the idea was too new to him and asked for time to consider it.[104] The next day, perhaps sensing that any attempt to avoid it would be futile, he agreed to the appointment of a British agent at Gilgit. At the same time, however, he asked for permission to write to the Government of India to seek certain assurances. This was given.[105]

Accordingly, he addressed a letter to seek a *Sanad* giving in it various assurances. The assurances he wanted clearly indicate that they were aimed at stopping any impairment of the integrity and dignity of the State and the erosion of his powers within it.[106] The Governor-General assured the Maharaja in his reply that the Agent at Gilgit would 'abstain from all interference in the internal administration or trade of your Highness' territory, in the affairs of your subjects, or in the conduct of your official servants'. He was also assured that the measure was not 'intended to form a precedent for enlarging or altering the arrangements that now exist in respect to the position of the "officer on special duty" at Srinuggur'.[107] Thus, with Capt. Biddulph as the first Agent, the British Agency at Gilgit was established in 1877.

Lytton did not stop at the establishment of the Agency at Gilgit. He revised the procedure of communication with the Officer on Special Duty in Kashmir. Henceforth, he was asked to correspond with the Government of India directly in all matters that were political.

Thus, a feudal state, limited in every possible way, was required to fulfil the objectives of an Imperial Power. Lord Hardinge, in 1846, considered that 'the Territories [of the State], excepting Cashmere, are comparatively unproductive, and would scarcely pay the expenses of occupation and management'.[108] Since then the State had lost, as a result of the ruin

104. Ibid.
105. Ibid.
106. Ibid., Maharaja to Viceroy, 26 November 1876.
107. Ibid., Viceroy to Maharaja, 22 December 1876.
108. *FDP*, Governor-General's Despatch to Secret Committee, 4 March 1846, no. 7, NAI.

of the shawl industry in Kashmir,[109] one of the major sources of its income. Lytton gave the Maharaja just 5000 rifles to accomplish the task assigned to him at Madhopore.

The task assigned to the Maharaja at Madhopore meant an enormous drain on the meagre resources of the State. To an already precarious situation was added a long famine in Kashmir in which about three-fifths of its population perished. From the account given by a contemporary native historian, it is apparent that the requirements of the Madhopore settlement surrely aggravated, if not initiated, the famine.[110] However, both the Anglo-Indian and the British Press held that it was a case of 'misgovernment' on the part of the State officials and held them responsible for it. Some pleaded the annexation of the 'Happy Valley' in the name of humanity. Others wanted the prompt intervention of the British Government to afford the people some immediate relief.[111] Official opinion also reacted the same way. Lytton did not find these proposals palatable. For him it was more important to have a 'very considerable consideration as a whole' and not merely interfere at the time of a famine.[112] He was against any move that would amount to annexation. His opposition was not based on any love for Ranbir Singh but rather his desire to avoid a heavy burden on British time, energy and money, and to avoid the effect of such an action on the other feudatories of India.[113]

The Madhopore settlement proved to be a failure because of the obvious difficulties in the way it was proposed to be carried out. This was clearly understood by Lytton, the man who had sponsored it. In view of this and the outcome of the second Anglo-Afghan War of 1879, he decided to ask the

109. For a fuller discussion of the state of the shawl industry, see ch. 5.

110. Hassan (1957), pp. 58ff.

111. See *Civil and Military Gazette*, 5 September 1878, 5 September 1879; *The Pioneer*, 31 December 1878, 17 January 1879; *The Statesman and Friend of India*, 16 and 30 September 1878; *The Times*, 25, 27 and 30 August 1879, 4 September 1879, as cited in Ghose (1975), pp. 15-16.

112. *Lytton Papers*, 518/4, pp. 845-46, 979-86, Lytton to Cranbrook, 2 October 1879 and 5 November 1879, as cited in Ghose (1975), p. 16.

113 *Lytton Papers*, 518/6, fp. 979, Lytton to Cranbrook, 15 November 1879, as cited in Alder (1963), p. 136.

Maharaja to stop his trans-frontier activities. However, before he could do so he had to go.

Lord Ripon, his successor, considered the establishment of Gilgit Agency to be a 'mistake'.[114] But before he could take any final decision, hostilities started on the frontier. It was obvious that neither the State nor the British Indian Government could provide adequately for the personal safety of an Agent in such a remote spot as Gilgit. Thus, the Agency at Gilgit was abolished in July 1881—but was re-established later in 1888. The Maharaja was informed that the Government of India still regarded

> the affairs of the Gilgit frontier with attention, and had no desire that His Highness the Maharaja should recede from the position which he took up in 1877. On the contrary, His Highness should maintain his influence unimpaired over the frontier Chiefs.[115]

Ripon told the Maharaja in a communication that 'in all questions of importance connected with your external relations, Your Highness will refer to me through my officer on Special Duty in Kashmir'.[116]

By withdrawing the Gilgit Agency there was no way in which the objectives it was expected to achieve could be attained. It was quite obvious to the concerned persons that the State apparatus was no longer strong enough to meet the new requirements. The necessity for reforms was felt during the operation of the forward policy itself. Lytton had decided to meet the Maharaja in order to impose upon him a programme of reforms and a Resident.[117] But his departure from India aborted such an eventuality. However, he left a note on record for his successor to such an effect.

114. *Ripon Papers*/2, p. 40, Ripon to Hartington, 27 July 1880, as cited in Alder (1963), p. 138.

115. *FDP*, Secret Branch, July 1881, nos. 314-99, Henry to Lyall, 18 May 1881, NAI.

116. Ibid., Viceroy to Maharaja, 18 June 1881.

117. Ghose (1975), p. 18.

The biggest drawback was the lack of means of communication within the State.[118] The condition of the Maharaja's army was also not thought to be proper to serve the new requirements.[119] A need was also felt to have a land settlement introduced. All these were, undoubtedly, interlinked and essential for British requirements. Therefore, it is not surprising that shortly after his arrival in India in 1880 Lord Ripon urged upon Ranbir Singh to introduce the reforms.[120] Only a year later the officer on Special Duty at Srinagar was asked to remind the Maharaja again.[121] It is significant that the first school to impart modern education was started by the Christian Missionary Society at Srinagar in 1880.[122]

The British Government wanted the 'reforms' to be introduced to enable the State to serve British imperial interests. It was natural then for it to keep itself abreast of the progress which the State was making in this direction. This implied interference in the internal affairs of the State. Such interference had always been resisted by the Maharaja, as we have seen, and the British Government had been at pains to assure him that it would not be resorted to. The British Government obviously could no longer afford this stand in the changed circumstances. At the same time, as expected, the Maharaja could not fulfil the task swiftly with his limited means and a medieval agency to operate with. These considerations, coupled with the reports sent by two successive Officers On Special Duty and a tour to the State to see things for himself, convinced Ripon that the political arrangement with the State had to be altered. But it was decided to withhold any such move till the death of Ranbir Singh who had not been keeping well for some time. In April 1884 Ripon asked the Secretary of State for India to sanction the appointment of a Resident—a measure which Ripon thought was

118. Alder (1963), pp. 133-34.

119. Ibid., p. 135.

120. *FDP*, A. Pol. E, September 1882, nos. 266-72, Viceroy to Maharaja, 13 July 1880, NAI.

121. *FDP*, A. Pol. E, September 1882, nos. 273-306.

122. See the section on Education and Intellectuals in ch. 5.

> called for, not merely by the need for assisting and supervising administrative reforms, but also by the increasing importance to the Government of India of watching events beyond the North-Western frontier of Kashmir. Any disturbances which continued misgovernment might create in Kashmir would be acutely felt on the frontiers of Afghanistan; the connection between Kashmir and its dependent Chiefships would in all probability be severed; and grave political complications might easily ensue.[123]

Ripon's communication makes it clear that the measure was prompted by the compulsions of the Paramount Power at the time and not by any sympathetic concern for the betterment of the people of Kashmir. While accepting the proposal, the Secretary of State, the Earl of Kimberley, made an observation that indicates the setting in of a new trend in the dealings of the Government with the State. He wrote :

> It may, indeed, be a question whether, having regard to the circumstances under which the sovereignty of the country was entrusted to the present Hindu ruling family, the intervention of the British Government on behalf of the Muhammadan population has not already been too long delayed; but, however, this may be, Her Majesty's Government are satisfied that, upon a fresh succession, no time should be lost in taking whatever steps may be requisite in order to place the administration upon a sound footing.[124]

Such a puerile argument had been tendered earlier when there was a lobby for the annexation of the State in the aftermath of the Queen's Proclamation of 1858. Undoubtedly, then they had done so in an attempt to recover the Vale of Kashmir which had been lost to them by Hardinge in 1846, rather than concern for the 'Muhammadan population'. The accounts given by them vividly reflected the distress to which the mass of

123. *FDP*, Secret Branch E, May 1884, nos. 354-57, Govt. of India to Secretary of State, 7 April 1884, NAI.

124. Ibid., December 1885, nos. 192-245, Secretary of State to Government of India, 23 May 1884, NAI.

peasants of Kashmir had been subjected largely as a result of the British imperialist obligations on the State.[125] Instead of placing the blame at the doorstep of British interests, the proponents of annexation used the 'native administration' as the flogging horse as is clear from the account written by an official of the Government—H.W. Bellew.[126] Then the Government was

125. See Arthur Brinckman, 'The Wrongs of Cashmere' and Robert Thorpe, 'Kashmir Misgovernment' in S.N. Gadru, ed., *Kashmir Papers* (Srinagar, 1973).

126. Bellew was one of the important members of the Embassy sent by the Government to Kashgar in 1873-74 to make a treaty of Commerce with the ruler of the short-lived kingdom of Yakub Beg in Chinese Turkistan. The observations made by him, of what he found in Kashmir while returning from Kashgar, are quoted here at some length: 'We passed several families on our way down from Sona Marg (where since our passage last year a couple of new houses had been built by the Kashmir authorities for the British Commissioner), who were delayed in their camps for want of carriage. I felt less pity for the plesure-seekers than for the unfortunate men who are pressed into their service during six months of every year, and on this occasion into ours.

Between three and four hundred European tourists roam this country during six months of every year, and as a rule none of them make any provision for their carriage. They are all dependent on the country for their means of transport within its limits. This necessitates the abstraction from their homes and fields of something like six thousand men during half the year, in order to carry their camps about from place to place; and of the amount of oppression it leads to few can have an idea.

Of the hundreds of English officers and their families who, during six months of every year, visit the Kashmir territory and enjoy the hospitality of the Maharaja, there are few, very few, who appreciate the benefits and privileges they are freely accorded within the territories of this most hospitable of Indian princes.

It is the fashion to abuse the native administration of Kashmir, and charge it with every species of oppression and corruption. Whether this is just or unjust I will not take on me to say. But this I do say, that of those who join in the outcry against the authorities of this tributary state, there are few, if any, who consider the part they themselves play in bringing about the very oppression they complain of.

I resided in the valley on duty during the season of 1869, and had ample opportunity of ascertaining the effects of our annual invasion on the country upon the people, as well as the impression our conduct in it made upon the strangers who, in pursuit of their commercial business, frequented the capital from all the outlying countries on the north, west

reluctant to intervene or even interfere in the affairs of the State because such an act stood in contravention of their paramount interests. But when the same paramount interest demanded intervention in the affairs of the State, the identical arguments which the Government of India had felt awkward about earlier[27] were used without compunction by the Secretary of State. Such a contention was clearly to be used now as a lever for the rationalization of the interference that was intended. Adoption of such a contention as an official argument at this juncture, and by so important a person, clearly reflects a conscious attempt at setting in motion the trend of using the *Muslim majority as a lever against the State.* That the Foreign Department of the Government never lost sight of the Secretary of State's remarks is evident from the long official note of the department on the

and east—men who carried away their opinion of the English man from what they had seen of him in Kashmir, and spread it as the character of the nation in the cities of Afghanistan, Turkistan, and Tibat. I observed also the benefits and privileges we enjoyed in the country. and the benefits we are satisfied that we confer upon it; and as to the last it is my positive conviction that they are outweighed by the evils attending them. It is needless here to enter into detail. It is enough to say that the roaming of hundreds of Europeans, independent of each other all over the country, necessitates a vigilant activity on the part of the authorities, and the employment of a large body of police officers, purveyors, clerks, coolie drivers, and others to look after their safety, attend to their wants, supply their carriages, procure their provisions, & C & C, in all parts of a thinly populated and wild mountainous country. How well this is done is proved by the fact that instances of insult, robbery, or assault, are never heard of.

For my own knowledge and observation, I can state that in no other part of India with which I am acquainted (and I have travelled in the three presidencies), not even in territory under our own administration, is the European so promptly and cheerfully served, and so safely protected, as he is in Kashmir, and nowhere else does he exercise the liberty of the subject to the extent that he does in that same territory.

Yet, notwithstanding these facts, there is a chronic outcry against the governors of the country, and the local English press rails at their shortcomings with a vehemence unbefitting the occasion, and altogeter forgetful of their claims upon our forbearance.' H.W. Bellew, *Kashmir and Kashgar: A Narrative of the Journey of the Embassy to Kashgar in 1873-74* (London, 1875), pp. 415-18.

127. See Ghose (1975), p. 6; Alder (1963), p. 101.

'Inauguration and Constitution of the Kashmir State Council' prepared in 1904 in connection with the official proceedings for the appointment of a successor to a deceased member of the State Council, Khan Bahadur Ghulam Ahmed Khan, who died in April 1904.[128]

1885—1889

The event of fresh succession which the Government anticipated did not take long to materialize. Maharaja Ranbir Singh died on 12 September 1885. Without losing any time, Oliver St. John, the Officer on Special Duty in Kashmir, set out to put into effect the scheme of action that had been already planned between him and the Government. Even before the mourning was over, Pratap Singh, the eldest of the three sons of the deceased Maharaja, and his heir-apparent, was informed by St. John personally about the recognition of his succession to the 'Chiefship'. Simultaneously, he was informed about the reforms that the Government desired him to introduce and about the decision of the Government to appoint a Resident in his territories. According to St. John, the message referring to the introduction of reforms was received 'without any mark of surprise' but the announcement of the immediate appointment of a Resident was evidently 'an unexpected blow'.[129]

As a logical corollary, the Maharaja was soon asked to withdraw his Vakil from the headquarters of the Government. There was no necessity for the Vakil now as the Resident was to be recognized as the accredited representative of the Government for the transaction of all political relations.[130]

The Maharaja was also informed about the Government's intention of establishing a British cantonment or more within his territories. This, he was told, was necessary to enable the Government to fulfil the obligation enshrined in the Treay; it was to protect the State from any outside aggression and

128. The note was a summary of the developments regarding the institution of the State Council—an administrative measure that was introduced in 1889 when Maharaja Pratap Singh was virtually deposed. See *FDP*, Int. A, January 1905, nos. 82-94, NAI.

129. *FDP*, Secret Branch E, December 1885, nos. 192-245, St. John to Durand, 16 September 1885, NAI.

130. Ibid., Durand to Resident, 5 October 1885.

likewise to preserve the general interest of the Indian Empire.[131]

This was not all. The question of providing all facilities to all classess of British subjects for trade in Kashmir was also taken up. These included the power to acquire premises for their business. The making of such arrangements, as was fair and proper, was left to the State. But a warning was given at the same time that if it was found by the Government that while the principle laid down by it was accepted but the actual transfer of buildings and lands was thwarted, the Government would be compelled to take measures 'which may be extremely unpalatable to the Darbar'.[132]

These demands on Pratap Singh elicited a two-fold response from him. On the occasion of his formal accession, he began by announcing a number of reforms.[133] Besides, as an edict of his general policy, he declared:

> I shall adopt such measures only as are calculated to secure to my subjects their greatest good and the fullest enjoyment of their rights and privileges, and shall conduct my administration, so that the tiller of the soil will enjoy a fair share of the produce of his labour, and manufacturer the fruit of his skill and industry; that every facility will be given to commerce by improving the means of communication and removing unnecessary and vexatious restrictions; that every encouragement will be offered to get all the resources of the country properly developed; that adequate measures will be taken to give my subjects the benefits of sound and useful education; that ample provision will be made for the relief of the sick and the suffering; and that real merit and worth in my subjects will be recognised and fostered without any distinction of race or rank, creed or color.[134]

131. Ibid., Durand to Resident, 19 October 1885.

132. *FDP*, Secret Branch E, July 1886, nos. 423-24, Memorandum of conservation between the Viceroy and the Maharaja, 15 January 1886, NAI.

133. *FDP*, Secret Branch E, December 1885, nos. 192-245, St. John to Durand, 27 September 1885, NAI.

134. Ibid., St. John to Durand, 27 September 1885, enclosure B, NAI.

So far as the other demands were concerned, he did not take them as *fait accompli*. On the contrary, he offered resistance But only one concession was made to him: that a British cantonment would not be established in his territories. He failed to get approval on the others because the Government willed otherwise.[135]

Lord Randolph Churchill, the Secretary of State for India, was even inclined to see such measures taken as would prepare for the future annexation of the State territories.[136] Besides, the Government's concern for reforms had emanated from their specific needs and it was mainly worried about the speedy construction of roads, revamping of the army and land settlement. Under these circumstances, it is not unnatural that a tussle between the successive Residents and the Maharaja should ensue. The political drama which took place till the Maharaja was finally virtually deposed in 1889 with a fixed privy purse was, so it seems to us, a natural outcome of this tussle. The whole drama was staged systematically.

To begin with the first two Residents concentrated on the Maharaja's Counsellors and what were known as his 'personal followers'. They were supposed to be hurdles in the way of introduction of reforms. This assessement was made soon after the Maharaja had begun the introduction of the suggested reforms and was duly implementing them. However, it is not difficult to understand why they were regarded as a hurdle. One of the Councillors was Babu Nilamber—a Bengali. St. John wrote about him in a letter to the Foreign Secretary to the Government as follows:

> . . . Babu Nilamber is rightly believed to be a mere theorist anxious perhaps for reforms, but ignorant how to carry them out, whose influence over the Maharaja is solely due to his ready invention of plausible pretext for resisting the supremacy of the British Government and for evading compliance with its advice.[137]

135. See Ghose (1975), pp. 26ff.

136. Ibid., p. 25.

137. *FDP*, Ext. A, June 1886, no. 90, St. John to Durand, 20 March 1836, NAI.

St. John's successor, J.C. Plowden, reported to the Government in June 1886 that 'the introduction of the Bengali element into Kashmir, and the high position which Nilamber has been permitted to occupy, has caused, and is causing, great dissatisfaction'.[138] Hence he believed that his departure was 'an essential preliminary' to the accomplishment of the policy of the Government.[139] The Foreign Secretary to the Government, H.M. Durand, expressed the same sentiments: 'The greatest obstacle to progress of any kind is the presence of so many useless and mischievous Bengalis . . . we must, I think, take some steps to put an end to the reign of Babu Nilamber.'[140]

The importance attached by the Government to the exclusion of Bengali elements from the State structure is further illustrated by the fact that later, in the note on the 'Inauguration and Constitution of the Kashmir State Council,' it was considered to have been one of the landmarks in the Council's history.[141]

All this goes to confirm that the agents of the Government were out to deprive the Maharaja of all possible props and exclude those elements from the State service who, because of historical reasons, were at that time politically the most advanced section of Indian society.

A two-pronged policy of first excluding these elements and then intimidating the Maharaja to associate with the State administration elements which were inimical to him and would derive their powers from the Resident's support was pursued by Plowden. The latter objective was achieved by forcing the Maharaja to appoint his brothers, Rajas Ram Singh and Amar Singh, as his Councillors and Dewan Lachman Das as his Prime Minister. This was followed by further alignments, the exclusion of Lachman Das, and the introduction of new elements—Pandit Bagh Ram and Pandit Suraj Kaul of the British Indian Service who were again the nominees of the Government. Some

138. *FDP*, Secret Branch E, October 1886, nos., 235-300, Plowden to Durand, 14 June 1886, NAI.

139. Ibid., Plowden to Durand, 15 August 1886.

140. Ibid., K.W. 1, Durand's note, 27 July 1886.

141. The Note was prepared in the Foreign Department in 1904. See in *FDP*, Int. A, January 1905, nos. 82-94, NAI.

letters supposed to have been written by the Maharaja, and attested to as such by his brother Amar Singh but disowned by the Maharaja, were produced so as to implicate him for having been in league with Duleep Singh, the erstwhile Sikh Maharaja of Punjab, and the Russians. This resulted in the extortion of an edict from the Maharaja by the new Resident, Col. R.P. Nisbet and his accomplices, by which he was to resign for five years and entrust his powers, subject to a few conditions, to a Council that would include, besides his two brothers, Pandit Bagh Ram, Pandit Suraj Kaul and an European. The edict was addressed to Amar Singh. The Government, however, acted unilaterally and unceremoniously divested the Maharaja of his ruling powers. It took note of the 'Maharaja's wish to retire from the control of affairs' but was cautious not to base its decision on that. The reason for this was that it was not prepared to make the settlement 'a matter of compact with the Maharaja'. The unilateral decision of the Paramount Power was conveyed to the Maharaja personally by Nisbet on 17 April 1889 as 'definite orders of the Government of India'.[142]

The Maharaja was to retain only his 'rank and dignity' and a privy purse. The 'powers of administration' were to lie with the Council. And Council had to work 'under the guidance of the Resident'

1889-1891

The State council, in its very first meeting held on 18 April declared:

> The Resident shall be the final referee in all matters and may veto any resolution passed by the Council or suspend action thereon pending further explanation.[143]

Further, it adopted a constitution for itself. According to it, and obviously subject to the above quoted resolution, the position and powers of the State Council officially were as follows:

142. See Kapur (1968), pp. 123ff; and Ghose (1975), pp. 34ff.
143. Quoted in Kapur (1968), p. 168.

> The members of the Council are appointed by the Government of India, and hold independent charge of their respective Departments subject to the general control of the Council which has power to veto or alter any orders passed by an individual member. The annual Budgets of income and expenditure and all legislative measures or schemes of general State reform, require the previous sanction of the Council.

Amar Singh's position was secure in the new arrangement; he was to be the 'executive head of the Administration'. He was to be the 'channel of communication in all important state affairs between the Council and the Resident'.[144] After keeping the situation vague for a few months, he was finally appointed President of the Council.

With this arrangement at the top and British and Eurasian officers heading the various departments below, it was virtually direct British rule that was established in place of the Maharaja's rule. It is only appropriate to refer to the administration after this as the State Administration or Residency Raj in place of the State.

While the Residency Raj set out to speed up the 'reforms' which in fact had been initiated in 1881, the Maharaja made efforts to retrieve his lost powers instead of retiring into oblivion. Within less than a month, he sent a lengthy impassioned letter to the Viceroy, Lord Landsdown, wherein he complained that he had been 'extremely misrepresented' to the Government by his enemies, in particular, Amar Singh. Amar Singh, he wrote, had been intriguing for long to destroy him. He repudiated the lettters, the authorship of which had been attributed to him, as 'most daring forgeries'. At the same time, he accused the Resident of obtaining his letter of resignation by 'a great and many-sided pressure'. He appealed to the Viceroy to give him a 'fair trial' with complete independence of action.[145]

The Maharaja received a communication from the Viceroy in which the latter justified the action of the Government.

144. Constitution of the State Council, *Administration Report of Jammu and Kashmir State, 1889-90*, pp. 4-5.

145. Ghose (1975), p. 90.

However, the communication assured him that the arrangement was not a permanent one and would be changed to associate him in the administration. This could be done only if the Maharaja could justify by his manners and dignity that he had not altogether lost the qualities of a wise ruler. This was nothing more than a suggestion to quietly endure what had been effected under the circumstances and desist from agitating.[146]

While the Maharaja was busy in making appeals, the nascent Indian Nationalist Movement came to his aid. The Indian press severely criticized the action of the Government and accused it of annexationist designs. A suggestion at this time by Sir Lepel Griffin[147] to the Government to colonize Kashmir with British settlers only confirmed the fears expressed by the press. It was not the cry of a solitary insane person. Such an idea had been coveted by the British earlier and also been expressed clearly. As already noted, the Maharaja had been asked to make arrangements for all British subjects to buy land and other immovable property in Kashmir.

Official secrets of the Government 'leaked through the waste-paper basket' and found their way to the Indian Press.[148] There was such an upsurge of feeling that the Viceroy considered contradicting what were termed as 'misrepresentations' of the Indian Press. He felt uneasy and wanted to avoid giving the impression that he intended annexation.[149]

The Maharaja's cause was also espoused by the British parliamentarians. Charles Bradlaugh, a 'free-thought' advocate and politician, pleaded his case in the House of Commons. He wanted a fair opportunity to be given to the Maharaja to defend himself.[150] Bradlaugh, who had come on a visit to India towards the end of 1889, was persuaded by Motilal Ghosh during

146. Ibid., p. 95.

147. The famous Punjab administrator; then a civil annuitant.

148. For this and the Indian press reaction in general, see *The Tribune*, 13, 16, 20, 23, 27 March, 3 April, 4, 11 May, 5, 8, 12, 19 June, 20, 24 July, 14 August 1889; *The Bengalee*, 16, 23 March, 15, 29 June, 6, 13 July; *The Indian Mirror*, 14, 21, 23 April, 1 May 1889; *The Hindoo Patriot*, 6 May, 4 June, 15, 22 July, 19, 26 August 1889.

149. Ghose (1975), p. 89.

150. Ibid., pp. 111-12.

the fifth session of the Indian National Congress to stand by the Maharaja.[151] William Digby of the Indian Political Agency addressed a letter to the House of Commons in which he criticised the action of the Government.[152]

In 1981, an administrative change was effected by the Government. The Maharaja was associated with the State Administration by appointing him as the President of the State Council. This change was probably introduced because of two reasons: The Maharaja was now considered to be amenable to the Resident's guidance; and despite his abdication the Maharaja was 'still a power in the State' and was able to some extent 'to thwart the action of the Council'. The former is explict from the conditions which were imposed when the new arrangement was made. These were:

—that Pratap Singh would become the President of the State Council, with Amar Singh as Vice-President;
—that the constitution of the Council would otherwise remain unchanged;
—that all measures of reform approved by the Council would be accepted by the Maharaja, and the latter would make no effort to change them without the consent of the Government of India;
—that all future differences of opinion between the Maharaja and the Council should be referred to the British Resident;
—that the administration would be guided in all matters by the British Resident; and
—that the Maharaja's personal expenditure should be reduced to six lakhs of rupees a year.[153]

1891-1905

The Maharaja's induction into the State Council by the Government must have helped to dispel the notion that it had

151. Par amananda Dutt, *Memoirs of Motilal Ghose* (Calcutta, 1935), pp. 68-72.
152. See William Digby, 'Condemned Unheard', in Gadru (1973).
153. Ghose (1975), p. 142.

any intention of annexing the State territories. To the Maharaja, however, it meant little more than the fact that he was the figurehead of the State Administration. That he was dispossessed of ruling powers was writ large in the existence of the State Council itself. But what was more frustrating was that he did not even have any effective voice in the State Administration. Consequently, his struggle took many directions. On the one hand, he struggled to have his ruling powers restored. On the other hand, he sought the cooperation of the members of the State Council. This implied the inclusion of those elements in the State Council who would be loyal to the Maharaja rather than to the Paramount Power. But such a contingency was generally precluded because of the very procedure for their appointment. Hence, there was a constant struggle between him, supported by his private staff and supporters, and the members of the Council. This struggle became intertwined with yet another element that was sought to be introduced into the politics of the State by the Secretary of State for India while approving the new arrangement that was intended to be put into practice by the Government at the time of the new succession. This was, as stated in the 'Inauguration and Constitution of the Kashmir State Council',[154] 'the desirability of Muhammadan interests in Kashmir being attended to'. In his struggle with the other members of the Council, the Maharaja was driven to champion the cause of his 'subjects'.

In the Maharaja's attempts to retrieve his ruling powers the first imperative was the abolition of the State Council. From a demi-official letter dated 18 March 1895, it is clear that the Maharaja sustained his efforts to have the State Council abolished. The Government's accredited representative made him understand that this could be done if he was prepared to accept the Government's nominees as his councillors and be guided by the advice of Amar Singh and the Resident.[155]

The Maharaja did not reply to this proposal, but instead

154. *FDP*, Int. A, January 1905, nos. 82-94, NAI.

155. *FDP*, Secret Branch E, July 1895, nos. 345-52, Barnes to Cunningham, 18 March 1895, NAI.

went on clamouring for the dissolution of the State Council. He speeded up efforts to attain his desired end, so at least it appeared to the Resident, on the eventuality of trouble for the Government in Chitral in the frontier region.

It was at about this time that the issue of his claim on certain forests as his private property came up. From his correspondence on the subject, it is evident that he resolutely fought a war of letters by combining the issue of forests and his ruling powers. The Government, however, responded by sending a Memorandum which strongly reprimanded him:

> It is essential that Your Highness should recognise the obligations, as distinguished from the privileges, of an hereditary ruler. Your Highness has advanced untenable claims to the exercise of unlimited powers as absolute owner of the state: and you have exercised the full powers you claim to possess in respect to some of the forests. The ruin Your Highness has permitted to be wrought in these particular forests must be regarded as an index of your fitness for exercising unrestricted authority. Your Highness does not appear to have learnt that power entails responsibility. It would be impossible to countenance your dealing with the Kashmir State, with all its wealth and resources as a toy which your birthright entitles you to break or spoil as you choose.
>
> Should your Highness, in spite of all warnings, continue to show that your chief care is to fill your own pockets regardless of the interests of the State, it will be my duty to report that neither the words of warning of the Government of India, nor a knowledge of the Secretary of State's wishes and opinion have any weight on Your Highness with whom only efficient measures of restraint can have any effect.[156]

The Maharaja raised the question of investment of 'full powers' in him in an interview on 25 April 1902 at Peshawar with the Viceroy, Lord Curzon. This time he exhibited his willingness to have Amar Singh as his Prime Minister. He also

156. *FDP*, Secret Branch E, February 1898, no. 183-286, NAI.

undertook to support the reforms that had been introduced and to refer to the Resident all matters of grave importance for advice where a difference of opinion arose between him and the Prime Minister whose advice and suggestions in all measures of importance was to be duly respected and attended to. The Viceroy in turn promised the Maharaja that the matter would be considered sympathetically but was categorical in making it known to him that 'no change could be considered which would affect the power of control and supervision then exercised by the Resident'.[157]

In the spring of 1903, a Memorandum was submitted in which an 'essential condition' laid down by the Viceroy had been 'disregarded'. Hence, the Government directed the Resident that the Maharaja was to be told that the Government was not prepared to pursue the matter further.[158]

The Maharaja was, however, much more amenable to the essential condition of 'maintenance of the *status quo* between the Darbar and the Resident' when the acting Viceroy, Lord Ampthill, visited Kashmir in November 1904 and the Maharaja had two interviews with him. Ampthill undertook to represent the case to Curzon.[159]

It was only then, as could be expected, that the Government initiated the process of the reversal of the arrangement made in 1889. It addressed the Resident in December 1904 to review the whole situation and asked for his final opinion. He reported to the Government that the change was both 'desirable and practicable'.[160] Consequently, after the sanction of the Secretary of State was secured, the Government issued a press communique on 8 August 1905 wherein it undertook to entrust to the Maharaja in 'large measure administrative responsibilities than he at present possesses. Under the new arrangements the existing State Council will be abolished, and its administrative powers will be transferred to His Highness'. It further stated

157. *FDP*, Secret Branch I, May 1905, nos. 19-20, Resident's Confidential Note on Jammu and Kashmir Affairs, 1901-5, NAI.

158. Ibid.

159. Ibid.

160. Ibid.

that the Viceroy 'may possibly visit Kashmir later on in the year, in order to confer the additional powers on the Maharaja in person'.[161]

At the time of the introduction of the State Council, as has been seen, the Maharaja's Councillors—Amar Singh, Ram Singh, Suraj Kaul and Bagh Ram—were all nominees of the Government. One more addition to this was made. Khan Bahadur Ghulam Mohy-ud-Din Khan, as a matter of deliberate policy, was included not only as a person loyal like the others but as a Muslim. It was inherent in the method of the appointment of the members and the constitution of the State Council that there would be no cooperation on their part with the Maharaja after he was inducted as its President.

Khan died in 1892. With this there arose the question of appointing a new member in his place. The Resident discussed this with the Maharaja who asked for Sardar Mohammed Hyat Khan. After his appointment as a member of the State Council contrary to what was expected of him as a Muslim, he cooperated with the Maharaja and consequently lost the goodwill of Amar Singh who intrigued against him. This resulted in the Government recalling him.

The Government did not appoint another Muslim member to succeed him. Suraj Kaul also left in 1896. No new member was appointed till 1899 when Ram Singh died. Meanwhile, the Maharaja's relations with Amar Singh continued to be strained, and he even made efforts to have Bagh Ram ousted.

At Ram Singh's death in 1899, the question of the appointment of a new member in the Councll arose. From the proceedings of the Foreign Department available and its correspondence with the Resident in Kashmir at that time, it becomes clear that the Government set out to enforce a three-dimensional policy *vis-a-vis* the State Administration. This policy was the re-introduction of a Muslim into the State Council; limiting the tenure of its members to only five years; and help to the natives of the State to be employed as subordinate officials of the various departments of the State Administration that were headed by Englishmen. With reference to the last, the Viceroy

161. *FDP*, Secret Branch I, August 1905, nos. 35-37, NAI.

wanted A. Talbot, the British Resident in the State, to be informed that

> it should be the duty of the various Englishmen, who are in positions of responsibility in the service of the Kashmir State, to endeavour to train up as subordinate officials of their various Departments the natives of the State, who in many cases possess great aptitudes for such employment, instead of bringing in men exclusively from the outside, whether these be Englishmen, or natives of the Punjab. Our duty in Kashmir is not merely administration, but political and administrative education; and our officials there will be judged by the Government of India not merely by their individual work or abilities, but by the permanent impress that they leave upon the native character and upon the internal development of the State. He should be instructed to bear these views in mind and to communicate them to the principal British officials in question.[162]

That the Government could not have taken recourse to the formulation and pursuit of the above stated policy without any pressures or motives related to certain desired goals or ends is a safe assumption though there is very little conclusive evidence to establish what these pressures or motives were due to. It seems that the policy was dictated by a desire to deny the Maharaja an opportunity of using a newly found ground in his manoeuvres against the Government and its nominees in the State Council. Maharaja Pratap Singh had taken to projecting himself as the champion of the interests of his 'subjects' and had espoused their cause. This and other connected postures adopted by him, believed Talbot, were chiefly under the guidance of Dr. Suraj Bal—'who is about the worst of the lot as being the best educated'.[163] The Maharaja pleaded on behalf of the natives of Kashmir and the Dogras for their appointment to official posts, which, he said, were held by 'aliens'.[164] Probably

162. *FDP*, Secret Branch E, March 1900, nos. 127-75, NAI.

163. *FDP*, Secret Branch E, February 1898, nos. 183-286, Talbot to Cunningham, 9 June 1897, NAI.

164. Maharaja pleaded that '. . .higher officials have filled all

more crucial than this was his role with regard to the mass demonstrations of the petitioners at Srinagar on 29 and 30 July 1897. The petitioners were seeking redressal of the wrongs faced by them in connection with 'the question of rice & c'. The episode, whether a natural development, as claimed by the Maharaja, or the result of an intrigue by him as believed by his opponents, clearly revealed the capacity and willingness of the Maharaja to use the mass discontent in his struggle against his adversaries.[165] While the Maharaja involved himself in these issues, the Government, in response to the other moves of the Maharaja—his claims over certain forests and his ruling rights and the strong action suggested thereupon against him by the then Resident—showed its unwillingness to have a show-down between the Maharaja and the Resident. In a demi-official letter to the Resident, the Secretary to the Government in the Foreign Department gave clear expression to the fact that the Government was constrained in its dealing with the Maharaja by 'the political affairs in respect to Native States generally'. He recalled the instructions of the Viceroy sent to the Resident on 28 September 1896 in which he was asked 'to avoid risk of a breakdown in the present arrangement whereby the Maharaja retains his personal dignity of head of the State while the Resident has the real power'. The Secretary wrote that the Government could not afford to deal with the Maharaja in a way that would make his position unbearable and push him to create a 'crisis'.[166] Thus, it is clear that the Government had to

appointments with their own relatives and friends, and whenever I recommend any one for appointment, I am told he is not properly qualified for it. Thus instead of what was intended, for instance in cancelling the contract for State customs and bringing them under direct State management, i.e, to give employment to Kashmir natives, all official posts are held by aliens. The Jammu district is worked by Jullunder people, and the Kashmir district by Sagris, while Amar Nath has his own clique. The Dogras get no share in appointments'. Ibid., McMohan to Talbot, 8 July 1897.

165. Ibid., Resident to Foreign Secretary, telegram, 30 June 1897 Talbot to Cunningham, 1 July 1897, Manners-Smith to Talbot, 1 July 1897, McMahon to Talbot, 8 July 1897.

166. Ibid., Cunningham to Talbot, 3 July 1897.

evolve much subtler ways of dealing with him. It was inevitable that the Government should take recourse to finding ways and means to prevent the Maharaja from emerging as the advocate of the people's cause—an eventuality that was imminent and likely.

A few other developments pertinent to the case in point occurred around this period. The *Pioneer*, a spokesman for official British opinion, reported in the 10 September 1897 issue that a 'mullah' had been caught for preaching against the British and Hindu government in Kashmir and had been turned out of the State. The Maharaja, who was then at Jammu, showed concern that he had not been informed about it from any quarter and asked Amar Singh telegraphically to note as follows:

> . . . sedition and scheming and intrigue have become fashion in Kashmir and therefore it is necessary that a keen watch be kept by the authorities to turn out of my state those who may be found spreading disaffection against the British Govt. by preaching in public or otherwise religious fanaticism and circulation of seditious writing calculated to make mind of the audience feel enmity towards hatred against the British Govt. can under no circumstances persons guilty of such offences should be dealt with very severity . . . .[167]

The first effort to impart modern education themselves to 'Muslims' by a section of the Muslim elite was made in 1899.[168] And in the same year an enquiry was made by the British Resident as to the subjects of the State who had attended the fourteenth and fifteenth sessions of the Indian National Congress.[169]

Whether these particular incidents had a bearing on the policy that was adopted by the Government in 1899 is difficult to establish. However, what seems clear is that around this time some kind of ferment was brewing in Kashmir. Under such circumstances, there was a possibility that the Maharaja would present himself as the protector of the different interests of

167. *Old English Records* (hereafter *OER*), 1897, File No. (F.N.) 39, Jammu and Kashmir State Archives, Jammu (hereafter JKA).

168. The popular response to education will be considered in ch. 5.

169. *OER*, 1899, F.N. 122/P-5, JKA.

his 'subjects'. Hence, it was in the interest of the Government to pre-empt such a situation from developing and it is apparent that the new policy formed a means to that end : Preferential treatment by Englishmen of the native claimants for employment as subordinate officials; and the appointment of a Muslim on the Council, who projected himself as a defender of 'Muslim interests', could take the wind out of the Maharaja's sails. The former would mitigate the chances of the growth of anti-British sentiments amongst those aspiring for jobs in the State services and the latter by directing, what had now become a continual phenomenon with the bourgeoning of the food distribution system in urban centres,[170] the mass distress at Srinagar into channels least harmful for the British.

1905-1921

In 1905, the Government enacted, and it was publicly impressed by Lord Curzon in a Durbar held for the purpose at Jammu, the 'enhancement or restitution of powers' of the Maharaja. The State Council was dissolved and the power hitherto enjoyed by it was transferred to the Maharaja under 'proper guarantees'. He was to be assisted in the discharge of his 'duties' by his brother (Raja Sir) Amar Singh, who had already occupied so prominent a position in the administration, as his 'chief minister and righthand man'. Further, the role of the British Resident was emphasised and defined thus : 'In all important matters you [Maharaja] will be able to reply [*sic*] upon the counsel and support of the British Resident . . . .'[171]

What was done was not even the formal investiture of the position and power that the Maharaja had held before the appointment of the first Resident or even before the State Council was instituted. It was a mere 'administrative change'

170. As a concomitant of land settlement measures introduced under the Residency Raj, the age-old food distribution system by the Government was abandoned and there was restlessness as a consequence. Some demonstrations against lent officials took place and the Maharaja was said to have instigated these. See *FDP*, Secret Branch E, February 1898, nos., 183-286, Talbot to Cunningham, 20 July 1897, NAI.

171. *His Highness' Private Records*, 1905, F.N. 6, Lord Curzon's speech at Jammu on 26 October 1905, JKA.

aptly defined so by Curzon himself.[172] The 'conditions' on which the Maharaja was to assume the powers of the State Council make it evident that this was so.[173]

The new arrangement did not entitle the Maharaja to 'rule' even in a circumscribed manner. It only entailed an enhancement in his 'prestige' by an improvement in his position in the State administrative structure. This seems to have been only a corollary to the policy pursued by Curzon towards the Princes. It was tantamount to 'exalt rather than to minimize' the 'role' of the Princes in the 'Indian system'.[174] In other words, '. . . he removed, without weakening paramountcy, unnecessary trammels on their administration'.[175] In his speech at Jammu, while inaugurating the new arrangement, sentiments expressive of such an intent were repeated.

After the new arrangement or 'regime'—as defined by the Maharaja soon in a letter to the Resident—was formally inaugurated by the Viceroy, the Maharaja, whether labouring under a misconception about its real nature and content or as a deliberate move to use the opportunity created by the new circumstances, set out to initiate such measures as would retrieve his ruling powers and restore the State to its initial status. On 6 November, he argued, in a letter to the Resident for the use of the designation of Prime Minister for his Chief Minister, and in doing so he sought support from precedent—the practice that was in vogue during the reigns of his father and grandfather.[176] As is evident from the practice that was followed subsequently, this was not allowed.

172. *OER*, 1905, F.N. 90, Curzon to Maharaja, Confidential, 30 August 1905, JKA.

173. The conditions were such as retained for the Government of India complete control over the finances of the State, the armed forces, taxation, *jagir* grants, appointments to administrative services and the foreign relations. The powers of general supervision and control that the Resident had come to acquire were left with him intact. For the conditions in detail see ibid., Confidential Note on the new arrangements for the administration of the Jammu and Kashmir State, Resident to Maharaja, Confidential, 31 October 1905.

174. Gopal (1975), p. 255.

175. Ibid., p. 252.

176. *OER*, 1905, F.N. 90, Maharaja to Resident, Confidential, 6 November 1905, JKA.

By October 1906, the Maharaja was still insisting that he wanted

> a Chief Minister upon whom I can place absolute confidence, who could work in harmony with the spirit with which I am determined to rule over, and to promote the welfare of my subjects, and who would be possessed of the capacity to carry into execution the ideas I have as to the manner in which the administration of the State should be carried out. It is only then that I will feel that the enhanced powers which the Government have been pleased to confer on me have been really allowed to have their effect.[177]

That was not all. The Maharaja had already begun to rely upon his private secretary, Daya Kishen Kaul, rather than upon Amar Singh, in the conduct of the State administration. On this, the Resident remarked

> . . .the Chief Minister in this State, under present conditions, exercises very little authority. All business is in theory submitted through him to the Maharaja, but in practice he has very little power.[178]

He further remarked: 'It came to this, therefore, that Kashmir was being ruled by the Maharaja's Private Secretary, and the Chief Minister was a non-entity'.[179] The fact, however, is that the Maharaja was only utilizing the services of Kaul, about whom the same Resident wrote at another place: 'He is decidedly anti-European in his tendency and might conceivably do us a [good] deal of harm'.[180]

The Government did not oblige the Maharaja in his attempts to replace Amar Singh by some other person as Chief Minister. But this did not deter the Maharaja from continuing his struggle against Amar Singh. In 1908, he even came out with the suggestion that a European be appointed as the Chief Minister

177. *FDP*, Secret Branch I, February 1907, no. 9, Confidential Note 29 October 1906, NAI.

178. Ibid., no. 12, Younghusband to Secretary, 24 August 1906.

179. Ibid.

180. *FDP*, Deposit—I, October 1908, no. 24, Resident to Secretary, 14 July 1908, NAI.

which the Government refused to accept.[181] Thereafter, whether as a last bid or in helplessness, he pleaded that if 'he [Amar Singh] is considered indispensable for the State', then the Government may 'declare him straightway the ruler of the State in place of me and order me to clear out'.[182] In reply, the Resident informed the Maharaja that the Viceroy desired him to leave the Chief Minister 'free, as the Emperor leaves the Prime Minister of England free to perform all the minor duties of a Chief Minister, while Your Highness performs all the larger and the more important functions of a Ruler'.[183]

The same fate met the Maharaja in what seems to have been his effort to have his adopted son approved as his heir-apparent by the Government. He had a son in November 1904 but the baby survived only for a few months. In 1906, he adopted a son of his second cousin on the paternal side, Raja Baldev Singh—the State feudatory in Poonch. Lord Minto, the Viceroy, who visited Kashmir in October-November 1906, approved the adoption for private and religious purposes only. The claim for succession, the Maharaja was informed in January 1907, was reserved for Amar Singh and his son, Mian Hari Singh.[184]

Nor was the Maharaja permitted to effect such measures as would provide him with the instruments to retrieve the economic power of the State or to reinforce his 'hegemony' over his subjects. The reaction of the Government to the Maharaja's attempt to assert the economic power of the State is visible from the Government's response to the 'Jammu and Kashmir State Companies' Regulation, 1906', that the Durbar had prepared and sent for the approval of the Government. Commenting on the draft, the Resident, Sir Francis Younghusband, remarked that, while the proposed Act incorporated provisions from the British Indian Act and from the English Law of 1900, it contained certain new provisions which 'considerably limit the power and independence of Directors—as Managers of

181. Cited in Hassnain (1974), p. 92.

182. *His Highness' Private Records*, 1908, F.N. 13, Pratap to Younghusband, 8 July 1908, JKA.

183. Ibid., Younghusband to Pratap, 11 July 1908.

184. See *FDP*, Secret Branch I, February 1907, nos. 1-11, NAI; ibid., April 1907, nos. 55-56; *FDP*, August 1907, nos. 89-95; and *Minto Papers* (microfilm), Younghusband to Dunlop Smith, 19 May 1907, NAI.

Companies—and entail a corresponding increase in the responsibility of the Darbar'.[185] He did not as yet doubt the intentions of the Darbar. What perturbed him was that

> in seeking to guard the State and people from certain dangers the Darbar may have run to the opposite extreme and made the Regulation of Companies so stringent that Foreign investors may be thereby discouraged from placing their money in Kashmir industrial enterprises.[186]

What worried him and the Foreign Department personnel was that the proposed Act would prohibit and restrict British industrial enterprise and exploitation in Kashmir and other territories of the State.

The Government did not approve of the draft and asked for the application of the British Indian Act (The Indian Companies' Act, 1882) *mutatis mutandis* with the exception of the omission of certain sections thereof. While forwarding a revised draft by the Darbar to the Government, Younghusband pleaded:

> The point then for the consideration of the Government of India is, whether the Darbar should be allowed to retain the means of obstructing the development of the country and the growth of British industrial enterprise. In my opinion it should not. Two years' experience of the working of the Darbar has shown me that by dilatoriness and procrastination and by direct opposition on the part of officials, most of whom are not Kashmir subjects at all, British enterprise is constantly, incessantly, and needlessly thwarted. The progress of the country is arrested and British subjects who might reasonably expect to obtain a living in Kashmir find it impossible to do business here. I hope then I may be authorized to inform the Darbar that the British Government . . .cannot therefore permit the Darbar to place British subjects trading in Kashmir under restrictions which are

185. *FDP*, Int. A. April 1909, nos. 37-46 Younghusband to Secretary, 31 August 1906, NAI.

186. Ibid.

not imposed upon Kashmir subjects doing business in India.[187]

The rection against the Maharaja's attempt to assert his hegemony over his subjects is visible from the note of the Resident on the 'scheme' for imparting education to the masses that was submitted to him after it had been formulated by the Committee appointed for the purpose by the Maharaja vide his Order number 256 dated 28/31 October 1907.[188] He remarked:

> Every one of the suggestions which they have made is not only sound but urgent. The better inspections of schools is a pressing need. The provisions of better and therefore more highly paid teachers is if anything more pressing. Not a day ought to be lost in giving better school accommodation. Kindergarten teaching is of the greatest value. Technical instruction is urgently required. At least a hundred more primary schools are an acknowledged necessity. And to give consistency and cohesion to the whole, to unify efforts, to keep all tending steadily in one direction, and to prevent the dissipation of energy and money, a Director of Education should be engaged forthwith. There is not one measure which the Conference has considered which the Durbar ought not to adopt immediately, *if funds were available.*[189]

Amar Singh was taken ill in January 1909. The Government arranged 'the best medical attendant' for his treatment. S.H. Butler, the Secretary to the Government of India in the Foreign Department, believed that in 'the present political situation in Kashmir it is of first rate importance that Amar Singh's life should be saved if possible'.[190] The efforts to save Amar Singh were unsuccessful and he died on 25 March 1909. The next day,

187. Ibid., Younghusband to Secretary, 16 June 1908.

188. *OER*, 1907, F.N. 101/P-102, JKA.

189. Ibid., Resident's Note, 22 February 1908. Emphasis in the original.

190. *FDP*, Int. B, April 1909, nos. 46-49, Butler to Duke, 17 March 1909, NAI.

in his communication to Butler, Francis Younghusband lamented his death and remarked: 'He will be an immense loss to the State for he was a business-like man and he was always well-inclined towards the British.'[191]

However, Amar Singh had already passed on what he believed to be his 'last message' to Younghusband. This was to put his son, Mian Hari Singh, in his guardianship as he did not think anyone else fit for the job. Further, Younghusband was desired to 'impress upon the Mian Sahib that he was to be loyal to the British Govt., loyal to the Maharaja, loyal to his servants and loyal to his country'.[192]

Even after Amar Singh's death, there was no basic shift in the policy of the Government towards the Maharaja. They had 'declined' to sanction any change in the post of Chief Minister during Amar Singh's lifetime because, as Amar Singh told Younghusband at the time he received the last message from him, he had worked 'conscientiously' and with 'thorough loyalty to the British Government'.[193] After his death, Younghusband lost no time and imformed the Maharaja that the Government had come to the 'conclusion' that 'Daya Kishen Kaul should not be appointed Minister here at present'. The Maharaja, whether humbled by now or sensing the mood of the Government, showed his full disinclination to have Kaul.[194] A few days later the Maharaja proposed the name of Dewan Amar Nath for the appointment to the post of Chief Minister. Younghusand recommended Amar Nath to the Secretary to the Government of India in the Foreign Department and opined: 'I think he will do his best to assist the Residency, although he too was at one time reported to me from the Punjab as possessing anti-European inclinations.'[195]

A survey of the records makes it clear that the hallmark of the criteria for the appointment of a minister was loyalty to the

191. Ibid., Younghusband to Butler, 26 March 1909.

192. *FDP*, Secret Branch, Int., March 1909, nos. 16-19, Younghusband to Secretary, 26 Februry 1909, NAI.

193. Ibid.

194. *FDP*, Secret Branch, Int., July 1909, nos. 6-7, Younghusband to Butler, 6 June 1909, NAI.

195. Ibid., Younghusband to Secretary, 14 June 1909.

Government. And this was maintained by appointing trusted men and, as aptly put in the case of one Rai Bahadur Diwan Bishandas by the then Resident, S.M. Fraser, making them 'still feel that there is a bit in his mouth and that he must still work for the good opinion of the Government of India'.[196] This was achieved by making the appointment for a short period of one or two years and if their behaviour was found to be satisfactory of renewing it. The letters to the Government of Raja Sir Daljit Singh, who held the post of Chief Minister for about four years, throw ample light on how the new 'regime' ushered in 1905 worked upto 1921.[197]

It has been mentioned earlier that the State had assumed importance for the British Imperial system in India because of its specific geographical location, apart from other reasons, and this had led to the Government's intervention. One of the manifestations of this was the reorganization of the State army and extension of control over it.

Colonel Neville Chamberlain, an officer of the British

196. *FDP*, Pol. D, Est—B, February 1916, nos., 69-70, Fraser to Wood, Confidential, 19 January 1916, NAI.

197. These were made by him while commenting on the way his tenure came to an end. Apparently not being convinced that the Maharaja wanted him to go and not the Government, he observed: 'As regards the so called wish of His Highness for this change who knows better than yourself how such wishes are created, how they vanish, and how similar wishes have invariably been treated? While discussing the question of His Highness' full powers last year, it was with a view to keep a check on such wishes that you proposed certain conditions to be undertaken by His Highness. I cannot help saying that in this particular instance this wish of His Highness, if it was in reality genuine, received extraordinarily prompt compliance. The past experience is somewhat different from this. In the matter of removing or re-employing even second or third class officials, His Highness' wishes were respected in a way well known to yourself.' *FDP*, 1922, File No. 121A, Daljit Singh to Sir John, 8 June 1921, NAI.

Subsequently, in response to a communication from the Government, he wrote: 'I may also point out that the period during which I held the office of the Chief Minister, according to the constitution, H.H. was not the sole judge of my work. On the other hand it was the Resident who was the final authority in all important matters.' Ibid., Daljit Singh to Sir John, 9 January 1922.

Indian Army, was appointed as Military Secretary to the State. Under him the State forces were thoroughly reorganized. One specific feature of the reorganization scheme was that a section of it was separately organized as the War Service Troops or Imperial Defence Troops. These were placed at 'the disposal of the Imperial Government' and came to form a part of what was known as Imperial Service Troops. Thereafter, these were stationed at the frontier post of Gilgit and employed there.[198]

During the earlier phase of the State Council, the command of the army was placed under Raja Ram Singh with Chamberlain as Military Secretary. Later, the appointment of a British Military Secretary was done away with and in his place Colonel Bishen Das was appointed. After Ram Singh's death in 1899, the command was placed under Amar Singh and he continued to have it till his death.

With Amar Singh's death, the question of appointing a successor to him as Commander-in-Chief also came up. The Secretary to the Government in the Foreign Department asked Younghusband:

> In view of the peculiar position of Kashmir politics you will no doubt let me know unofficially, for His Excellency's information, any proposal as to the appointment of Chief Minister and Commander-in-Chief before you commit yourself in any way.[199]

In reply Younghusband informed Butler that the Maharaja was inclined to appoint Mian Sahib as Commander-in-Chief, and so long as the Mian remained a minor the Maharaja would attend to the job himself.[200] While this was still under discussion, the Maharaja informed the Resident about the appointment of Mian Sahib Hari Singh as Commander-in-Chief.

198. *Administration Report of Jammu and Kashmir State, 1889-90*, Military Department, Report submitted by Colonel Neville Chamberlain, Military Secretary, for the first year of the State Council Administration, JKA.

199. *FDP*, Secret Branch, Int., September 1909, nos. 30-31, Butler to Younghusband, 16/19 April 1909, NAI.

200 Ibid., Younghusband to Butler, 23 April 1909.

Further, he specified that so long as the Mian was 'unable' to carry on the duty, he himself would attend to it, and Colonel Bishen Das, who had worked as Commender-in-Chief's Military Secretary during the tenure of Raja Ram Singh and after him Amar Singh, would continue in his job. Lastly, as the Resident had been informed previously, Major Rose—Inspecting Officer, Kashmir Imperial Service Infantry—would be consulted and his advice sought in important matters.[201]

The intention and then the proposal to appoint Hari Singh to the post was received well both by the Resident and the Government. This was solely on account of imperial considerations and not for any of the services rendered by Amar Singh. The Resident believed that the

> appointment of the Mian Sahib to the nominal command is highly desirable both for the sake of the Army and on political grounds. The Army are very anxious for it, and politically it is desirable as a sign that the Maharaja had become reconciled with his brother.[202]

F.H.R. Drummond, Inspector General Imperial Service Troops, who was sounded, agreed with Younghusband; in his opinion the 'appointment of the Mian Sahib would be popular with the Kashmir Army and that it is desirable from a political point of view'.[203] Both Butler and Lord Minto, the Viceroy, concurred with Younghusband and Drummond and finally Butler conveyed their concurrence to Younghusband.[204]

However, the arrangement that the Maharaja had proposed—that he look after the Army during Mian's minority—was not accepted. There was complete unanimity amongst all those concerned that the Maharaja was not to be permitted to control the Army. The Resident wrote in his first communication that he sent to Bulter in reply to his query: 'It will not do to let the Maharaja have too much say . . . .'[205] Opinions to the same

201. Ibid., Maharaja to Younghusband, 18 June 1909.
202. Ibid., Younghusband to Butler, 23 April 1909.
203. Ibid., Drummond to Butler, 28 April 1909.
204. Ibid., Butler to Younghusband, 12 May 1909.
205. Ibid., Younghusband to Butler, 23 April 1909.

effect were either expressed or supported by others before and after the Maharaja's proposal was received. The sole reason, it comes out clearly from their arguments, was their distrust of the Maharaja.

The policy of the Government was expressed succinctly by Butler: 'It is most important to secure proper control of the Kashmir Army, which holds an important section of our frontier.'[206] But at the same time a semblance of the command to rest in the State was also to be maintained; for that was the general policy of the Government *vis-a-vis* all Native States.[207] The two objectives were combined by approving the appointment of Mian to the post of Commander-in-Chief and by devising an arrangement to control the military affairs during his minority. A Council of three members was to be appointed for the purpose. It was to be assisted by advice from a British military expert in his capacity as Military Secretary to the Council and his 'duties' were clearly defined. While conveying this decision of the Government the Resident was asked to impress upon the Maharaja that this scheme was devised to keep the 'efficiency' of the army 'unimpaired' as the Maharaja could not be expected to devote time to that.[208]

1921-1931

On 5 March 1921, prior to which he had already given a confidential undertaking that firstly the 'advice of the Resident will be accepted whenever offered in State matters' and secondly that the 'Resident will be informed of any important changes to be made in the existing rules and regulations and the laws of

206. Ibid., Butler's Official note, 10 August 1909.

207. Minto, while rebutting the suggestion of Kitchener, the Commander-in-Chief of the British Indian Army, to replace Amar Singh by a British Officer, remarked: '. . .the proposal that such an officer should *control* the Maharaja's forces, which practically means should command them, appears to me contrary to the accepted principle that such forces should be under the command of the State concerned.' Ibid., Official note, 19 May 1909.

208. Ibid., Secretary to Younghusband, 8 September 1909.

the State, and in regard to Frontier matters',[209] the Maharaja received an intimation from the Viceroy about his decision to remove the restrictions placed by Curzon in 1905 in the way of the Maharaja enjoying 'full powers of administration'.[210] The Viceroy conferred publicly upon the Maharaja 'full powers of administration' and the authority which his 'ancestors enjoyed'.[211] The Viceroy, obviously as a gesture to woo the Princes, declared that in taking recourse to it he had 'followed the traditional policy of His Majesty's Government which is, to use the words of my distinguished predecessor, Lord Curzon, "to safegurd the prestige and the authority of the rulers" of the Indian states'.[212] These were not empty words but a reflection, and a true one, of the policy.

The Viceroy, after flattering Pratap Singh that 'it has been your Highness' constant endeavour to secure the happiness and contentment of your people', contemplated:

> It may be that in pursuit of this endeavour, and a consequence with the spirit of the time, you may decide to place your system of Government upon a broader basis, with a view to associating your subjects, both Hindu and Mohammedan, more closely with the administration'.[213]

Nor was the role of the representative of the Paramount Power, the Resident, ignored. Rather, it was better defined than had been done by Curzon in 1905. The Maharaja was told that should he 'elect' to do what was contemplated by the Viceroy, he would find in his Agent, Colonel Windham, as in the case of his predecessor, a 'sincere friend' on whose judgement the Maharaja 'may safely rely'. Further, the Viceroy stated that he was confident that 'in all matters of difficulty, and particularly in regard to frontier affairs and important changes in administration, you [Maharaja] will avail yourself freely of his advice'.[214]

209. *OER*, 1920, F.N. 104, Maharaja to Resident, 7 January 1921, JKA.

210. Ibid., Chelmsford to Maharaja, 30 August 1905.

211. Ibid., Chelmsford's speech at Jammu on 5 March 1921.

212. Ibid.

213. Ibid.

214. Ibid.

The Maharaja in return declared that the Government's decision was 'a practical vindication of the solicitude of the Government to faithfully carry out the behest of its august sovereign to keep inviolate and inviolable, the solemn pledges embodied in the treaties and engagements made with the princes of India'.[215]

With regard to the question of giving his government a broader base, he showed the realization that

> the affairs of this world are in a constant course of transition and that policies of State must also be moulded according to the proper requirements of the times. . . . The trend of events in the territories under the direct control of the British Government must necessarily affect a change in the angle of vision of the peoples inhabiting the Indian States. As Ruler of the Jammu and Kashmir State, I welcome the change.
>
> I hope to be able to make an announcement shortly in this connection; and, I am sure, the measures taken will, in their practical application, be fruitful in promoting the public good and in affording better opportunities for the association of my subjects in the government of the State.[216]

Within two months of the Maharaja's pronouncement to associate his 'subjects' with the government, a full-fledged draft of the proposed 'Reform Scheme'—The Sri Pratap Reforms Regulation 1978—was prepared and sent to the Resident for his approval. It envisaged the establishment of an Executive Council, Representative Assembly and High Court of Judicature.[217] After the draft had received the Resident's full consideration and that of the Government, and after the alterations thus suggested had been incorporated in it, he conveyed the Government's approval of the Reform Scheme to the Maharaja by the middle of September.[218] The Government's approval

215. Ibid., Maharaja's address delivered in response to that of the Viceroy.

216. Ibid.

217. *FDP*, Secret Branch, Int., November 1921, nos. 34-43, First draft of the 'Reform Scheme', NAI.

218. Ibid., Thompson to Resident, 3 September 1921; *OER*, 1921, F.N. 239/10, Resident to Maharaja, September 1921, JKA.

thus received was for the scheme minus the provisions for Representative Assembly—that part of the draft which pertained to the institution of a Representative Assembly had been held back by the Resident.[219]

The Maharaja, however, showed great enthusiasm for the institution of a representative assemly and official orders to that effect were issued by him.[220] This was not all. A public pronouncement regarding it was also issued at Srinagar on 11 October 1921.[221] He wanted to have it instituted along with the appointment of the Executive Council. But the Resident was keen only about the immediate appointment of the Executive Council. This is not surprising. The appointment of an Executive Council was essential to accord a predominant position to Hari Singh in the administration. That this was the intention of the Government is borne out by the correspondence that ensued between the Resident and the Government after the Maharaja had sent in the draft of the Reform Scheme. The Resident concluded his lengthy comments in his demi-official communication on the position of Hari Singh in it. According to him, the scheme had one 'radical fault', that it 'ignores the outstanding feature of the position and the end in view'.[222] Hence, he had conveyed to the Maharaja the alteration in the provisions concerned. Wood approved because this was essential 'in order to safeguard the position of Raja Hari Singh'.[223]

The Government had all along looked at Hari Singh as the 'probable heir' to the Maharaja and had a 'particular interest' in his 'proper training'. Hence, care was always taken that he had a suitable person as his tutor. Such was the case both during

219. *FDP*, Secret Branch, Int., November 1921, nos. 34-43, Windham to Wood, 10 June 1921, NAI.

220. *OER*, 1921, F.N. 239/10, Maharaja's Order to Chief Secretary, Srinagar, n.d., (connected papers and the contents of Order suggest that it must have been issued in October or November 1921); and Maharaja's Order to Raja Hari Singh, Senior Member of the Jammu and Kashmir State Council, 30 January/6 February 1922, JKA.

221. Ibid., Maharaja's Order to Hari Singh, 30 January/6 February 1922.

222. *FDP*, Secret Branch, Int., November 1921, nos. 34-43, Windham to Wood, 6 May 1921, NAI.

223. Ibid., Wood to Windham, 12 May 1921.

his stay at home and later when he was at Mayo College, Ajmer, and at the Imperial Cadet Corps, Dehra Dun. The one essential qualification for those who were entrusted with the job was their capacity to groom the boy to develop loyalty towards the British. That such was the case is evident from what one Resident, H.V. Cobb, had to say to Wood about Major Barr who had been Hari Singh's tutor for four consecutive years—and had been given an extension of three more years but was called to the front after the outbreak of the First World War. Cobb considered it a 'misfortune' to lose his services and wrote:

> Barr is neither a qualified educationist nor a brilliant scholar or administrator. On the other hand, he has the knack of winning not only the respect but the genuine affection of young Indians of whom he is in charge. And this asset will, I venture to submit, be of the highest value to us hereafter when Hari Singh becomes Ruler of Kashmir. Already, as I have seen for myself, Hari Singh, as the result of Barr's friendship and influence, likes and trusts British officers and looks to us for help and support. If this attitude of mind continues and grows stronger, it will mean much for Kashmir in years to come.[224]

Born in September 1895, Hari Singh was appointed in 1909, as successor to his father, to the post of Commander-in-Chief of the State forces with the local rank of General. In 1918, he was made K.C.I.E. for services rendered in connection with the war and in the same year was gazetted by the War Office with the honorary rank of Captain. In 1921, at the time of conferring full powers of administration upon the Maharaja, the Government initiated a process of providing him with a berth in it. And on 24 January 1922, i.e., less than a year from the day of initiating the process, he was appointed to the ceremonial position of the 'Senior Member' of the proposed Executive Council[225] which was inaugurated formally by the Maharaja

224. *FDP*, Est.-B, July 1915, nos. 150-75, Cobb to Wood, 13 January 1915, NAI.

225. *OER*, 1921, F.N. 239/10, Order No. 104-C, 24 January 1922, JKA.

on 28 January.[226] The Maharaja, who had placed himself as the President of the Council, under pressure from the Resident, issued an order on 23 January 1924 by which he virtually gave away the exercise of full powers of the State to Hari Singh. Pratap Singh ordered: 'I shall not in future ordinarily attend the meetings of Council.'[227] It was not long before Hari Singh became the Maharaja as Pratap Singh died on 23 September 1925.

The new Maharaja—Hari Singh—had already proved his devotion and loyalty to the British. In an official note of the Government dated 17 April 1917, he was said to have 'not only personally asked to be allowed to go to the Front shortly after war was declared but was genuinely most anxious to go. . . .'[228] In 1919, perhaps to please the masters, he had even gone on a trip to Europe.[229] The correspondence available reflects how well he kept the men concerned in Britain in good humour by writing flowery letters to them.[230]

This was not all. An official note of the Government dated 2 June 1917 described him as a 'youth of more than average intelligence who gives evidence of considerable strength of character and a capacity for forming his own opinion on men and matters'.[231] It is not surprising, in view of this assessment, that he became conscious of the growing Indian Nationalist Movement and how it had come to the aid of the Princes. Shortly after Pratap Singh had declared that he would not attend the meetings of the Council, Hari Singh wrote to Windham, the ex-Resident:

> It was interesting meeting Bikaner [Maharaja of that State] again though I did not see very much of him as he seemed to

226. Ibid., Order No. 134-C, 27 January 1922.

227. *Political Records* (hereafter *PR*), 1924, F. N. 19/E-67, Order No. 1794, 23 January 1924, JKA.

228. *FDP*, Pol., Int.-A, October 1918, nos. 115-20, NAI.

229. The trip, however, proved a fateful one for him for he became involved in a scandal that cost him heavily. The scandal remained unknown till 1924, when it was disclosed and publicized as the 'Mr. A affair'.

230. *PR*, 1923, F. N. 116, JKA.

231. *FDP*, Pol., Int.-A, October 1918, nos. 115-20, NAL.

> be very much occupied with Canal Committees and a long note for the Govt. of India. He writes very good notes and must be rather a thorn in the side of those political officers who do not realise that the time has come to radically alter their method of dealing with Indian Princes.[232]

Perhaps in order to restrain Hari Singh from developing such tendencies, or to gain leverage against him since he had virtually reached the apex of power in the State and had to be curbed, the Resident engineered a petition by a section of the elites amongst Muslims to the Viceroy, Lord Reading, who visited Kashmir in October 1924.[233] The action of the State against the petitioners was surely bound to aggravate, if not create, the estrangement between it and the petitioners.

After he was entrenched in power as the Maharaja, Hari Singh started a gradual process of undoing the restraints that had been imposed on his predecessor. Quite contrary to both the letter and the spirit of the confidential undertaking given by Pratap Singh, as noted earlier, the new Maharaja committed acts that were not only inimical to the established interests of the British but also ran counter to the very essence of the fact of British paramountcy. A fundamental question concerning the State's relationship with the British Crown—whether that was to be based on the Treaty of Amritsar or governed by what was by then the well established canon of British Paramountcy—was raised. It was the former that was sought to be emphasized.

To start with, many facilities which the Resident used to enjoy at Srinagar were withdrawn.[234] He also started hitting at the vested interests of the British officials in the State service and in doing so withstood pressure from the highest authorities.[235]

232. *PR*, 1923, F.N. 116, Hari Singh to Windham, 25 February 1924, JKA.

233. G.A. Hamadani Zuhara, *A Brief History of Shah-Hamdan-Mosque, known as Khanquah-i-Moualla, Srinagar—Kashmir and Mir Sayyid Ali Hamdani* (Srinagar, n. d.), p. 20; Rasheed Taseer, *Tahrik Huriyat Kashmir; 1931 ta 1939* (Urdu) (Srinagar, 1968), Vol. 1, p. 71.

234. Bamazi (1973), p. 712.

235. See, for example, how he withstood pressure from the Secretary of State for India in the case of Colonel Ward. *Halifax Collection* (micro-

Most important of all was the change in his attitude towards the accredited representatives of the Crown—the Residents. Hari Singh 'did not get on very well',[236] with J.B. Wood, who happened to be the first officer to hold the post after he ascended the throne; the 'relations between the two were considerably strained'.[237] Wood's successor, Howell, believed that his 'personal relations' with Hari Singh were 'pleasant enough' and that the latter had on occasion gone 'out of his way' to show him 'friendliness and courtesy' but he was no less dissatisfied with Hari Singh's conduct towards him as the Resident. The Viceroy, Lord Irwin, wrote in a private letter to the Secretary of State, The Earl of Birkenhead:

> . . . Hari Singh has been so moved by his experience of Residency control in his earlier years as to be now almost obsessed with a passion for divesting himself of all traces of it. He consequently tries to exalt himself and his Government in various minor ways at the expense of the Government of India and their representative, and to hold the Resident, qua-Resident, at arms length, and to avoid contact with him, especially contact on a plane of equality.[238]

Birkenhead, who felt equally concerned about such tendencies on the part of the 'Maharaja of Kashmir' and wanted to know as to how he was 'shaping', remarked on receiving the aforesaid communique:

> . . . I should say that there is an element of the bully in him [Hari Singh] . . . when he has only the Resident to deal with, he tends to assert himself in a domineering way, or worse. . . .[239]

In short, the men concerned were much bothered about, to use Birkenhead's own words, Hari Singh's 'tendency to assert

film), Birkenhead to Irwin, 19 January 1928; Irwin to Birkenhead, 21 March 1928; Peel to Irwin, 29 November 1928; Peel to Irwin, 14 March 1929; Peel to Irwin, 17 April 1929 and its enclosure—Hari Singh to Peel, 7 March 1929, Nehru Memorial Museum & Library (hereafter NMML), New Delhi.

236. Ibid., Birkenhead to Irwin, 12 May 1927.
237. Ibid., Birkenhead to Irwin, 19 January 1928.
238. Ibid., Irwin to Birkenhead, 21 March 1928.
239. Ibid., Birkenhead to Irwin, 26 April 1928.

himself at all costs' and were eager to bring him 'back to the strait path'. They exercised their ingenuity to understand the problem from a 'psycho-analytical point of view' and find some remedy 'to cure' him. Apparently they found none as sometime, by the end of 1930 or early 1931 during his stay in London, we find Hari Singh exhorting an important person 'to persuade the Indian Government to do away with British Residents from the native states as they were expensive and the Rajas could manage their states without any help'.[240]

Furthermore, Hari Singh also exhorted the Government to withdraw the British political Agency in Gilgit. It is not difficult to see, in view of the antecedents known to us now, that the Government could not have been willing to do so, the more so because of the existence of a socialist state just across the frontier. That this might have been so is evident from the precautions it had taken in not allowing the dissemination of Bolshevik ideas in Kashmir and other territories of the State.[241] A long correspondence ensured between Hari Singh and the Government. Ultimately, the Resident sent a Memo to the Durbar and in it a proposal was made by which

> the appointment of political Agent, Gilgit, should be abolished and in his place a Political Officer should be lent to the Kashmir State to hold the appointment of Governor of Gilgit and to conduct political relations on behalf of the Government of India and the Kashmir Government with the Political Districts. The Political Officer would be a lent State servant and not under the orders of the Government of India.[242]

But before this was done the upsurge took place in Kashmir and the proposal was withdrawn by the Resident at the instance of the Government.[243] Later, in 1935, Gilgit was taken over by the Government on a '60-year lease'.[244]

240. Tyndale Biscoe, *An Autobiography* (London, 1951), p. 228.
241. See, for example, *PR*, 1924, F.N. CS/PB 56/HP-11, JKA.
242. Quoted in Bamzai (1973), p. 712.
243. Ibid.
244. Ibid., p. 713.

The growing tendency on the part of the Maharaja to clash with the paramount power culminated at the First Round Table Conference held in London when he spoke as a representative of the Princes:

> Allied by Treaty with the British Crown and within our territories independent rulers, we have come with a full sense of responsibility to our States and to all India. As allies of Britain, we stand solidly by the British connection. As Indians and loyal to the land whence we derive our birth and infant nature we stand as solidly as the rest of our countrymen for our land's enjoyment of a position of honour and equality in the British Commonwealth of Nations.[245]

Keeping in view the policy pursued by the Government *vis-a-vis* the Princes since 1858 and the attempt to buttress the princedoms as a bulwark against the growing Indian Nationalist Movement, particularly since 1921, this tendency could hardly have been platable to the Government. This was bound to have been even less so in this case as the prince concerned was governing territories situated in the strategic zone of the northern extremity of India. Therefore, there was a pressing need to forestall an eventual confrontation. Only the means to be employed for this purpose remained to be chosen.

245. Maharaja Hari Singh's reply to the opening address of His Majesty the King Emperor, George V, on 12 November 1930, as reproduced in H.L. Saxena, *The Tragedy of Kashmir*, p. 110.

4

PLURAL SOCIETY: SOCIO-ECONOMIC STRUCTURE OF KASHMIR ABOUT 1846

At the time of its incorporation into the State, Kashmir had evolved a plural society.[1] There existed at that time three socio-religious segments in the population of the region.[2] The

1. For an excellent recent treatment of Kashmir as a plural society, see T.N. Madan, 'Religious Ideology and Social Structure: The Muslims and Hindus of Kashmir', in Imtiaz Ahmad, ed., *Ritual and Religion Among Muslims in India* (Delhi, 1980), pp. 21-64.

2. See Walter R. Lawrence, *The Valley of Kashmir* (Reprint Srinagar, 1967), p. 284. Lawrence, later Sir Lawrence, was the second Land Settlement Officer of the State. It was he who introduced the first land settlement in Kashmir. As such he had the opportunity of extensively touring the place and knowing it during his long stay of six years (April 1889-March 1895) in the State. The above work, which is almost a treatise on Kashmir, is based on firsthand information collected by him. There is no detailed account available to us which dates earlier than his. However, as is evident from his narrative, things do not seem to have changed much for long before he started his work there. The span of about fifty-three years (1846-89) could not have resulted in much change in those days of comparative stagnation. Therefore, after taking due note of the earlier available accounts and evidences and making a comparison with later evidences, this work remains the best source and has been

large majority of the population was Muslim comprising of those who had adopted Islam as their creed during the long span of about five hundred years of the successive reigns of different Muslim rulers (1320-1819).[3] To this multitude of local converts to Islam were added some Syeds, Mughals, Pathans (Afghans) and others. Even though they had retained their identity, they had become largely integrated with the local converts, except for some Afghans.[4] The second segment consisted of those who had resisted conversion and had continued to remain within the Brahmanical Hindu fold. The third section was that of the Sikhs. They are supposed to have settled in Kashmir during the tenure of the first Afghan Sirdar, and later during the reigns of the different Sikh rulers.[5] They have retained their Punjabi origin and culture up to this date.[6]

It is not possible to ascertain the exact proportion of these segments in the population of the region. The first Census of Kashmir, which can be taken to be at all accurate, was carried out in 1891. When compared with earlier evidence of G.T. Vigne and Henry M. Lawrence, the figures returned by it give a fair idea of the possible distribution of the population among the three segments.[7] According to it, out of the total population

extensively relied on in this chapter. It was originally published then and is now available only in the reprint edition.

3. Up to 1586, when Kashmir was annexed to the expanding Mughal Empire, it was ruled by different locally placed Sultans. Thereafter, it was ruled by various Mughal Subhedars till its incorporation in 1753 in the newly emerged Afghan Empire. Different Afghan Sirdars ruled it until its annexation to the rising Sikh Kingdom in 1819.

4. Walter R. Lawrence, op. cit., pp. 306ff.

5. Ibid., pp. 300-1, 305. Cf. G.T. Vigne, *Travels in Kashmir, Ladak, Iskardo and the Countries Adjoining the Mountain Course of the Indus, and the Himalaya North of the Panjab* (London, 1842), Vol. 2, p. 29.

6. Our personal observations show that it is commonplace to find that in Kashmir the Sikhs still retain Punjabi as their spoken language at home.

7. Vigne, who travelled in Kashmir in 1835 and again passed through it in 1837, wrote: 'There are Musalmans and Hindus: the former predominate in proportion of 3 to 1 in the city and 9 to 1 in the villages. The Musalmans are almost all Sunis, the number of Shiahs being very inconsiderable'. Vigne (1842), p. 137.

of 814,241, there were 52,576 Hindus and 4,092 Sikhs, the rest were Muslims.[8] This indicates that Muslims formed over 93 per cent of the total population.

These segments did not constitute cohesive communities. The available evidence suggests that the members of the three segments, the Muslims in particular, did not form a homogeneous mass but were stratified into various occupational categories based on terrain or geograhpical factors, economic production, and the socio-historical and political background. There is evidence to suggest that these categories had tended to crystallize into different hereditary and endogamous caste-like groupings.[9] There was little, if any, intermarriage between these groupings. 'Custom'—*Rawaj*—reigned supreme. This helped to further reinforce such groupings. The groupings situated at the top and the bottom of the social pyramid tended to be more closed in their membership. It was generally as members of these groupings that social interaction took place among different segments in society.[10]

Henry Lawrenc, as said earlier, entered Kashmir with Maharaja Gulab Singh in November 1846. While giving his first impressions about the land and its people, he wrote that the people were 'all Mussulmans or Brahmins' and about four-fifths of them were 'Mahomedans'. *Foreign Department Proceedings*, Secret Branch, 26 December 1846, nos. 1240-1, Lawrence to Currie, 9 November 1846. National Archives of India (New Delhi).

For earlier rough estimates, see also Water R. Lawrence, op. cit., pp. 223-25.

8. *Census of India, 1891*, Kashmir (Lahore, 1893), pp. 6, 14, 15; see also Walter R. Lawrence, op. cit., 284.

The figures given above for Hindus and Sikhs are those given by Lawrence. In the Census, the figures for these two sections have been given for the administrative division of the Kashmir Province, which included Muzfarrabad district also.

9. W. Wakefield, *The Happy Valley* (London, 1879), p. 101. Cf. Madan who states that '. . . . both Muslims and Pandits recognize the notion of *Zat* as the crucial factor in identity specification and in determining an individual's natural or moral conduct'. See in Ahmad (1980), p. 59.

10. See, in particular, Walter R. Lawrence, op. cit., pp. 9, 306-7; *Census of India, 1891*, p. 172; and C.E. Tyndale Biscoe, *Men in the Making in Kashmir* (Oxford, 1914), p. 17. Also see Madan in Ahmad (1980), pp. 25-27. Even at present, when the traditional occupational structure has been disturbed to a large extent and the old classification has lost much of its meaning, people are seen taking note of their lineage

PEOPLE, TERRITORY AND OCCUPATION CORRELATION

Before an attempt is made to portray the elaborate degree of segmentation of Kashmiri society, it would be desirable to have a general view of the geographical distribution of the members of the three socio-religious segments and to ask whether there was any specific correlation between religious sections or sub-sections and the occupations pursued by the majority of their members.

Of the three socio-religious segments of the population, the Muslims, preponderant in number, were naturally scattered all over the region. However, the Shia Muslims, who according to a rough estimate formed about five per cent of the total Muslim population, were chiefly found in Hasanabad, Nandpur and Zadibal near Srinagar and the rural areas of Saidpura and Ahmadpura in Kamraj district.[11] Of the total population of Hindus in 1891, a little more than half (28,695) lived at Srinagar and the small towns while the rest were scattered in the rural areas.[12] The Sikhs were found in the rural areas of Tral, Hawal, Kirohan, Biroh and Ranbir Singh Pura.[13]

Sunni Muslims were not found to be particularly concentrated in any specific occupations but appear to have been members of almost all occupational groupings. The same seems to have been true of the Shia Muslims as well, except that there were certain peculiarities with respect to them. The craft of papier-mache was monopolized by Shia men and most of the shawl manufacturers were also Shias.[14]

and thus the place occupied by their forefathers in the traditional social structrue.

Cf.: 'All types of surname are called *Zat* and enquiries about them are made in the effort to obtain identity specification. The important question is what does *Zat* denote? Apparently it points to birth, as does the well known word *jati* used elsewhere among Hindus. The Kashmiris, however, use the word *Zat* in a broader sense to connote essence or inherent nature. . . . When used as part of a person's name, *Zat* has the narrower meaning of birth . . . or hereditary occupation.' Ibid., pp. 25-26.

11. Walter R., Lawrence, op. cit., pp. 284-85.
12. Ibid., p. 296.
13. Ibid., p. 305; *Census of India, 1891*, p. 140.
14. See and cf. Walter R. Lawrence, op. cit., pp. 284-85; Horace

All the Hindus in Kashmir, except for the small segment of *Buhur*, were Brahmins.[15] This fact had a direct bearing on the callings pursued by most of them for their livelihood. The *Buhur* were a community of grocers dealing in some special commodities like herbs, etc. Brahmins—known locally as *Bhatta* and popularly as Pandits—were further divided into two sections: *Karkum* and *Bechi Bhattas*. This division was of long standing and was the result of the replacement of Sanskrit by Persian as the court language.[16] The *Karkum* were those Brahmins who had taken to Persian learning to enable them to enter state service. The *Bachi Bhattas* were those who had continued with the learning of Sanskrit and the religious scriptures and acted as priests.[17] They are popularly known as *Gour*.[18] *Karkun* Pandits can be said to have formed the equivalent of the Kayasthas found elsewhere in India. As a class, deviants and exceptions apart,[19] *Karkun* Pandits provided the clerical establishment[20]

Hayman Wilson, ed., *Travels in the Himalayan Provinces of Hindustan and the Panjab, in Ladakh and Kashmir, in Peshawar, Kabul, Kunduz, and Bokhara by Mr. William Moorcroft and Mr. George Trebeck, from 1819 to 1825* (Reprint New Delhi, 1971), Vol· 2, p. 116; Charles Ellison Bates, *A Gazetteer of Kashmir and the Adjacect Districts of Kashmir, Badrawar, Jamu, Naoshera, Punch and the Valley of the Kishen Ganga* (Calcutta, 1873), p. 31; *Gazetteer of Kashmir and Ladakh* (Reprint Delhi, 1974), pp. 467-68, 778-79; and Prithivi Nath Kaul Bamzai, *A History of Kashmir, Political, Social, Cultural: From the Earliest Times to the Present Day* (New Delhi, 1973), 2nd revd. edn., p. 677.

15. Walter R. Lawrence, op. cit. 302; *Census of India, 1891*, p. 139.

16. This division occurred during the reign of Sultan Zain-ul-Abiden, popularly known as Badshah (1420-70). R.K. Parimu, *A History of Muslim Rule in Kashmir, 1320-1819* (New Delhi, 1969), p. 144.

17. Ibid.

18. It seems to be a corrupted form of Sanskrit *Guru*—the spiritual teacher.

19. As reported by Lawrence, many, during his sojourn in Kashmir, were in business. Others worked as cooks, bakers, confectioners, and tailors. Acting and music was also adopted by some as their profession. And at least one person is reported by him to have worked as a cavalry soldier in the army of Maharaja of 'Oodepore'. In 1894 many were working as daily labourers on the river embankments. Walter R. Lawrence, op. cit., p. 303.

20. Cf. '. . . at present the Karkun Pandit regards the pen as his

and were employed in the State service,[21] as Patwaris[22] by the village communities, and to maintain their accounts by the traders.[23] There is evidence that even the village Pandits—*zamindars*—had the inclination to read and write.[24] Thus, it can be assumed that *Karkun* Pandit was largely identifiable with a quill-driver[25] while a *Gour* Pandit was a priest. This is probably why over half of the Hindu population was urban-based in Kashmir.

Sikhs, it is certain, were rural-based. There is no indication that they worked as artisans. On the contrary, it is known that they lived by 'cultivation or service'.[26] They must have been largely *Zamindars*; or it is probable that they might also have been a part of the State militia. They had a strong tendency to look to service as their source of livelihood and were recruited during the early Dogra rule in the Nizamat regiment, employed to back up the tax-gathering agency.[27]

According to the Census of 1891, which provided the data base for Lawrence while working on the land settlement, the rural population was estimated at about 83 per cent of the total population.[28] It lived in the various villages and the small towns

natural destiny, . . . they would infinitely prefer to spend their lives as clerks in some offices'. Walter R. Lawrence, op. cit., p. 303.

21. Ibid., pp. 303, 401. Cf. The Baron Erich Von Schonberg, *Travels in India and Kashmir* (London, 1853), Vol. 2, pp. 100-1, 105; Lt. Col. Torrens, *Travels in Ladakh, Tartary, and Kashmir* (Londod, 1862), p. 302.

22. Walter R. Lawrence, op. cit., p. 400.

23. It was reported in 1931 that the pandits were employed then as clerks by the Muslim traders and that this connection was 'ancestral'. See His Highness' Government, Jammu and Kashmir, *Evidence Recorded in Public by Srinagar Riots Enquiry Committee, 1931* (Jammu, 1931), p. 201 (hereafter *Evidence SREC*).

24. Walter R. Lawrence, op. cit., p. 327.

25. The efficacy of this identity is indicated by the following fact. One Afghan Sirdar (1813-19), Muhammad Azim Khan, fearing the Pandits to be intransigent, wanted to dispense with their services. But, he still had to retain them because no local substitute was available. See Schonberg (1853), Vol. 2, p. 105; and Hassan, *Tarikh Kashmir* (Political Section), Maulvi Mohammed Ibrahim, trans. (Urdu) (Srinagar, 1957), p. 505.

26. Walter R. Lawrence, op. cit., p. 301.

27. Ibid., p. 305.

28. Ibid., p. 225.

and was divided into a number of distinct social categories. First of all, there was the category of *Zamindars*—the agriculturists.[29] Most of them were Sunni Muslims. And in the villages where Shia Muslims, Pandits and Sikhs lived, there were *Zamindars* from each group.

Then there were the *Nangars*—the artisans or menials. They did not have any hereditary rights to land, save the garden plots adjoining their houses. For the services rendered to the *Zamindars,* they were entitled to receive remuneration at the time of harvest and payment in kind according to fixed scales. A big village also had carpenters, blacksmiths, potters, weavers, butchers, washermen, barbers, tailors, bakers, goldsmiths, carriers, oil-pressers, dyers, milkmen, cotton cleaners and snuff-makers and their families.[30] Besides, there were *Galwans* (horse-keepers), *Chaupans* or *Pohls* (shepherds), and *Bhaggats* or *Bands* (minstrels).[31] *Nangars*, with few exceptions, seem to have been Muslims.

At the bottom were *Dums*[32] and *Watals*.[33] *Dums* were the village watchmen who, in addition to their police functions, were entrusted by the State to look after the crops. *Watals* have been equated with gypsies. They were a wandering people who would occasionally settle in a village. They were divided into two categories. Those belonging to the first category abstained from eating carrion; their occupation was to manufacture boots and sandals. They, as also *Dums*, were admitted to mosques and to the Muslim religion. The second category comprised of those who performed the job of scavengers, ate carrion and manufactured winnowing trays of leather. They were not admitted to the Muslim religion.

According to the Census of 1891, the urban population was estimated at about 13 per cent.[34] Of the urban centres that had developed in Kashmir, Srinagar was the only major town. Its population in 1891 was estimated at 139,410 but the real

29. Ibid., p. 310.
30. Ibid., p. 315.
31. Ibid., pp. 311-12.
32. Ibid., pp. 311.
33. Ibid., pp. 314-15.
34. Ibid., p. 225.

city population, after deducting the suburban population, was only 118,960.[35]

For centuries, Srinagar had been the capital of state power in Kashmir. Besides the various urban luxury-item crafts and industries shawl manufacture in particular were carried on here. This is the reason why the population of Srinagar was mainly categorized according to the functions performed in the different industries or the services necessary to support them.

As is already known now, a conspicuous category of quill-drivers—*Karkun* Pandits—lived in Srinagar.

A wealthy class of *Karkhanadars*—the shawl manufacturers, merchants and bankers had also grown here.[36] It has been indicated earlier that most of the shawl manufacturers were Shia Muslims. The same is believed to have been the case with regard to the bankers and merchants.[37] However, it needs to be made clear that the ratio of Shias in this class of shawl manufacturers, bankers and merchants could not have been overwhelming; it seems that a good number of men of this class were Sunni Muslims.[38]

Apart from *shawl-bafs*—shawl-weavers—who were employed by the *Karkhandars* as wage earners, there was the usual affiliated complement of dyers, washers and brokers. According to the Census of 1891, these people formed a 'large population of the inhabitants.'[39] Most of the *shawl-bafs* were Sunni Muslims and the remainder were Shia Muslims and Hindus. According to the estimate of one who spent six summers, from 1865 to 1872,

35. Ibid., p. 241.
36. *Census of India, 1891*, p. 7. Cf. Wilson, op. cit., p. 116.
37. Bamzai (1973), p. 677.
38. The place occupied by this class of people is given to us by Moorcroft as the area 'between the bridges called Saraf-Kadal and Kazi-Kadal, and on each side of the canal [Nala Mar]'. This area is identifiable even at present. The buildings there still speak for their past grandeur and bear a testimony to the description given by Moorcroft. According to him, 'the best houses in Kashmir' were situated in this area, 'Sheikh Mahal'. It is only on one side of the canal that the Shias lived; and this part is known as Kumangarpur. Wilson, op. cit,, p. 116.
39. *Census of India, 1891*, p. 7.

in Kashmir, 28,115 shawl weavers were Sunni Muslims, 1,000 were Shia Muslims and 315 were Hindus.[40]

Besides the *shawl-bafs* there were artisans engaged in the manufacture of other handicrafts. Of all these, it was only in papier-mache work that Shia Muslims were predominant. It can safely be presumed that the men engaged in the other crafts were mostly Sunni Muslims.

Finally, there were the categories of people that can normally be expected to be necessary for the upkeep of such a big population. Except *Buhur*, these categories seem to have been comprised predominantly of Sunni Muslims.

In addition to the categories that have been broadly enumerated above there were a few others that were conspicuous both in rural and urban centres. Situated at the apex socially were Pirzadas—the Muslim priestly class.[41] They performed what can be broadly categorized as the various functions of 'Intellectuals' in a feudal society. Their counterparts among Hindus were *Gour*. In view of the social structure existing then, it is not surprising that *Gours* as compared to Pirzadas were insignificant both in number and social significance.

In the various urban centres and the big villages was found the *wone* or *wani*. He was the shopkeeper who functioned as a middleman in whatever little merchant trade existed in articles other than luxury crafts and industrial products. He was usually a Muslims.[42]

An important and prominent category was that of *Hanz* or *Hanji*—the boatmen. This was divided into various strata. At the top were the *Demb Henz*—the boatmen of the Dal Lake near Srinagar who lived near or on the lake and were really vegetable-gardeners who cultivated the small islands. They were followed by the *Gari Hanz*—the boatmen of the Wular Lake, who gathered the *singhara* nuts. Next were those who lived in the large barges, known as *Bahats* and *War*, in which cargos of 800 maunds of grain or wood were carried. Below

40. This was Dr. Elmslie, the Christian Medical Missionary. Bates (1873), p. 30. Also see Bamzai (1973), p. 677.

41. See Walter R. Lawrence, op. cit., pp. 307-8.

42. Ibid., pp. 5, 387.

them were the owners of *dungas*—the passenger boats. And last were the *Gad Hanz*—the fishermen, and *Hak Hanz* who made a living by dredging for driftwood in the rivers. They were all Muslims.[43]

AGRICULTURE

Agriculture formed the main source of production. This is well illustrated in the accounts of the period available to us. According to the Census of 1891, 581,966 persons (roughly three-quarters of the population) were occupied in agriculture then.[44] In addition to the crops raised on the land, of which rice was the main one, cultivation was also carried on 'floating gardens' found in the different waters.[45] Besides, *Gaer* or *Singhara*—a waternut—grew abundantly in the lakes.[46] Fruits, of which there was abundance, grew wild.[47] All these products formed a source of revenue for the State.[48]

Agricultural implements used were 'few and simple'. The plough was light and made of wood and the ploughshare was tipped with iron. For clod-breaking, a wooden mallet was used. The land was fertile and there was no problem of irrigation for

43. Ibid., pp. 313-14.

44. This is calculated on the basis of the figures given in *Census of India, 1891*, pp. 123-24.

45. 'They [floating gardens] are common on the city lake, where they produce abundant crops of fine cucumbers and melons. For forming these islands, choice is made of a shallow part of the lake overgrown with reads and other aquatic plants, which are cut off about two feet below [*sic*] the surface, and then pressed close to each other without otherwise disturbing the position in which they grow. They are subsequently moved down nearly to the surface, and the parts thus taken off are spread evenly over the floats, and covered with a thin layer of mud drawn up from the bottom, on the level thus formed are arranged, close so each other, conical heeps of weeds, about two feet across and two feet high, having each at top a small hollow filled with fresh mud.' Bates (1873), p. 49.

46. Ibid., p. 50.

47. Walter R. Lawrence, op. cit., pp. 348-55.

48. Cf. 'It has been pointed out by many writers on the subject that nearly everything in the valley was brought under taxation.' Ibid., p. 417.

it could easily be carried out with water from the various mountain streams, wells, etc.[49]

Tenure, Land-holding and Zamindar's Rights

To understand the nature of the land-tenure existing in Kashmir then, it is essential to first ask who could possibly have any rights over land? There appear to have been two such parties. Firstly, the *Zamindars*,[50] to whom a reference has been made earlier, and secondly the ruler or his assignees—a not inconsiderable number. The *Zamindar* in Kashmir, it should be added, was the peasant and not one who enjoyed any superior rights over land. There was no such intermediary class there. Why this was so is not our direct concern here. Suffice it to say that there seem to have been some definite historical reasons for this. These could be that (*a*) it had been a consistent policy of the different reigning powers over Kashmir since 1586 that Kashmiris should be excluded from the state military structure; and (*b*) the state employed its own tax-gathering agency to collect the revenue directly from the *Zamindars*. The assignees were of different types and their number when Gulab Singh finally occupied Kashmir was quite sizeable. These were in the nature of *dhurmurth*, *jageers*, *mustumurree* grants, *nukdee dhurmurths*, and *jinsee dhurmurths*. It seems that the term *maufeedars* was used en bloc for all grantees other than those who held *jageers*. There were 3,115 cases of land granted under *dhurmurth*. Besides these there were the grants of other types and very many cases were *Kharij az juma o duftar* or totally unregistered.[51]

Ownership

Pronouncements on the 'ownership' of land in Kashmir are available to us first from European travellers. These do not

49. Ibid., pp. 319, 323, 324.

50. In the sources that have been consulted, the terms *Zamindar*, Cultivator, Farmer, Peasant, Ryot, *Raiyat* and *Assami* have been used interchangeably to convey the same meaning. Our choice to use the term *Zamindar* has been dictated by the consideration that it is the most meaningful and comprehensive and the least confusing of all the terms.

51. *Punjab Government Records*, Political Diaries (Lahore, 1915), Vol. 6, p. 61 (hereafter *PGR*).

differ from what was stated by Europeans to have been the case in the rest of India during the pre-British period. It was unanimously held by them that the 'proprietorship of land vested with the king alone'.[52]

The earliest pronouncement made on the nature of land tenure in Kashmir was by Moorcroft, who travelled there for about one year during the early Sikh rule (1822-23). He wrote:

> According to the prevailing notions on the subject the whole of the land in Kashmir is considered to have been, time out of mind, the property of ruler . . . . The Khalsa lands are now, as heretofore, let out for cultivation.[53]

The same observations were echoed by others, who went there during both Sikh and Dogra rule.[54] Lawrence, in the same fashion wrote that the status of the *Assamis* (*zamindars*), from the point of view of the state, during the Mughal rule and thereafter 'in theory meant nothing more than a tenant-at-will'.[55]

There is no evidence to suggest that the land was parcelled out to the *Zamindars* every season or year. On the contrary, it is known for certain that the *Zamindars* in a village held the customary hereditary right of *miras* to certain plots of good and irrigated land within the boundaries of the village. Lawrence himself observed that the 'Changes of dynasty and changes of system, earthquakes, floods, and famines, have alike failed to

52. Our understanding of the conception of 'ownership' in pre-British India is derived from a comprehensive discussion on the subject by Irfan Habib, in *The Agrarian System of Mughal India, 1556-1707* (Bombay, 1963), p. 111.

53. Wilson, op. cit., p. 125.

54. Cf. 'A Zemindar, who wishes to rent and cultivate a tract of land, is never refused permission to do so.' Schonberg, 1853, Vol. 2, p. 109. Also see Mrs. J.C. Murray Aynsley, *Our Visit to Hindostan, Kashmir and Ladakh* (London, 1879), p. 72; W. Wakefield (1879), p. 89; Bates (1873), p. 100; E.F. Knight, *Where Three Empires Meet* (London, 1905), p. 62; *Gazetteer of Kashmir and Ladak*, op. cit., p. 104; *The Imperial Gazetteer of India* (reprint Faridabad, n.d.), Vol. 15, p. 138.

55. Walter R. Lawrence, op. cit., p. 428. At yet another place, he wrote that land during the Mughal rule was 'apparently regarded as the absolute property of the State, and every year allotments were made to cultivators'. Ibid., p. 402.

obliterate the hereditary principle in land tenures in Kashmir. . . .'[56] A holder of such a hereditary right in land was known as *mirasdar*.[57] Thus, it can be said that the *zamindars* already possessed such prescriptive rights as were later conferred juridically at the time of land settlement on those who agreed to pay the assessment that was fixed at that time on the field entered in their respective names. This was the right of 'occupancy' which was to be 'permanent' and 'hereditary'.[58]

The prescriptive right enjoyed by the *zamindars* does not seem to have been free of the obligation to have his land cultivated, either with the help of his family members or by engaging labourers. It seems only logical to deduce such a thing because of the fact that the State worked as an active organizer of cultivation. For example, a certain quantity of rice seed was provided to the *Zamindar* or the labourer working in the field and a definite quantity of produce was expected in return.[59]

It seems unlikely that the *zamindars* possessed the right of alienation of land—or practiced it. There is enough evidence to show that much land that was cultivable was lying waste.[60] There was not much pressure on land because the population was not large enough to give rise to such pressure. The nature of taxation, which was heavy[61] and had been so before also,[62] rendered the production system as one of 'production for use'. In view of these facts and the available conditions for carrying on cultivation, the alienation of land by sale does not seem to have been possible either for an agriculturist or a non-agriculturist.

However, it is possible that such a practice had developed at Srinagar. This assumption has been made on the basis of

56. Ibid., p. 428.
57. Ibid. Cf. *The Imperial Gazetteer of India*, op. cit., p. 138.
58. See also ch. 5.
59. See Vigne (1842), Vol. 1, pp. 310-11.
60. Moorcroft found that 'not more than about one-sixteenth of the cultivable surface is in cultivation. . . .' Wilson, op. cit., Vol. 2, p. 124.
61. See ibid., pp. 124-26; and Vigne (1842), Vol. 2, pp. 310-11.
62. *Report on Revenue Arrangements under Indian Rulers*, C. 1788, British Museum, MSS, 6586, f. 164a. This reference was made available to us by the courtesy of Irfan Habib, to whom we feel greatly indebted.

the following facts: the lands nearer the city were valued higher than others for revenue consideration during the early Sikh rule;[63] a tax on any sale of land was maintained in Kashmir around the early 1870s;[64] and after the land settlement, alienation of land by sale was permitted at Srinagar.[65]

Assessment

Assessment was based on crop-sharing and was taken in kind. Such was the case prior to Dogra rule, and also under early Dogra rule until the land settlement. The assessment was generally heavy but the Pandit and Pirzada *Zamindars* were charged less.[66]

Village Functionaries

The two important functionaries in the village were the Muqqadam (Headman) and the Patwari (Accountant). The men appointed to these posts were selected by the villagers themselves. The Muqqadam was chosen from amongst the *zamindars* of the village and the Patwari, it is significant to note, was a *Karkun* Pandit.[67] By whom they were selected and to which appointment naturally would determine their position and attitude. They were bound both to the villagers as well as to the State.

HANDICRAFTS AND INDUSTRY

Although agricultural production formed the occupation of the majority of the people, it was not the sole occupation of all those who followed it. In the 1891 Census, the people who were returned as agriculturists by caste numbered only 158,074 as against 581,966 who were agriculturists by profession. The

63. See Wilson, op. cit., Vol., 2, p. 125.

64. Robert Thorp, 'Kashmir Misgovernment', in S.N. Gadru, ed., *Kashmir Papers* (Srinagar, 1973), p. 79; Bates (1873), p. 100.

65. See *OER*, 1902, F.N. 199/0-87, Judicial Members' Note on Settlement Commissioner's Memo.

66. *Gazetteer of Kashmir and Ladak*, op. cit., p 106.

67. Walter R. Lawrence, op. cit., pp. 400, 446-47.

anomaly existed because for many agriculture was an additional occupation.[68] A considerable section of this population involved themselves in various handicrafts and art manufactures. It was the same with a great majority of the urban population.

Artisans such as weavers, carpenters, blacksmiths, potters, and basket-makers, who produced the articles of common consumption, were found in rural and urban areas. The spinning wheel was an essential property of every household, both in the villages and in the urban centres,[69] particularly Srinagar. Islamabad (Anantnag) was famous for embroideries, Kulgam for lacquered woodwork, Bijbihara for wood-carving, the villagers of the Zainagir circle for soft woollen cloth, and Nava Shahr for paper. Apart from the crafts manufactured at other places, silver work, sword-making, leather work, fur work and shawl-making were carried on at Srinagar. Boat-making was also an old industry in Kashmir.[70]

Shawl manufacture was the major industry in Kashmir. Apart from Srinagar, this industry was carried on at Islamabad (Anantnag) also. The raw material for the manufacture of shawls was formerly supplied exclusively by the western provinces of Tibet and Ladakh but subsequently large quantities were procured from the neighbourhood of Yarkand, Khoten, etc.[71] From a detailed account about this industry in Kashmir by Moorcroft,[72] it appears that a considerable section of the population of Srinagar was connected with it at one or the other stage and thus it was a principal source of livelihood. Even the *Karkun* Pandit families benefited directly from this industry.[73]

68. This is calculated on the basis of the figures given in the *Census of India, 1891*, pp. 122-24.

69. A glimpse to this effect is available in a pertinent observation made by Prem Nath Bazaz in one of his earlier cited works. He wrote: 'The *charkha* which was a prominent part of the household property in Kashmir, is rarely visible now and has been turned out from the cities and towns for good.' Prem Nath Bazaz, *Inside Kashmir* (Srinagar, 1941), pp. 77-78.

70. Walter R. Lawrence, op. cit., pp. 370ff.

71. Wilson, op. cit., Vol. 1, pp. 346-47; Vigne (1842), Vol. 2, p. 126.

72. Wilson, op. cit., Vol. 2, pp. 164ff. Also see Vigne (1842), Vol. 2, pp. 124ff.

73. This was at the stage of spinning, so goes the tradition.

There is sufficient evidence to show that along with agricultural production, shawl-manufacture was an important and rewarding source of revenue to the state.[74]

A class of *Karkhanadars* who owned workshops had grown in Kashmir. They were the people who employed *shawl-bafs* to work on the looms. *Shawl-bafs* were the wage earners and were completely dependent upon the *Karkhanadars* for their livelihood. This was inevitable because having adapted to this occupation they were left completely unfit for agriculture[75]. The *Karkhanadars* were mostly Shia Muslims while the *shawl-bafs* were mostly Sunni Muslims. There is an indication that apprentices were bound to work for the same master.[76] It can be assumed that such a rule could not be enforced without the backing of the state because there is no evidence to suggest that the *Karkhanadars* had their own authority to enforce it. The interest of the State in this industry is apparent because we know that a shawl, after it was woven, could not be cut from the hook unless the inspector, who was employed by the State, was present. But even such strict vigilance by the State and a 25 per cent duty on the price of shawls did not prevent a class of 'merchants and bankers' from emerging. This class of people was concentrated in Sheikh Mahal, a place situated on the both sides of the 'Nala Mar' canal between the 'Saraf Kadal' and 'Kazi Kadal' bridges. Their position can be assumed to be reflected in their houses which have been reported as 'the best' in the whole of Kashmir by the travellers on whose accounts we depend for information about that period.[77]

Around 1846 the shawl industry was not in its former state of health. It was on the decline but had not yet been wiped out. There is evidence to show that during the period, when Kashmir was under the Sikhs, many Kashmiris were found living outside Kashmir. They were mostly *shawl-bafs*.[78] Their

74. Wilson, op. cit., Vol. 2, p. 126; Vigne (1842), Vol. 2, p. 120.

75. Walter R. Lawrence, op. cit., p. 316.

76. See and cf. *FDP*, Secret Branch, 18 November 1843, nos. 13-17, Leech to Assistant to Governor-General's Agent, NAI; and Hassan (1957), p. 554.

77. Wilson, op. cit., Vol. 2, p. 116.

78. For example, there was a great colony of Kashmiri shawl-weavers

migration has been attributed to the heavy taxation by the Sikhs, but other evidence suggests that the main reason was the vicious circle that had arisen in Kashmir by the extension of the British imperial possessions in India. Unemployment in Kashmir forced them to move out. This was caused by two reasons: first, the destruction of the market that had become extensive after the rise of Mughal Empire in India,[79] and, second, diverting of the raw material to the territories occupied by the British, thus depriving Kashmir of the traditional monopoly of its use.[80]

TRADE

External

Kashmir enjoyed a virtually self-supporting economy, but nevertheless there existed through it a long route trade in luxurious items such as shawls with the outside world. The wool was traditionally brought from Tibet and more recently from Sinkiang.

Active trade in the products had existed earlier with far-off places and on an extensive scale. 'Kashmir was formerly resorted to for shawlgoods by merchants from Turkey, both in Asia and Europe, by Armenians, Persians, Afghans, Uzbeks and by traders from Hindustan and from Chinese Turkistan', but it had declined much at the time when Moorcroft visited Kashmir:

> Political events had largely reduced the trade with Persia, Turkey, and the Panjab, and that with Hindustan had sustained much detriment from the prevalence of British rule, and the loss of wealth by the Native courts, in which costly shawls were formerly a principal article of attire. The

---

at Ludhiana in 1857 and they rose and were in the forefront in the revolt against the British. Bates (1873), pp. 36-37.

79. See section on Urban Arts and Crafts in ch. 5.

80. Cf. Wilson, op. cit., Vol. 1, p. 347 and Walter R. Lawrence, op. cit., p. 375.

> trade with Turkistan was on the increase, in consequence of the extending demands of Russia.[81]

The extension of British possessions in India had also caused the prices of the shawl wool to be increased.[82] That this was of great consequence for this old industry in Kashmir is clear from the fact that the Kashmiri merchants had tried to thwart the movements of Moorcroft at Ladakh before he left for Kashmir. He was fully aware of 'their undoubted activity in frustrating my projects . . .'[83] and wrote that they feared greatly the 'loss of their monopoly of the shawl-wool trade through European interference'.[84]

However, the loss of earlier markets and the British interest in this industry had not killed the industry. This was because a new market had been thrown open in France. This happened after Napoleon brought the first shawls, at the time of the campaign in Egypt, as a present for Empress Josephine. They soon became an article of fashion; the European generals in the Sikh army were probably responsible for giving a boost to this export trade with France.[85] Kashmir imported tea, salt, sugar, tobacco, etc.

Internal

Internal trade was not of large dimensions. This was possibly due to the fact that in Kashmir almost every village had a self-sufficient economy. Moreover, it had been the custom for centuries for the state to sell grains to the city people. This had naturally not permitted a class of people dealing in surplus produce to grow and act as genuine middlemen. However, there existed in the larger villages a *Wani* or *Bakal*, who was a Muslim huckster. He dealt in salt, oil, spices, snuff, sugar and tea. He would sometimes lend money to his customers under the system known as Wad and receive things like cloth, etc., in

81. Wilson, op. cit., Vol. 2, pp. 194-95.
82. Ibid., p. 167.
83. Ibid., Vol. 1, p. 454.
84. Ibid., pp. 451-52.
85. See Walter R. Lawrence, op. cit., p. 376.

return at a later date.[86] Generally speaking, men with both enterprise and capital were by and large absent.[87] The 'Banya of India' was practically unknown in Kashmir as late as 1895.[88]

ECONOMY

As late as 1895 Lawrence wrote:

> The Kashmir valley, owing to its remoteness from the railway and to its difficult approaches, has been thrown on its own resources, and is to a great extent a *self-supporting country*. In normal years the food supply of the valley is ample for its inhabitants; for clothing the people have wool and a certain amount of locally-produced cotton of a fair quality. There is a wealth of fibres, ample timber, and with the single exception of salt there is no necessity of life which needs to be imported. Iron locally produced used to suffice for agricultural implements, and clay vessels serve all the purposes of copper and brass in domestic life.[89]

Money economy does not seem to have acquired a foothold as to play a significant role in the people's day-to-day life. Wingate, the first Settlement Officer in Kashmir who started his work in 1887, wrote in his preliminary report that prices were non-existent.[90] Lawrence made the same observation in 1889:

> . . . money prices did not exist. Salaries were paid in grain, ... Oil-seeds were looked upon as an appreciated currency, while maize and singhara nuts, with which many persons were paid, were regarded as a depreciated medium. Not only did the State pay its officials in grain, but private persons paid their servants in the same fashion, ... The

86. Ibid., p. 387.
87. Ibid., p. 390.
88. Ibid., p. 387.
89. Ibid., p. 383, (emphasis added).
90. A. Wingate, *Preliminary Report of Settlement Operations in Kashmir and Jammu* (Lahore, 1888), p. 12.

currency was to a great extent shali, and silver played a subsidiary part in the business of the country.[91]

COMMUNICATIONS

Means of communication both within Kashmir and with the outside world were not developed. Wheeled carriage was unknown. The situation continued to remain so for a few decades more thereafter.[92] Water transport formed the only means of communication that was available and where it was not possible, men carried their loads on their backs. The same course was naturally resorted to while carrying loads both within and out of Kashmir. This was an old institution in Kashmir and was the result of the physical features of its terrain.

EDUCATION

There is no evidence to show that the state took any direct part in the education of the people or even in the training of those who were needed to perform various clerical jobs. From C.E. Tyndale Biscoe, a British Christian Missionary who became intimately connected with the imparting of modern education in Kashmir from 1891 onwards, it is evident that there were indigenous schools attached to the mosques. There the Muslim boys were taught to read Arabic so that they would be able to read the Koran. Likewise, there were schools where Sanskrit was taught to enable Hindu boys to read their religious books. Besides, the teaching of Persian was also practised. At the time when Biscoe wrote his account, a certain amount of arithmetic was also taught.[93]

CULTURE

All the writings produced by the different British authors in the nineteenth century tend to aim at showing the Pandits and the

91. Walter R. Lawrence, op. cit., pp. 243-44.

92. See ibid., p. 23.

93. C.E. Tyndale Biscoe. *Kashmir in Sunlight and Shade* (London, 1922), p. 253.

Muslims as two homogenous groups in separate water-tight compartments. And, based upon this wrong assumption about the material and mental disposition of the members of the two major religious segments of society in Kashmir, they were treated as two comparable categories.[94] Such a view was also adopted by the leaders of the agitation in 1931 and has dominated the thinking of the writers on the struggle for freedom in Kashmir.[95] Whether this was a conscious or unconscious act on the part of these writers is irrelevant here; the fact remains that it helped in the perpetuation of a distorted picture and contributed greatly to confusing the issues under discussion.

It has already been noted that Pandits along with the small community of *Buhurs* formed the only Hindus in Kashmir. As against this, the Muslims comprised, because of historical reasons, of a hierarchy of different social strata with the Syeds and Pirzadas at the top and the higher of the two strata of *Wattals* at the bottom. Even if culture be narrowly identified with the formal symbols and prescriptions of the different religious scriptures, a point of view to which we do not subscribe, a comparison would be feasible only between Hindu

94. David Lelyveld has in his recent work traced the consequences of the British view of Indian society. His observations can be said to apply equally to Kashmir. Lelyveld writes: 'Whether based on regional, religious, or racial divisions, most of the official analysis proceeded from a theory of history that saw Indian society as a museum of evolutionary layers, each composed of separate, birth-defined social groups that were unable to relate to each other as constituents of a larger whole. If the differences were based on region, as with Ibbetson, education and improved communication might eventually override them. If they were based on race, as with Wise, the only possible consolidation would be a uniformly inferior "breed" permanently subjected to foreign rule. And finally, if they were based on adherence to one of the great world religions, as with most common understandings of Indian society, consolidations would tend to separate Hindus from Muslims.' David Lelyveld, *Aligarh's First Generation: Muslim Solidarity in British India* (Princeton, 1978), p. 16.

95. See, for example, how Naseer-ud-Din counterposes and compares the material disposition of 'Pandits' and 'Muslims' while seeking an explanation for the trust and faith that the Pandits were said to have had in Muslims prior to the disturbances in 1931. Munshi Naseer-ud-Din, *Tarikh Jang Azadiye Kashmir* (Urdu) (Srinagar, 1971), pp. 29-31.

Gour and Muslim Pirzada representing the two religious doctrines. For others, some religious symbols and features had become a part of their habitual observance but they formed only one part of their complete culture.

A comparison between the members of the two religious sections, with regard to their mental disposition, can be made at two levels. Firstly, at the level of faith as the common man understands it. Secondly, at the level of the social occupational ethos. It has been already noted that '*Rawaj*' played a significant role in the day-to-day life of the common man.[96] The conduct of the common Muslim was such that Lawrence labelled him as being a 'Hindu at heart'.[97] The majority of Muslims were as attached to *rishis* and *fakirs* as the Hindus were and both believed in the common stock of superstitions and myths. Even after becoming Muslims, they were not able to achieve a complete break with their past; in some respects they were nearer to Hindus. Lawrence has vividly reflected on the idolatrous tendencies exhibited by them for which they were known by outsiders as '*Pir-Parast*'—saint-worshippers. This epithet, he says, they 'well deserved'.[98]

The cultural differentiation between the segments of society in Kashmir was based upon the nature of various hereditary occupational persuasions and the different occupational categories rather than on the faith they followed. This is supported by a comparison of an anthropological view of present-day Kashmiri society with the few but all the same relevant observations made in this connection in our sources.[99] It is unfortunate,

96. Walter. R. Lawrence, op. cit., p. 9.

97. Ibid., p. 286.

98. Ibid., pp. 286-89. Muhammad Yusuf Saraf has completely ignored the social aspect highlighted here and has brought forth only those features and facts, such as dress etc., which differentiated Hindus and Muslims of Kashmir. Such an action on his part was obviously necessary to support the underlying presumption in his work that the Hindus and the Muslims are two nations and were always so. See Saraf, *Kashmiri Fights for Freedom* (Lahore, 1977), Vol. 1.

99. See, for example, the following observations about *Karkun* Pandits and shawl-weavers:

'But at present the Karkun Pandit regards the pen as his natural destiny, and though many have taken to agriculture and many are

and surprising as well, that not much light has been thrown on this aspect of social reality by Walter Lawrence, the chief source for the period under review. This makes it difficult to understand the real working of the social mechanism but whatever little is available from him supports our contention. For example, Pandits representing a traditional category of 'Intellectuals', displayed a general tendency to perform those functions in society which did not involve manual labour. So for that matter did the Pirzadas. It is a fact that the rural Pandits engaged themselves in cultivation. But that seems to have been a result firstly of the structural constraints produced by their replacement by Pirzadas as the priests for the masses and, secondly, by an increase in their number to such an extent that all of them could not be employed in various clerical jobs. Even at present Pandits and Pirzadas despise traditional professional jobs as *kamina kaam*—menial work.

Another category, which was socially close to Pandits and Pirzadas comprised of those who did not perform the functions of the intellectuals but, at the same time, did not work themselves. They were either employers of workers, such as the *Karkhanadars*, or middlemen like shawl merchants or *Wanis* who were engaged in the merchant trade. Included in this category also were those who could earn superior rights over land from the rulers traditionally—and, as seen earlier, there were a good number of them.

Cultural differentiation within Kashmiri society, there are reasons to believe, was linked to the different occupational groups also at a more general level. This was the differentiation of the population into non-working and working segments. Such an assumption is based upon certain specific features of Kashmiri society that have been handed down to the present

---

looking to land as a means of employment and subsistence, they would infinitely prefer to spend their lives as clerks in some offices.' Walter R. Lawrence, op. cit., p. 303.

'The shawl-weavers possess a language of their own, which although essentially Kashur [Kashmiri], differs materially from modern Kashmiri, in which corrupt Persian words so greatly prevail,' Bates (1873), p. 95.

generation as relics of the past but which are now dying out fast. These features are the differentiation of the Muslim population into two categories—*andrem* and *nebrem*—and its symbolization through certain specific differences in the dress worn by their respective womenfolk.[100] These differences existed with regard to the headgear and the outer garment (*pheran*) worn by them. The headgear worn by the *andrem* women, known as *thoud kasab*, and the sleeves of their garment, called *Qourab nour*, were special and denoted their higher status.

The classification of the population into *andrem* and *nebrem*, though historically known for Muslims only, can be said to apply to the whole of Kashmiri society for analytical purposes. The *andrem* can be said to have included the Pandits as well besides those who are known to have been so categorized from amongst the Muslims. It would be appropriate to mention here that the headgear worn by the Pandit women—*tarange*—was to a large extent analogous to the *thoud kasab* of the *andrem* women. The *andrem*, then, can be said to have included the intellectual groups of Pandits and Pirzadas and those who were socially close to them in the sense that they did not themselves work such as the *Karkhanadars*, or the middlemen who were engaged in whatever little merchant trade there was, and those who enjoyed superior rights over land and to whom the land revenue was alienated in one form or the other.

The foregoing account suggests that only a drastic reshaping of the existent socio-economic structure or an intensive mobilization of the social segments along religious lines could have made it possible for Hindus and Muslims to behave as two different and organized camps hostile to each other. There were marks of identity, other than religion, that were more relevant to the people in their mundane affairs. The truth of this contention is best illustrated by how, for example, *Karkun* Pandits studying in Christian Missionary School at Srinagar in 1891 perceived their privileged hereditary position in society: it was

100. No mention has been made about this aspect of social life in Kashmir by an author who lays claim to have dwelt upon the social life in Srinagar from 1846-1947. See Mohammed Ishaq Khan, *History of Srinagar, 1846-1947: A Study in Socio-Cultural Change* (Srinagar, 1978).

by virtue of being *sufed posh*[101]—a category which seems to have been equivalent to that of *andrem.* They did not perceive themselves in strictly religious terms.

101. Cf. Biscoe, who spent almost his entire life-time teaching in Kashmir, wrote about his first experiences in the school:

'. . . I inspected them [the students who were almost all Brahmins] more closely, I noticed that their finger-nails were abnormally long and all in the very deepest mourning. On inquiry I found the possession of long nails to be one of the signs of gentility, as it was an incontestable sign that they never disgraced themselves with doing manual labour of any kind, and therefore belonged to the 'sufed posh'—i.e. white flower, or tip-top class, as they were by birth the highest caste. When I had been in the school a few days, I told them I thought that black nails were hardly in keeping with white flowers, and insisted that clean nails should be the complement of the white-flower class.' Biscoe (1922), pp. 263-64.

5

TRENDS IN THE DEVELOPMENT OF SOCIO-ECONOMIC STRUCTURE: 1846-1931

It has been shown that British political influence had started penetrating the territories which came to constitute the State much before its formation in 1846. Similarly, the extension of the British possessions in the north started affecting the socio-economic structure in these territories. We have already seen this in the case of the shawl industry in Kashmir. A continuous process of change, apparently faint in the beginning but which became bolder and bolder with the passage of time, was taking place in the socio-economic and the politico-administrative structure of Kashmir from 1846 up to 1931. The year 1880 became a landmark in this process of change. That year a qualitatively different set of trends arising out of the Government's objective of reorienting the whole structure of the State was set in motion. The immediate motivation for this was to make the State serve the new imperial demands. The changes began the process of modernization in Kashmir which received added impetus after the establishment of what we have preferred to call the Residency Raj. The process brought about a relatively new complex of economic and social relations and produced stresses and strains that were hitherto unknown. Since an elaborate account of these developments and their implications is beyond the scope of this study, we will content ourselves to attempt to trace the trends merely in what seem to have been the major aspects of these changing relationships. This has been attempted by contrasting the emerging situation with the situation as it obtained before 1880. The emphasis all along is on depicting the changing] forms of the relationships rather than on seeking an explanation for the mechanisms underlying those changes.

MEANS OF COMMUNICATIONS

The most important change that took place was the construction of a cart road, namely the Jhelum Valley Road, which connected Kashmir with the outside world by wheeled traffic. The construction of this road was begun in 1880 and it was completed in September 1890[1] This ended the relative, age-old isolation of Kashmir because of its natural geographical features. At about the time of the completion of Jhelum Valley Road, the construction of a road from Srinagar to the frontier post of Gilgit was undertaken.[2] Later, another road, namely Banihal Cart Road, was constructed from Srinagar to Jammu. The work on it began in 1909 and it was completed in 1922.[3]

LAND AND AGRICULTURE

The history of different questions relating to land and agriculture from 1846 to 1931 falls into two periods: pre-settlement and post-settlement. The preliminary survey work relating to settlement operations was conducted by A. Wingate for about two years from 1887 to 1889. He was succeeded by Walter

1. Prithivi Nath Kaul Bamzai, *A History of Kashmir, Political, Social, Cultural: From the Earliest Times to the Present Dav* (New Delhi, 1973), 2nd revd. edn., p. 693; E.F. Knight, *Where Three Empires Meet* (London, 1905), p. 9.
2. Ibid., pp. 2, 286.
3. Bamzai (1973), p. 693; Gwasha Lal Kaul, *Kashmir Then and Now* (Srinagar, 1967), 8th end., p. 92.

R. Lawrence, who carried out the first land settlement in Kashmir from 1889 to 1895. The work was continued thereafter by others. An account of the changes that occurred in the post-settelment period is given below. The features of the settlement itself will not be dwelt on but will be referred to while discussing the changes caused and in order to show the inter-linkages.

The situation in the pre-settlement period was by and large the same as existed around 1846 and, except for the issue of land ownership and tenure, will not be discussed here. The question of ownership needs further elaboration because it is linked with the fact of the payment of money by Gulab Singh to be British—something that had happened with the establishment of the Dogra rule itself. The question of tenure calls for elaboration because with the advent of the Dogras a new governing power was established.

Land Ownership

There exists a widespread impression, which has also received authentication at the hands of certain writers,[4] that under Dogra rule the people of Kashmir were deprived, for the first time in their history, of the right of 'proprietorship' over land. This seems to be a popular prejudice rather than a well-established fact. We have found nothing to confirm such a belief or to suggest that Gulab Singh or, after him, Ranbir Singh assumed rights over land that had not been exercised by their predecessors in Kashmir. That no such thing was done by Pratap Singh either on his succession to the *gaddi* is suggested by the fact

4. Prem Nath Bazaz, *Inside Kashmir* (Srinagar, 1941), p. 72; Prem Nath Bazaz, *The History of Struggle for Freedom in Kashmir* (New Delhi, 1954), p. 140; F.M. Hassnain, *British Policy Towards Kashmir, 1846-1921: Kashmir in Anglo-Russian Politics* (New Delhi, 1974), p. 32.

Bazaz, however, gives a different account in his later work: '. . . Mughals arbitrarily deprived the Kashmiris of the ownership of their land; the emperor was declared as sole proprietor of all cultivable land in the Valley and the Kashmiri landlords were entered in the revenue registers as tenants. This practice too was continued by the successive rulers . . . .' *Kashmir in Crucible* (New Delhi, 1967), p. 21. Hassnain has ignored this, and to support his contention, has cited Bazaz's earlier work.

that even the author of *Cashmere and its Prince*,[5] a partisan account that was published in 1889 to enable Pratap Singh to retrieve his ruling powers and to safeguard his rights as the rightful descendent of Gulab Singh, does not proclaim any prerogative over land for the Maharaja that did not belong to the predecessors of the Dogra rulers. There is no record of the title used, if any, by Gulab Singh, Ranbir Singh, and, in the beginning of his reign, Pratap Singh to denote right over land in Kashmir. This occurs for the first time in the 'Preliminary Report on Settlement Operations in Kashmir and Jammu' submitted by the first Settlement Offlcer, A Wingate, to Pratap Singh on 1 August 1888. *Inter alia* it states that Pratap Singh had been firm on the point that the *Hak Malikana*, which is transcribed by Wingate as 'proprietorship' over land in Kashmir belonged to the Maharaja.[6] What the exact connotation was of such a title and the basis on which it was founded is not available in the report. If it is granted that the title—*Hak Malikana*—had been used by the Dogra rulers earlier also, the evidence available otherwise makes it clear that the connotation of the title could not be the same as that of the bourgeois juridical right of 'proprietorship' and therefore Wingate's transcription is wrong. The evidence alluded to here is as follows: (a) Gulab Singh acknowledged the possibility of persons other than himself also as 'owner' (s);[7] (b) persons other than

5. Jogendra Chandra Bose, *Cashmere and Its Prince: An Authentic Exposition of the Recent Imbroglio in Cashmere* (Calcutta, 1889). Bose was one of the Bengali officers who had been appointed by Maharaja Pratap Singh and remained in the service of the State for about four months. The said publication by him was a partisan one and was written in defence of the Maharaja.

6. A. Wingate, *Preliminary Report of Settlement Operations in Kashmir and Jammu* (Lahore, 1888), p. 44.

7. This is evident from the fact that Gulab Singh, while engaged in settling the various land grants in consultation with the Government's representative, R G. Taylor, in 1847, laid down as one of the conditions that 'when a man had received the *ijarah* or contract of a village he was not in the second year to become the owner of it and call it *hunood* or *zer-i-niaz*; . . .' *Punjab Government Records* (hereafter *PGR*). Political Diaries (Lahore, 1915), Vol. 6, p. 92.

the Maharaja possessed rights such as *Malikana*;[8] and (c) the right to sell land was entertained and recognized by law during the reign of Ranbir Singh.[9]

What really is at issue here is whether Pratap Singh claimed the title of *Hak Malikana* simply by virtue of succession as the sovereign of Kashmir or because his grandfather Gulab Singh had to pay money, according to the terms of the Treaty, for the transfer of the territories to him. Lawrence, who succeeded to Wingate's position in April 1899, does not touch upon this point directly. However, there are statements by him,[10] the veracity of which might be debated now, which clearly imply that such a title was claimed by him as an inheritance by virtue of his being the ruler of Kashmir and not otherwise. The contention of the author of *Cashmere and its Prince* is similar. Bose says : 'The Maharaja is by immemorial custom the owner of the soil.'[11] There was nothing unique in this. The rulers of other Native States, as we know from a British authority of those days on agrarian history in India, B.H. Baden-Powell, were also said to stake such a claim.[12]

The scope of such a title, or the extent of its application *vis-a-vis Zamindars*, can be understood by the practice that was followed under Dogra rulers in Kashmir uptil the time of the

8. *Old English Records*, 1911, File No. (F.N.) 134/L-168, Revenue Minister to Chief Minister, 26 June 1913, Jammu and Kashmir State Archives (Jammu), (hereafter *OER*, JKA).

9. This is evident from the fact that a tax on any sale of land was charged by the state. See Robert Thorp, 'Kashmir Misgovernment' in S.N. Gadru, ed., *Kashmir Papers* (Srinagar, 1973), p. 79; Charles Ellison Bates, *A Gazetteer of Kashmir and the Adjacent Districts of Kishtwar, Badrawar, Jamu, Naoshera, Punch and the Valley of the Kishen Ganga* (Calcutta, 1873), p. 100. Robert Thorp made the above observation in Kashmir in 1868 and his *Kashmir Misgovernment* was published in 1870.

10. 'The land in those days [Mughal era] was apparently regarded as the absolute property of the State, and every year allotments were made to the cultivators'. Walter R. Lawrence, *The Valley of Kashmir* (Reprint Srinagar, 1967), p. 402. '. . . in the Mughal times and thereafter, from the point of view of the State, status of assami (zamindar) in theory meant nothing more than a tenant-at-will.' Ibid., p. 428.

11. Bose (1889), p. 83.

12. B.H. Baden-Powell, *The Land-Systems of British India* (Reprint Delhi, 1974), Vol, 1, pp. 320-32, 246; Vol. 3, p. 122.

first settlement. However, first we must ask whether the *Zamindars* enjoyed any rights over land. Lawrence states that they did enjoy a right known as *miras*.[13] This word is commonly understood in Kashmir even now and denotes hereditary possession. Thus Lawrence affirms categorically the uninterrupted use of such a right by the *Zamindars* till the time of land settlement in Kashmir.[14] And this is well corroborated by Baden-Powell.[15]

With the land settlement carried out under Residency Raj, bourgeois juridical forms of property came to be introduced in Kashmir. As elsewhere in India, the concept of absolute property was thus introduced in Kashmir too. Once the title of *Hak Malikana* got metamorphosized into proprietorship, and was reserved in this form for the Maharaja, its logical outcome was the ascription of the status of tenant to every landholder under it. And that is what actually happened. Every landholder, whether *Zamindar* or *Chakdar*, was given the status of a tenant with 'Permanent hereditary occupancy rights'.[16] These were at the same time made non-alienable by sale or mortgage.[17] It has to be remembered here that the right to alienation by sale or mortgage was not denied to the landholders because such denial was taken to be a corollary to proprietorship but for quite another consideration. Lawrence believed that the 'right to sell and mortgage would in the end injure the Musalmans of Kashmir, [*sic*] . . . it would also injure the State, by the introduction of a large class of powerful middlemen, who would intercept the land revenue due to the Darbar'.[18] In substantia-

13. Walter R. Lawrence, op. cit., p. 428.

14. 'Changes of dynasty and changes of system, earthquakes, floods, and famines, have alike failed to obliterate the hereditary principle in land tenures in Kashmir . . . .' Ibid., p. 428.

15. 'They [Rajas of Chamba, Kashmir, and those of the Simla Hill States] respect occupancy—rights of old cultivators, and certainly admit the heritable nature of the right; but they do not allow of alienation, without permission and payment of a fee, or 'nazrana', to the chief.' Baden-Powell, op. cit., Vol. 1, p, 232.

16. Walter R. Lawrence, op. cit., p. 429.

17. Ibid., p. 6.

18. Ibid., p. 432.

tion of his contention, he recalled the outcome of the grant of such a right to the peasants in the British Indian provinces and wrote : '. . . every year Musalman proprietors are becoming the servants of Hindu Banias.'[19]

Having shown that the question of 'proprietary right' over land in Kashmir came into being only as a concomitant of the settlement operations, it would be worthwhile to investigate what really gave birth to this question at all and, more important, how it developed further. It may be suggested in passing that since the Maharaja was under pressure from the Government to provide land to European/British subjects, a fact to which we have alluded earlier, he may have put forth the claim and then insisted on it to thwart the Government from distributing land in the 'Happy Valley' to British colonizers.[20] The basis for his claim lay probably in the difference in the history of land tenures in Kashmir and other territories of the State.[21]

Evidence exists to suggest that till as late as 1897, there was no change in the way that the Maharaja's right over different territories in the State were perceived. The Maharaja, who became involved in a dispute with the Resident in 1897 over the issue of his rights over some forests in Jammu province, expressed his ideas and beliefs about the nature of his rights, both 'private' and otherwise. The Maharaja does not seem to have had any inkling until then of linking up the question of his rights over land in Kashmir and the payment made by Gulab Singh to the British.[22]

It was in 1901 that the claims of the Maharaja's rights over Kashmir and some of the other territories of the State in those terms became evident. This is explicit from the Memorandum drawn up by the Settlement Commissioner in 1901 regarding

19. Ibid.

20. See Bose (1889), p. 83.

21. This difference in land-tenures was most probably an outcome of the difference in the histories of the two regions. Kashmir, unlike other territories of the State, had been declared *Khalsa* by Akbar and was continued as such by later Mughals, Afghans, and Sikhs.

22. *See Foreign Department Proceedings*, Secret—E, February 1898, nos. 183-286, National Archives of India, New Delhi (hereafter *FDP* NAI).

transfer of lands by mortgage in Kashmir. It laid down that the '*Sarkar*' (Ruler) possessed not only '*Haq Shahi*' (Ruling Right) in Kashmir Province but also '*Haq Milikiyat*' (Proprietary right); and that these rights belonged to him by virtue of '*Kharid*' (Purchase).[23] Who the propounder of this theory was, whether the Maharaja or the Settlement Commissioner, is not known. However, once such a theory had been propounded, the Settlement Commissioner set out to introduce some changes. He wanted to withdraw

> the right which the residents of Srinagar at present enjoy of executing deeds of transfer with respect to the right of occupancy or permanent residence in regard to the land in their possession without previous reference to the authorities, & proposing rules laying down the manner in which permission to the transfer of such right of occupation or permanent residence shall in future be accorded.[24]

Another change sought to be introduced by the Settlement Commissioner was to levy a ground rent from the occupiers of land. The Judicial Member of the then State Council, Narayan Das, however, refused to countenance such proposals. With regard to the proposal of levying ground rent, he wrote that

> the measure would cause considerable heartburning & discontent & I am not in favour of its adoption. The people understand the unwritten law that the State is the proprietor of all land in the country & as long as no special necessity exists for the levy of ground rent as proposed I would not adopt the proposal as made with the object merely of making the people realise the existence of that proprietary right.[25]

Although the old occupiers of land and residents at Srinagar were thus saved from paying ground rent, such rent nevertheless

23. *OER*, 1901, F.N. 71-H-18, Settlement Commissioner's Memo, JKA.
24. *OER*, 1902, F.N. 190/0-87, Judicial Member's Note on Settlement Commissioner's Memo, JKA.
25. Ibid.

came to be levied on those who received land from the State for construction purposes within the then recently extended parts of Srinagar.[26]

The logical outcome of these developments was that, unlike earlier, the right of alienation now came to be taken to be a corollary of proprietary right over land, and it was claimed not as a prerogative of sovereignty but on the basis of the fact that Gulab Singh had to pay money for it to the British under Article 3 of the Treaty. This in turn implied another assumption the validity of which, however, seems questionable. It was that the money was paid not in respect of all the territories put under the State but only for those which had not constituted the fief which Gulab Singh held from Lahore Durbar which included Kashmir. All this was summed up by the Maharaja in 1918 in a directive to his Chief Minister. He wrote:

> . . . proprietary rights in all the lands of Kashmir belong to the Ruling Chief exclusively, for the simple reason that the torritories of Kashmir were purchased by my late lamented grandfather Maharaja Gulab Singh Ji and hence any sale of such land by any one else is illegal.[27]

Land Tenures

The predominant system of land tenure during the pre-settlement period was that of free hereditary peasant holdings.[28] However, a few big hereditary proprietary privileged landholders—the *chakdars*—were created under whom were a class of tenant cultivators.[29] These tenant cultivators had an obvious interest in accepting that position rather than be free peasants—it

26. *OER*, 1901, F.N. 134/B-20, State Council Resolutions no. 8 dated 7 September 1901 and no. 2 dated 16 June 1905, JKA.

27. *OER*, 1906, F.N. 191/H-75, Maharaja to Chief Minister, D.O., 14 December 1918, JKA.

28. This becomes visible particularly from what Wingate has to say about the land tenures in Kashmir. What he found there was characterized in short by him as 'ryotwari' in ruins. Wingate (1888), p. 33.

29. See, for example, the *patta* issued to one Diwan Nihal Chand, dated 23 Har 1919, in *OER*, 1911, F.N. 134/L-168, JKA.

freed them from the frequent call for *begar* (forced labour).[30] But there is nothing to suggest that there could have existed a class of landless peasants. In fact, measures such as would bind peasants to their holdings were adopted.[31] There was a lack of what has been termed a 'labouring class'.[32]

In the case of the assignees, the situation was as follows. On his takeover, Gulab Singh issued a *quo warranto* to all those who held land grants, of whatever nature, under the tenure of the different Sikh Nazims. The issue of their release was resolved by him in consultation with, and with the cooperation of, an agent of the Government, R.G. Taylor. These were of three categories. The first consisted of those who were given grants before the time of the last two Nazims—Sheikhs Ghulam Mohy-ud-Din and Imam-ud-Din. Such grantees, to quote Taylor, were 'the most respectable people of the country'.[33] The grants of 'nearly all' these persons, it is certain, were released.[34] Regarding the other two categories, i.e., those received under the tenure of the two Sheikhs, nothing definite is known. However, from the comments of Taylor that are pertinent to the question,[35] it seems that not many amongst these could have been released.

30. See Walter R. Lawrence, op. cit., p. 414.

31. These were the practice of forcing the peasants to cultivate land and the system of *Rahdari*. The latter was the system of preventing people from leaving the valley. It was removed during the famine in 1878. See Wingate (1888), p. 16.

32. Lawrence, op. cit., p. 411.

33. *PGR*, Political Diaries, Vol. 4, p. 60,

34. Ibid., p. 58.

35. 'The grants up to the time of the elder Sheikh embrace those given to the most respectable people in the country; and it is apparent that both the elder Sheikh and his son, Emamoodeen, were, the former unusually liberal and the latter rather careless in the amount bestowed in grants of this nature. When the enquiry is completed the question will be to what extent the grants of the latter two individuals are to be released; . . . The Maharaja will, I am persuaded, do whatever is distinctly recommended. At present I hold out little hopes to the claimants of grants received in the times of the two Sheikhs, and have not requested the Maharaja to allow the collection of revenue from them to be suspended pending a decision. The people are very exigent and require a little rough handling. The elder Sheikh received charge of the country

The question of releasing the various grants or withholding them, notwithstanding a later day statement of a native historian,[36] was not decided on communal considerations. It is possible that in a region where nearly the whole population comprised of Muslims many of the sufferers may have been Muslims. In view of the other facts provided by the same historian and the evidence found in Taylor's diaris, it becomes apparent that the issue was not settled along communal lines but that those in whose favour the grants were released included a substantial number of Muslims.[37] The deciding factor seems to have been the importance of the grantee. The sufferes, mostly those it is almost certain whose grants had been of very recent origin, seem generally to have been people of lesser social standing. Besides retaining the grants in favour of some of the ertwhile assignees, some new additions were made in the pre-settlement

in 1898 [*sic*], and surely men who have received grants of land within the last five years from a Viceregent confessedly weak and capricious in his latter days, and others within the last two years from his son, who, a youngman unused to business, would have given away anything to gain popularity (a quality that has earned for him the title of the "Nawab"), can afford to wait till the nature of their claims has been fully examined, and may, I should think, consider themselves very fortunate if their grants are eventually released.' Ibid., p. 60.

'Towards the end of the evening I mentioned the *dhurmarth* cases, and said that I thought I should have to request him to release part, at any rate, of the Sheikh's grants. I wished to prepare his mind for such a result, but I think it is very possible that I may not have to do so.' Ibid. p. 73.

36. Gulab Singh, says Hassan, confiscated forcibly the property belonging to top Muslim families. And this was done, so he says, on the advice of the Pandits. Hassan, *Tarikh Kashmir* (Political Section), Maulvi Mohammed Ibrahim, trans. (Urdu) (Srinagar, 1957), p. 568.

37. Hassan claims that Main Singh, the predecessor of Sheikh Ghulam Mohy-ud-Din, had the *jagirs* that had been confiscated in the wake of occupation of Kashmir by the Sikhs (1819) restored and granted by Maharaja Ranjit Singh amongst Brahmins, *Faqirs* and *Darveshs*. Ibid, p. 531. This statement, taken together with the fact that the noted family of Naqashbands had a further advance in its fortunes around this time (1835) suggests that the leading men or families were restored to their earlier status and position before the tenure of the two Sheikhs started. And, as we know from Taylor, the grants of 'nearly all' these persons were released by Gulab Singh.

period. First, there was a group of Dogra Mian Rajputs.[38] Second, there was a group of Pathans (Afghans).[39] Both groups received the concession in lieu of their military service to the State. In addition a few *Ahlkari Chaks* were also granted—to individuals who were high up in the civil service of the State.[40]

At the time of the settlement all those peasant proprietors who agreed to pay the assessment fixed on their holdings were recognized as *assamis*.[41] To extend cultivation and secure more revenue for the State, *chaks* were distributed freely to all those who applied for them at concessional revenue rates. This was done under what was known as Regulation No. 6. They were recognized as *Chakdar assamis* and had the same status as ordinary *assamis* except that they paid revenue at concessional rates.[42] In 1894, Regulation No. 5 was enacted specially for Dogra Rajputs.[43]

The class of different kinds of assignees was not only maintained after the land settlement but means were also devised to keep them strong.[44] The rule of primogeniture was introduced under the Residency Raj to strengthen this class. The reason for this is stated clearly in a letter from the Assistant to the British Resident written to the Chief Minister in 1913:

> The policy underlying the state council decisions is the prevention of the frittering away of a Jagir into small portions with the consequent reduction of the status of Jagirdars to that of the ordinary indigent Zamindars, and the *establishment of a class of landed gentry, loyal to His Highness*

38. Walter R. Lrwrence, op. cit., p. 305.
39. Ibid., p. 309.
40. See *OER*, 1911, F.N. 134/L-168. JKA.
41. See Walter R. Lawrence, op. cit., p. 429.
42. *OER*, 1900, F.N. 96/H-11; ibid., 1911, F.N. 134/L-168, Revenue Minister's Memo, 22 August, JKA; and Walter R. Lawrence, op. cit., p. 426.
43. See *OER*, 1894, F.N. 67, State Council Resolution, 3 February 1894, JKA.
44. See Government of Jammu & Kashmir, Ministry of Revenue, *Jagirs, Muafis and Mukarraris* (Srinagar, 1956); and Government of Jammu and Kashmir, *On the Way to Golden Harvests: Agricultural Reforms in Kashmir* (Jammu, 1951).

the Maharaja, influential in their local districts, and capable of exerting a wholesome effect on the surrounding peasantry (emphasis added).[45]

Security of Tenures

The prescriptive rights enjoyed by the peasant proprietors, as noted earlier, and the facts of availability of waste land, lack of pressure on land, existence of crop-sharing as the form of taxation, system of *Rahdari*[46] and the evidence from Lawrence that force was employed to make the *Zamindars* till the land,[47] all suggest that there was no problem of lack of security of tenure for them in the pre-settlement period.

Lawrence claimed, and it has been accepted uncritically by later writers, that the land settlement introduced security of land for the *Zamindars*.[48] However, a careful study of the available official records does not suggest that this proved to be a boon for all those dependent on land for their livelihood nor was it assured for all time to come. Though an intensive treatment of this subject is out of place here a mention of the trends in this sphere is necessary.

Certain changes introduced along with land settlement obviously had their concomitant inconveniences for the peasant cultivators. Before the settlement, a peasant cultivator automatically earned prescriptive right to land which he tilled, and which was not in any other person's possession. This right, as has been seen, was equivalent to the right that was bestowed upon the landholders after the settlement. Subsequently, after the conception of juridical rights had been introduced, the mere breaking of virgin land or cultivation of land did not earn the tiller right over it. The right had to be secured formally from the State. Thus we find that the fact of having cultivated a particular tract of land did not necessarily nor always lead to

45. *OER*, 1913, F.N. 162/H-13, Assistant to the Resident to Chief Minister, 14 November 1913, JKA.

46. This practice has already been referred to earlier at f.n. 31.

47. Walter R. Lawrence, op. cit., p. 2.

48. See ibid., p. 4; Bazaz (1941), p. 71; Bazaz (1954), pp. 138-39; Bamzai (1973), pp. 690-91.

the recognition of right over such land by the State. There is evidence to suggest that land broken or tilled by peasant cultivators was subsequently granted to others.[49]

The 'permanent' and 'hereditary occupancy right' that was conferred at the time of the settlement was subject to one condition, namely, that the person concerned undertook to pay the revenue fixed at the time of assessment on his land.[50] Before the settlement, as is evident from the narrative of Lawrence, the taxation system was such that there could accumulate a big revenue deficit against the *zamindars* as '*bakaya*'.[51] But such accumulation never led to their eviction from the land under their possession. After the settlement, the non-payment by a person of revenue, that came now to be levied in cash, resulted in what was known as voluntary *dustbardari* by the person concerned. Sufficient evidence is available to suggest that the land so given up was passed on by the State to any other person who would volunteer to pay the revenue that lay outstanding against the earlier occupant of the land.[52] An order from Maharaja Pratap Singh in 1911, which refers to the fact of 'several transfers of land in the [Kashmir] valley' having taken place during the tenure of a late Governor and declares these invalid unless his proper sanction was secured, establishes beyond any doubt that the incidence of cases of voluntary *dustbardari* must have been numerous rather than just a few isolated cases.[53] This process was conducive to the creation of a large section of landless labourers such as existed by 1931.

Pressure on Land

Prior to the land settlement there was no pressure on land. A

49. See *OER*, 1911, F.N. 14/B-168, Petition from Sri Kanth Khazanchi to Maharaja, 12 August 1913, JKA.

50. See Walter R. Lawrence, op. cit., pp. 429-30.

51. Ibid., pp. 407-8, 448-50.

52. See *OER*, 1909, F.N. 112/H-1, Chief Minister to Resident, 5 January 1909, JKA.

53. See *OER*, 1910, F.N. 218/H-23, Maharaja to Chief Minister, 20/22 July 1910, JKA.

good deal of land was available for reclamation even at the time of the land settlement.[54]

After the settlement, the trend changed gradually. By 1921 the situation had taken a turn for the worse. The two important reasons to which such a change can be attributed were the population growth[55] and the increasing de-industrialization in the rural sector. Be that as it may, the fact remains that the pressure on land had increased and the Census Commissioner for 1921 recognized it thus:

> The existence of this surplus population though only for a few months in the year, is an evidence of the fact that agriculture is outgrowing its resources, and an increase in cultivated area at the recent settlement part of the population to other pursuits beyond the State boundary is a further indication of the necessity of finding fresh outlets for local employment of the cultivator.[56]

Conditions by the end of the next decade had deteriorated further. The Census Commissioner for 1931 described the State as a 'predominantly agricultural country'.[57] He declared:

> If agriculture is to form the principal source of livelihood of the State population it would appear that the pressure on the resources is already exerting itself in most of the districts . . . .[58]

About Baramulla, one of the two districts of Kashmir, he wrote:

> . . . practically every acre of land has been brought under the plough and the only remedy lies in increasing the yield

54. See Walter R. Lawrence, op. cit., pp. 411, 426.

55. The population of Kashmir Valley which in 1891 was 814,241 had gone up to 1,190,977 by 1921. *Census of India, 1921,* Kashmir (Lahore 1923), Pt. 1, p. 25.

56. *Census, 1921,* Pt. 1, p. 163.

57. *Census of India. 1931,* Jammu and Kashmir (Jammu, 1933), Pt. 1, p. 16.

58. Ibid., p. 62.

> from the land and not bringing new land under cultivation which is a wellnigh ruled out problem, unless the cultivable area is supplementcd either by enroachments on the forests or the drying up of the Wuller lake or breaking up the hill sides.[59]

Agricultural Indebtedness

Lawrence, who was at pains to elaborate upon the condition of cultivators, gives no indication that the phenomenon of agricultural indebtedness existed in the pre-settlement period. As a matter of fact, he is categorical that 'the Banya of India is practically unknown in Kashmir . . . .'[60] Of course, this does not mean that all terms of credit were totally unknown. In fact, he wrote that

> in all the larger villages there is found a *Wani* or *Bakal*, who is a Musalman huckster . . . . The *Wani* sometimes lends money to his customers under the system known as *Wad* . . . Although both lender and borrower repudiate the idea of interrst passing, as a matter of fact the profit made by the *Wani* represents a rate of interest varying from 24 to 36 per cent.[61]

However, he wrote that 'at present the cultivator, somehow or other, manages to cultivate his land without going to the moneylender . . . .'[62]

The situation changed in the post-settlement period. The *Wad* became a prominent and important part of village life. This development, generally the result of the need of the peasants to pay the revenue in cash, worked to the detriment of

59. Ibid., p. 55.
60. Walter R. Lawrence, op. cit., p. 387.
61. Ibid. Cf. 'The shopkeeper (*wani*) is a Musalman and must not take *interest*. He lends money to the peasants on a system known as *wad*. A man borrows 50 rupees, and promises to pay this within the year in blankets, ghi, apples, grain etc. The rate fixed by the *wani* for blankets will be 3 ruppes, whereas the market price at which thc *wani* will sell is 3 rupees 8 annas, or 4 ruppes.' Ibid, p. 5.
62. Ibid., p. 432.

their condition. It was perhaps to pre-empt the development of some serious situation for the State on account of the disconent prevalent as a result of the deplorable condition of the peasants that Maharaja Hari Singh promulgated an' Agriculturists Relief Act' in 1927.[63]

Demand on Land

The existence of a subsistence economy, the type of agrarian system existing then, lack of pressure on land and other related factors could not have produced much demand for land in the pre-settlement period. Nor was the case any different at the time of the settlment.[64] However, subsequent developments increased the demand for land both in and around Srinagar and in the countryside. Such an eventuality had been anticipated, in a way, at the time of settlement.[65] The fact that a proposal was made in 1901 to the effect that *Harjana* (penalty) should be demanded from a person who wanted to relinquish a *chack* granted under the current rules or under the former rulers,[66] suggests that agricultural land had not yet become a sufficiently valuable possession for non-agriculturists. However, the trend changed soon. This is clear from the contents of the petitions submitted by one Sir Kanth Khazanchi in 1911 to the Maharaja for grant of land to him. The petitioner was a native and belonged to the *Karkun* Pandit class. This fact coupled with the contents of his petitions suggest that the process of competition amongst the natives who were non-agriculturists for the possession of agricultural land had already begun.[67] The concept of differentiating between the natives and outsiders also

63. Cf. 'The Agriculturist's Relief Act specially relieved the cultivator from the clutches of the moneylender.' Gwasha Lal Kaul (1967), p. 101.

64. This becomes patently clear from the account given by Lawrence about the land and its settlement. Walter R. Lawrence, op. cit.

65. See, for example, Watler R. Lawrence, op. cit., p. 6; and *FDP*, Secret Branch E, July 1894, nos. 132-3, Secretary's Note, 3 May 1894, NAI,

66. *OER*, 1901, F.N. 48/R-45A, JKA.

67. See *OER*, 1911, F.N. 14/B-168, Petitions by Pandit Sri Kanth Khazanchi, 13 September 1911, 4 August 1912, 16 October 1912, 12 August 1913, JKA.

seems to have germinated at this time.[68] It had developed considerably by 1921 when expression was given to this feeling in the outside press by some *Karkun Pandits.*[69] By 1931 the notion had gained ground that *Zameen gao Krehne soun,*[70] which in Kashmiri means that possession of land was considered equivalent to the possession of gold. The same sentiment was echoed in a Persian phrase also.[71] Therefore it is hardly surprising that after proprietary right had been conferred on landholders in Kashmir in 1932, which was one of the main outcomes of the upsurge and which entailed permission for the alienation of land by sale, that there was a race among resourceful people to buy land from the *Zamindars.*[72] These adventurers included both Hindus and Muslims. The leaders of the agitation did nothing to stop such transactions.[73] It is possible that the Muslim commercial bourgeoisie developed a strong urge to own agricultural land and raised the issue of the bestowal of proprietary right over land to *Zamindars* for this reason. Proprietary right over land, it has already been seen, had become linked with the right of alienation by sale.

But even before the demand arose for agricultural land, there developed a demand for land for construction purposes at Srinagar and its suburbs. Rules for the grant of building sites at Srinagar were framed first in 1901. The State Council resolution pertaining to this says that this was done in view of 'the constantly increasing demand for superior house accommodation

68. See ibid., Petition dated 13 September 1911.

69. This is seen in the newspaper articles by 'Kashmiricus' and 'Satis Superque' in *United India and Indian States*, 22 September 1921. A copy of this issue is preserved in *OER*, 1921, F.N. 73/97-C, JKA. For an insight into what 'Kashmiricus' wrote, see ch. 6.

70. This information has been gathered by the author in interviews with a number of old natives of Kashmir.

71. Personal interview with Damoodhar Bhat, 22 November 1977 (Srinagar). Bhat, a lawyer by profession, is a public figure. He came first into prominence as Secretary of the Sanatan Dharam Young Men's Association formed in 1931. Later, he became a Marxist and was actively associated with the Communists in Kashmir.

72. Munshi Naseer-ud-Din, *Tarikh Jang Azadiye Kashmir* (Urdu) (Srinagar, 1971), p. 142.

73. Ibid., pp. 141-42.

in the town of Srinagar and elsewhere and the desirability of meeting the same'.[74] There is reason to believe that this demand must have arisen after the construction of the Jhelum Valley Road and the consequent influx of Punjabi traders whom the Government was keen to encourage to settle down in Kashmir in pursuance of its policy of encouraging trade there.[75] However, there is sufficient evidence to indicate that the demand for land for construction purposes at Srinagar did not come only from the Punjabis but also from the natives.[76]

This prompted the state to re-open in 1915 the question regarding the practice started in 1900 which entitled a tenant-cultivator to occupancy rights after having held land continuously for twelve years.[77] It was considered unfair that a cultivator 'should acquire right of occupancy either in land or in residential *ahatas* or in lands of which the value for building purpose far exceeds the agricultural value' [78] The Committee appointed to look into the question 'unanimously recommended that no right of occupancy should in future be created in the Srinagar city'.[79] The areas affected by such a measure were the twelve *zilas* of Srinagar, namely, Narsingh Garh, Haba Kadal, Maharaj Ranbir Ganj, Tashwan, Rainawari, Nawa Kadal, Mohi Guna, Kothi Bagh, Chatta Bal, Sangin Darwaza, Nauhatta and Khanyar.[80] The approval of the Resident for the introduction of such a measure was obtained in 1920.[81] That this measure undoubtedly gave rise to a lot of discontent amongst the cultivators of these lands is suggested by the fact that as far back as 1915 it was feared by the officials that if the 'proposal not to

74. *OER*, 1901, F.N. 134/6-20, Council Resolution no. 8, 7 September 1901, JKA.

75. See and cf. Walter R. Lawrence, op. cit., pp. 384, 387 and *OER*, 1901, F.N. 71/H-18, Settlement Commissioner's Memorandum (Urdu), paragraphs on trade.

76. See, for example, *OER*, 1906, F.N. 220/X-157, papers regarding grant of land for building purpose to one Aziz Ju Kausa, JKA.

77. *OER*, 1915, F.N. 259/H-68, Settlement Commissioner to Revenue Minister, 16 June 1919, JKA.

78. Ibid.

79. Ibid.

80. Ibid., Revenue Minister to Chief Minister, 4/9 September 1915.

81. Ibid., Resident, Col. Bannerman's D.O., 25 August 1920.

allow right of occupancy in Srinagar city lands gets known there will be a great rush of suits for acquisition of occupancy rights'.[82]

INDUSTRIES

Industry witnessed certain important developments during the period under consideration, both in the urban and the rural sectors.

Urban Industries

Shawl Industry

Despite the decline in the shawl industry by 1846, which was a consequence of the extension and consolidation of territories by the East India Company northwards, the industry still survived during the earlier part of the period under consideration. In fact, the industry came to flourish[83] for a little while (1865-72) on account of the availability of a new market in France where shawls had become a high status article of attire.[84] But the Franco-German war of 1870, which ended in the defeat of France and the heavy war indemnity demand from it by Germany, gave a 'deathblow' to this industry.[85] Any hope of its revival was 'dashed' by the famine of 1877-79 in Kashmir,[86] in which three-fifths of the population is supposed to have vanished. 'None suffered more heavily in that calamity than the poor weakly shawl-weavers'.[87] Lawrence, who perhaps felt shy of enumerating and admitting the principal cause of decline, nevertheless wrote that it was 'commonly reported that the fine wool of the Central Asian goats no longer finds its way to

82. Ibid., Revenue Minister to Chief Minister, 4/9 September 1915.

83. Walter R. Lawrence, op. cit., pp. 375-76; Sir Francis Younghusband, *Kashmir* (Reprint, New Delhi, 1970), p. 212.

84. Walter R. Lawrence, op. cit., p. 376; Younghusband, op. cit., pp. 210-11.

85. Walter R. Lawrence, op. cit., p. 375; Younghusband, op. cit., p. 211.

86. Walter R. Lawrence, op. cit., p. 375.

87. Ibid.

Kashmir, and the scarcity of the raw material, combined with the smallness of the demand, has reduced the shawl-trade to the smallest dimensions'.[88] This was undoubtedly a fall-out of British imperialism. The verdict on the fate of the industry as it was during Lawrence's stay (1889-95) in Kashmir, was succinctly expressed by him: 'The shawl industry is now unfortunately a tradition—a memory of the past'.[89]

The account given in 1909 by Francis Younghusband, who stayed long in Kashmir as the Government's representative—Resident, does not indicate that the industry was restored to its earlier shape even by that time.

The shawl industry, though it never gained the position it had enjoyed for centuries, was carried on right up to 1931. 'Thousands of adults and immatures' in Kashmir depended for employment then on the shawl and its accompaniment—fringe weaving.[90]

Carpet Industry

The carpet industry was organized at Srinagar by British entrepreneurs. Lawrence makes a mention of three persons who were engaged in 'business in Srinagar as manufacturers of carpets'. He does not, however, name them as being British but as Europeans.[91] Younghusband makes a mention of their enterprises as 'two European firms, Messrs Mitchell and Co., and Mr. Hadow'.[92] These firms were established at Srinagar immediately after the introduction of the Residency Raj and was evidently a concomitant of the demand of the Government to provide facilities to 'all' British subject to do business in Kashmir. The industry gave employment to a 'considerable number' of the shawl weavers who had lost employment because of the decline of shawl industry.[93] As early as 1891,

88. Ibid.
89. Ibid.
90. *Census 1931*, p. 216.
91. Walter R. Lawrence, op. cit., p. 377.
92. Younghusband, op. cit., p. 212.
93. Walter R. Lawrence, op. cit., p. 377. See also Younghusband, op. cit., p. 212.

between 800 and 900 of them were already employed in the manufacture of carpets.[94] New manufacturing firms of carpets were established during the decade preceding 1931.[95]

Silk Industry

It was in 1870-71 (Samvat 1927) that Maharaja Ranbir Singh had started the silk industry at Srinagar in a 'systematic way'.[96] In 1873-74 'an extensive establishment' giving employment to 400 men existed at Srinagar, and it was said that there was room for an additional 'four times the number'. There existed then itself a larger filature in one of the suburbs of Srinagar. The attempt in this direction, as suggested by our source, was warranted by the ruin of shawl industry.[97] The industry was in a 'flourishing condition' till 1878-79 (Samvat 1935) when it was abandoned because of worldwide plague of 1878 (Samvat 1934). However, it was revived in July 1888 (Samvat Har 1945).[98]

In 1901, 'no less than six or seven thousand inhabitants of Srinagar are to be found working in the [silk] factory'.[99] In 1931, the silk factory at Srinagar was said to be the 'biggest in the world' and gave employment to 'hundreds of persons';[100] the exact number is not stated.

Other Industries

During the decade preceding 1931 some other industries such as a match factory, and an oil factory, besides a few small scale industries were also established. The state appears to have taken an active interest in this new development. This is indicated by the fact of the establishment of a portfolio of Commerce and Industries in the State Government in 1922.[101] Besides,

94. Walter R. Lawrence, op. cit., p. 375.
95. *Census of India, 1931,* p. 36.
96. *Administration Report of Jammu and Kashmir State, 1889-90*, p. 63, (hereafter *ARJKS*).
97. H.W. Bellew, *Kashmir and Kashgar: A Narrative of the Journey of the Embassy to Kashgar in 1873-74* (London, 1875), p. 83.
98. *ARJKS, 1889-90*, p. 63.
99. *Census of India, 1901,* Kashmir (Lahore, 1902), Pt. 1, p. 10.
100. *Census of India, 1931*, p. 216.
101. Ibid., p. 36.

> Kashmir handicrafts and cottage industries too numerous to mention have side by side made a satisfactory all round progress which is evidenced by the birth of new manufacturing firms of carpets, puttos, lois, silks, shawls, embroideries, papier-mache works, silver-ware and wood-carving, etc.[102]

The foregoing makes it clear that a large population in Srinagar was dependent on the different urban industries all through the period under consideration. What is not so obvious is the fact that this population, and also their dependents, experienced the trauma of uncertainty with regard to their livelihood during this period triggered by the decline of the shawl industry. It is not likely that cause remained hidden from those who were dependent on it for their survival. It is probable that this knowledge was a contributory factor for colony of Kashmiri shawl weavers at Ludhiana in 1857 to be

> among the foremost in 'plundering the Government stores, in pillaging the premises of the American mission, in burning the churches and buildings, in destroying the printing process, and in pointing out the residences of Government officials, or known well-wishers of Government, as objects of vengeance for the mutinous troops'.[103]

In 1870, when the Franco-German war broke out, the shawl weavers in Kashmir 'watched the fate of France in that struggle—bursting into tears and loud lamentations when the news of Germany's victories reached them'.[104]

After the First World War broke out, and trade was dislocated as a result of it, 'most of these people' were seen 'selling off even their ordinary clothes in order to provide themselves with means of subsistence'.[105]

The world-wide economic depression which started in 1929 also produced adverse conditions for the trade and consequently

102. Ibid.
103. Bates (1873), pp. 36-37.
104. Walter R. Lawrence, op. cit., p. 375.
105. *OER*, 1915, F.N. 278/P-16, Revenue Minister's Note, 8 March 1915, JKA.

for the artisans. The prices of shawls fell 'considerably' and an era of cheap shawls set in.[106] The workmen and petty shop keepers were reduced to 'low straits'. 'The shawl embroiderers and the papier-mache artists were thrown out of job'.[107]

Given this background, it is not difficult to visualize the state of mind of these people. More so, if note is taken of the norms of behaviour prevalent among them during the contemporary period. In 1915, an official reported about these people: 'Nor would any of their class do manual labour of any kind, even as an alternative to starvation, as they regarded it as a disgrace and they would rather die than suffer that disgrace.'[108]

Rural Industries

There is no evidence available to suggest that there was a process of de-industrialization in the rural sector before the establishment of Residency Raj in the State territories. Rather it seems that with the opening up of Kashmir to British tourists after the creation of the State the demand for the locally produced *putto* must have arisen.[109]

The situation, however, changed later. This evidently followed the opening of Kashmir after the construction of Jhelum Valley Road and the active encouragement of the Government to increase trade. Indigenous goods gave place to machine-made goods from outside. The Census Commissioner for 1911 recognized this fact:

> In Kashmir, as in other parts of India, the older and indigenous industries have tended to decline; but for this the State can scarcely be held accountable. With a gradual change in the style of living and of the tastes of people, whose wants were once supplied by local industries, there has come a diminution of the demand for the various articles

106. *Census of India, 1931*, p. 216.

107. Bamzai (1973), p. 707.

108. *OER*, 1915, F.N. 278/P-16. Revenue Minister's Note, 8 March 1915, JKA.

109. '. . . the home spun cloth [pattu] woven by the villagers in the winter is highly appreciated both by Europeans and visitors.' Walter R. Lawrence, op. cit., p. 370.

and commodities upon the manufacture of which those industries depended.[110]

The effect of the development of such a trend on the producers of indigenous goods was vividly expresed by him: 'The decline of old industries has undoubtedly affected the population to some extent by throwing out of work the persons that once depended upon them for their livelihood.'[111]

The trend was further aggravated by 1921. This is self-evident from what the Census Commissioner for 1921 observed in this connection. He wrote that in comparison with 1911

> we find that there has been an increase in the proportion of the population subsisting on agriculture from 7,979 to 8,173 per 10,000. This increase of 19 *per mille* is counterbalanced by a corresponding decrease of 15, 2 and 4 *per mille* respectively in Industry, Transport and Trade.[112]

It appears that the population thus thrown out of their traditional callings turned to land. This and the trend of de-industrialization in the rural sector continued up to 1931.

> . . .artisans who have to face a severe competition of machine made goods have been severely hit and have turned to land. The agriculturist who was already in that calling sticks to it. Land is the only safety valve to which [all] castes look for an escape from the disaster facing them. The old economic division of society has to a very large extent disappeared. Most of the castes are cut off from their ancient moorings, which has led to unemployment and economic distress.[113]

TRADE AND COMMERCE

Urban Arts and Crafts

The long-route luxury shawl trade of Kashmir had been

110. *Census of India, 1911,* Kashmir (Lucknow, 1912), Pt. 1, p. 60.
111. Ibid., p. 65.
112. *Census of India, 1921,* Pt. 1, p. 162.
113. *Census of India, 1931,* p. 222.

reduced, after Kashmir's dismemberment from the waning Mughal Empire in 1756, to a 'declining and languid state' by 1783. Yet there were still seen in Kashmir 'merchants and commercial agents of the principal cities of northern India, also of Tartary, Persia, and Turkey, who, at the same time, advance their fortunes. . .' .[114] The situation had, however, deteriorated much by 1822-23. This, and the reason which led to it, is clear from what Moorcroft wrote about the situation existing then:

> Political events had largely reduced the trade with Persia, Turkey and the Panjab, and that with Hindustan had sustained much detriment from the prevalence of British rule, and the loss of wealth by the Native courts, in which costly shawls were formerly a principal article of attire.[115]

That the furtherance of British rule in India compounded the adverse effects on Kashmir trade is confirmed by what a British officer touring Kashmir wrote in 1862. After noting the complaint of the shawl dealers regarding the 'slackness of trade', he observed:

> The demand for Kashmir shawls has dwindled in extent proportionately as British supremacy has spread northwards from Bengal proper; . . . whereas in olden days, the native Courts were an unfailing annual source of revenue to the Shreenuggur manufacturer. The fall of Lucknow [The Native state of Oudh with its capital at Lucknow was annexed by the British in February 1856] had been his last and bitterest blow.[116]

114. George Forster, *A Journey from Bengal to England, Through the Northern Part of India, Kashmire, Afghanistan and Persia* (London, 1808), Vol. 2, p. 22.

Forster attributed the decline to 'heavy oppressions of the government, and the rapacious temper of the bordering states, who exercise an unremitting capacity on the foreign traders, and often plunder whole cargoes, ...'

115. Horace Hayman Wilson, ed., *Travels in the Himalayan Provinces of Hindustan and the Panjab, in Ladakh and Kashmir, in Peshawar, Kabul, Kunduz, and Bokhara by Mr. William Moorcroft and Mr. George Trebeck, from 1819 to 1825* (Reprint New Delhi, 1971), Vol. 2, pp. 194-95.

116. Lt. Col. Torrens, *Travels in Ladak, Tartary and Kashmir* (London, 1862), pp. 263-64. He continues to explain:

The sudden collapse of this trade was arrested by the opening up of the new market in France. This gave the industry a new lease of life and trade in it flourished until the Franco-German war of 1870. 'The best shawls ever made in Kashmir were manufactured in time of Maharaja Ranbir Singh, between the years 1865-72'.[117] From 1862 to 1870 the export of shawls averaged 25 to 28 lakhs of rupees per annum.[118] Because of the subsequent developments of the Franco-German war of 1870 and the severe famine of 1877-79 the export fell and in 1893-94 amounted to only Rs. 22,850.[119] That it did not assume its former state is illustrated by what one Christian medical missionary, who at the time of writing (1911) had stayed in Kashmir for a quarter of a century, wrote:

> The shawl trade, for which Kashmir used to be specially famous, has, however, to a large extent passed away. The industry received its death blow in the Franco-German war in 1870-71, after which the great demand in France ceased, and it has never really revived.[120]

'. . . for we are content with—in fact, rather prefer—tweeds and broadcloths, sombre suits of dittos, to the gorgeous colours of the Kashmir fabric; Ellwood's patent helmets, or the modest wide-awake, to the graceful folds of an embroidered turban; and are wont, either by elastic braces, or often simply by the nearer propinquity of button and button-hole, to support our nether garments, making the costly'Cummer-bund', or girdle, an *object de luxe* quite uncalled for; and even our ladies, much as they prize a real Kashmir shawl, are apt to think that one hundred pounds can be spent much more profitably than in the purchase of one; . . . .'

117. Walter R. Lawrence, op. cit., p. 376.

118. Ibid., pp. 376-77.

A traveller, who visited Kashmir in 1870, wrote: 'The French trade is represented by several houses, and their annual exports, chiefly of shawls, average in value four lacs of rupees; besides this they have establishments at Amritsar, where a larger trade is done by them.' Dugsal, *Letters from India and Kashmir: Written 1870* (London, 1874), p. 205.

119. Walter R. Lawrence, op. cit., f.n. on p. 377.

120. Ernest F. Neve, *Beyond the Pir Panjal: Life Among the Mountains and Valleys of Kashmir* (London, 1912), p. 236. Cf. 'The trade received its deathblow when war broke out between Germany and France in 1870 . . . .' Walter R. Lawrence, op. cit., p. 375.

A perusal of the census reports of 1921 and 1931 does not give any indication that the trade staged a comeback to its earlier dimensions. On the contrary, as reported by the Census Commissioner for 1931, 'economic depression' (probably the world economic depression of 1929 and after) had resulted in a considerable fall in the price of shawls and had ushered in an era of 'cheap shawls'.[121] This must obviously have resulted in a substantial cut in the earnings of those who were dependent for their livelihood on the shawl trade.

The accounts given by the various travellers during the nineteenth century illustrate that the attraction of Kashmir for the British as a summer resort provided for the luxury arts and crafts a market at Srinagar itself.[122] It was only natural that such an impetus should have resulted after the construction of Jhelum Valley Road and the further development of tourism. This is confirmed by the evidence provided in the Census Report of 1931.[123]

Consumer Goods

Salt had for long been imported into Kashmir. It was carried by a class of people known as *markhbans* over the high passes into Kashmir.[124] Later, and obviously after the famine of 1877-79

'The true Kashmir shawl is—alas!—almost a thing of the past hardly any being made now; and those that are made want millionaires to buy them. An inferior imitation is made in large numbers, but it does not appeal to me.' Oscar Eckenstein, *The Karakorams and Kashmir* (London, 1896), p. 18; and

'. . . (the old shawl manufacture is totally extinct) . . . .' T.R. Swinburne, *A Holiday in the Happy Valley* (London, 1907), p. 74.

121. *Census of India 1931*, p. 216.

122. Cf. 'The saluburbious (sic) climate, natural scenery, beautiful springs, pleasure grounds and health resorts annually attract a large number of European and Indian visitors who constitute a ready market for the products of Kashmir. Instead of the Kashmir manufactures going in search of the market it is the market itself which annually comes to Kashmir to carry way the products of the country.' Ibid., pp. 54-55.

123. See ibid., p. 36.

124. Walter R. Lawrence, op. cit., p. 383.

when the practice of *rahdari* was abolished, an export trade developed in a small way in consumer goods. This happened as a result of the annual migration of some peasant cultivators for the winter months to Punjab. They would carry 'local produce' on their backs and return with commodities which were light to carry and which would either be used by their families or sold to others.[125]

The real increase in import and export trade of consumer goods was achieved only after the introduction of wheeled traffic into Kashmir. The people who took to it were Punjabi traders and not any particular section or class of natives, a fact which should not be surprising. A territory, where until recently natural and subsistence economy was the order, was suddenly opened to the outside world. A class which possessed 'sufficient enterprise' and 'capital' and as such was in a position to benefit from the new opportunity did not then exist in Kashmir.[126] The *Wani* or *Bakal*, who could have naturally entered it, was found by Lawrence to be 'a man of no enterprise'; he allowed 'the export trade to pass entirely into the hands of the Panjabi traders of the city and towns, who have their agents busily buying up by the system of advances all articles of the export trade'.[127] The description given by Lawrence about the position of the *Wani*, however, shows that he, contrary to what Lawrence tells us, did possess enterprise.[128] What probably worked against him was lack of a sufficient degree of enterprise required under the circumstances and therefore the inability to

125. Ibid.
126. Ibid., p. 390.
127. Ibid., p. 387.
128. H. wrote:

'The Banya of India is practically unknown in Kashmir, but in all the larger villages there is found a *Wani* or *Bakal*, who is a Musalman huckster, with a stock-in-trade amounting to about Rs. 20 to 30 worth of salt, oil, spices, snuff, sugar, tea and sometimes a few rolls of European or Indian cotton piece goods. When these have been disposed of the *Wani* sets off to the nearest depot and replenishes his stock. The *Wani* sometimes lends money to his customers under the system known as *wad*, ... Although both lender and borrower repudiate the idea of interest passing, as a matter of fact the profit made by the *Wani* represents a rate of interest varying from 24 to 36 per cent.' Ibid.

compete with the Punjabi traders who were obviously not lacking in capital.

At the time of Lawrence's stay in Kashmir, Punjabi traders had opened up shops for business in various places, chief among which were Srinagar, Baramulla, Islamabad (Anantnag), Shupiyon and Bandipur, and were

> importing manufactured cotton and piece goods, brass, copper, and iron, salt, sugar, tea, tobacco and a certain amount, and that an increasing amount, of petroleum. These traders exported to the Panjab non-intoxicating drugs, fibres, fruits, hides and skins, ghi, linseed, rape-seed and *jingli*, wool raw and manufactured.[129]

With the introduction of land settlement and with it, on an increasing scale, cash-assessment, and encouragement from the Government,[130] a fertile ground was provided to these traders to operate and flourish. The nexus with the populace was provided by the native *Wani*.

Whom the development of trade in consumer goods benefited mainly is self-evident from what the Census Commissioner for 1931 has to say in connection with trade that had developed. He wrote for the State territories as a whole:

> The village shopkeeper carries on his precarious existence by selling general stores. The money-economy is generally absent in the village and barter system prevails which adds to the profit of the shopkeeper who in grading grains into different kinds generally assesses their value at a lower rate.[131]

Given the fact that money prices did not prevail at the time of the land settlement, it is clear that the middleman prospered at the cost of the *Zamindars*.

129. Ibid.
130. See *OER*, 1901, F.N. 71-H-18, JKA.
131. *Census of India, 1931*, p. 213.

EDUCATION AND INTELLECTUALS

The medieval educational system remained undisturbed till 1880, when for the first time a serious effort was made to introduce English education at Srinagar.

The Beginning of Modern Education

The first modern agency to have started educational work in Kashmir was the one-man effort of Dr. Elmslie[132]—a Scot, who arrived there as the first Christian Medical Missionary in the spring of 1865 and worked in that capacity for six summers.[133] But his seems to have been a stray attempt.[134] The real work was started by Rev. J.H. Knowles. He arrived there in 1880 and started the C.M.S. School with twelve Pandits handed over to him by Rev. Dixey at the Mission hospital.[135] Later, in 1891, Rev. C.E. Tyndale Biscoe arrived to assist him.[136] The state followed suit by opening a school in 1886. Both, Mission and State school were located at Srinagar.

The first to avail themselves of the new opportunity were the *Karkun Pandits*. In 1891, 'nearly all the 250 or so' of those attending the Mission School belonged to this class.[137] The data available about the state schools for the year 1891-92 does not indicate a blank for the Muslims but suggests the pre-eminent position secured by the *Karkun Pandits* in the attainment of new education.[138] The lead, which the *Karkun Pandits* had taken

132. Neve (1912), p. 244.

133. See and cf. C.E. Tyndale Biscoe, *Kashmir in Sunlight and Shade* (London, 1922), p. 240; and Neve (1912), p. 262.

134. '. . . educational work was started by the late Dr. Elmslie, the first medical missionary in Kashmir. But it was not until the time of the Rev. J. Hinton Knowles in 1884 that distinct progress was evident.' Neve (1912), p. 244.

135. See the obituary by C.E. Tyndale Biscoe on Knowles in the log-book for 1943, in the school. However, in an earlier work Biscoe gives the year of the arrival of Knowles in Kashmir as 1881. Biscoe (1922), pp. 260, 263.

136. Ibid., p. 263.

137. Ibid., p. 265.

138. 'No. of boys on roll : 1,585
Average daily attendance : 1,228

over others, was not confined to Kashmir only but extended to the whole of the State. This is clear from the observation made by the State Council in 1891 in one of its resolutions.[139] All the evidence available in this regard until 1911 points in the same direction.[140]

No. of scholars learning:	
English	: 299
Vernacular only	: 1,541
Sanskrit only	: 44
Religion:	
Hindus	: 1,327
Sikhs	: 21
Muhammadans	: 233
Others	: 4

That is to say, out of a population of 52,576 Hindus only 1,327 are receiving State instruction, while out of a population of 757,433 Muhammadans only 233 obtain any benefit from the State schools. These figures also show that though the Hindus from less than 7 per cent of the population, they monopolise over 83 per cent of the education bestowed by the State. Walter R. Lawrence, op. cit., p. 229.

139. '. . . competition is to be among the inhabitants of the State only, and the education of every sect, religion and grade of the subjects is in the same state (Kashmiri Pundits excepted who are comparatively more advanced).' *OER*, 1891, F.N. 9, Resolution No. 9, dated 26 & 27 June 1891, para 3, JKA.

140. 'Pursuing our way in the bazaar [at Srinagar] we notice many groups of school children carrying black wooden boards instead of slates. Most of them are Hindus.' Neve (1912), p. 239.

'As a class, for instance, they [Pandits] are eager for education. The Mohammedans are grossly illiterate.' Ibid., p. 256.

'Unfortunately Mohammadans have been less influenced by education than the Hindus. The Islamic brotherhood is very conservative in matters of education, and in Kashmir it forms more than ninety per cent of the population.' Ibid., p. 239.

'Barring ecclesiastical people of all the nationalities here the only literate community is that of the Kashmiri Pundit.' *Census of India, 1911*, p. 160.

'That the Kashmiri Pundit is the most literate community in the State will be realised from the presence within it of 325 literate persons *per mille* (580 males and 4 females). The Brahmans of Kashmir beat even the trading Arora (274), and service-hunting Khattri (247), and Mahajans (201) of the Jammu.' Ibid., p. 162.

'The position occupied by these castes (Arora and Khattri) in

Nothing in our researches suggested that any special inducements were given by the State to the *Karkun* Pandits to encourage them to take to the new education.[141] The only cogent factor responsible for the advancement of the *Karkun* Pandits not only over the different sections of Muslims but over the *Gour* Pandits and *Buhur* was their social origin and the circumstances which accompanied the introduction of new education in Kashmir. The new education was not the result of any spontaneous internal development in the socio-economic structure of Kashmir but an introduction from outside. It was literary and secular in content. To whom other than the *Karkun* Pandits, which was then the only secular intellectual class, could such an education have been of functional value in a hereditary occupational structure? This presumption is validated by the fact that the 'pupils', whom Knowles has gathered soon after his arrival, were 'eager to learn English, as that language began to supersede Persian in certain State offices'.[142] Acquisition of the new education was for them not only necessary to earn their livelihood in the changed circumstances but also to preserve their status as 'intellectuals'. There was also a strong cultural predisposition to become literate which is apparent even today with them, a trait which they share with the other two intellectual classes—Pirzadas and *Gours*. If *Karkun* Pandits were declared to be 'literate' in 1911, Pirzadas and *Gours* were no less.[143] The Pirzadas were an exception to the educational index of 1911 about the Muslims in general. As the Census Commissioner wrote:

> The Babazadas (52), to which class most of the *Pirs* and *Mullahs* of Kashmir belong, have returned a proportion of

public service here is very much akin to that of the Kayasthas in Hindustan.' Ibid., fn.

141. It is in the case of Dogra Rajputs that a special interest was taken and inducement offered to make them to take to education. For this see *OER*, 1894, F.N. 67, Pratap Code—A Regulation to ameliorate the condition of the Dogra Rajputs, JKA.

142. Biscoe (1922), p. 263.

143. 'Barring ecclesiastical people of all the nationalities here, the only literate community is that of the Kashmiri Pundit. *Census of India, 1911*, p. 160.

literate that looms largest in the literary list of Mohamedan races and tribes found in the State.[144]

The *Karkun* Pandits seem to have had an added advantage over the other intellectual categories in that they had nothing to fear about learning a new language under the circumstances that accompanied the introduction of the new education. They had for centuries learnt an alien language—Persian—which had no link whatsoever with their religious literature, and still continued to uphold their 'Dharma'. Moreover, they also attended *Maktabs* run by Pirzadas.[145] They did not shirk learning another such language nor did they have reservations about doing so from people who practised and propagated a different creed. But this was not the case with different sections of Muslims; their intellectual and spiritual leaders—Pirzadas—stopped their clientele from taking to the new education.[146]

Attitude of the State

During the first year (1889-90) of the formation of the State Council, there existed in Kashmir only one state school—Srinagar Middle School. No tuition fee was levied and class books were distributed free among the boys. Later the distribution of free books was restricted to those whose parents' income was below Rs. 35 per month. Scholarships were awarded on the basis of merit.[147] Apart from this and the increase in the number of schools subsequently, there is nothing to suggest that the State Council offered any inducements to attract more boys to the school. The sole purpose of the education seems to have been to prepare a class of men who could man the clerical ranks of the State Administration.[148]

144. Ibid., p. 163.

145. *Interview with Sri Kanth Toshkhani by P.N. Pushp and Others* (Kashmiri). This is preserved in the Srinagar station of the All India Radio and was broadcast in the *Myon Kar Myeani Zindgi* programme of the station on 27 September 1977.

146. Naseer-ud-Din (1971), p. 25.

147. *ARJKS, 1889-90*, pp. 103-7.

148. Lawrence, while commenting on the state of education as obtained in Kashmir at the time of publication of his account, wrote;

Notwithstanding a steady extension in the number of state schools and favourable response to the initiatives of the non-official agencies by granting state aid, there seems to have been no move to take, or even a discussion about taking, education to the masses during the tenure of the State Council as we shall see. However, after the dissolution of the State Council in 1905 and conferment of its powers on Pratap Singh, a 'Conference' was appointed by him in October 1907 'to formulate a scheme' to impart education to State subjects. The scheme was formulated and sent to the Resident for approval, who acknowledged that 'Every one of the suggestions which they have made is not only sound but urgent. . . . There is not one measure which the Conference has considered which the Durbar ought not to adopt immediately, if funds were available'.[149] Needless to say the scheme was shelved.

Pratap Singh did not, however, lose enthusiasm. In September 1909, he again took the initiative by issuing an order in this connection. After elaborating upon the necessity of mass education and his duty in this connection, he asked 'the Home Minister to draw up a scheme for making Primary Education compulsory and free throughout my State'.[150] The Minister

---

'. . . education is backward in Kashmir,. . . . The State is also old-fashioned and recognizes that the supply of educated Pandits is already far greater than the demand, and that the manufacture at State expense of a number of hungry students, for whom there is no employment, would be likely to cause discontent. If the Kashmiri Pandits would leave their country in search of work it might be well to extend education, but they prefer to stay in Srinagar. As regards the rural classes the State holds the view that those [who] want education will obtain it at their own expense, and it is doubtful whether in the present circumstances of the agricultural population it would be wise to educate the masses at the cost of the exchequer. I think that the best policy will be to leave the rural classes alone at present, and to use every effort to introduce technical education in Srinagar.' Walter R. Lawrence, op. cit., p. 229.

Lawrence, it has to be borne in mind, was one of the top officials on loan from the Government and as such must have been closely associated with the pursuit of official policy.

149. *OER*, 1907, F.N. 101/P-102, Resident's Note, 22 February 1908, JKA.

150. Ibid., Maharaja's Order No. 1348/m dated 21 September 1909.

'invited the views and opinions of all the Inspectors and Head Masters of the High Schools. They all hail [ed] with joy the gracious order of His Highness the Maharaja. . .and consider-[ed], it will inaugurate a new era in the History of Kashmir and its Rulers'.[151] Before any final decision was taken, another minister—A. Mitra—took over charge of the education department. In a memo to the Maharaja in this connection, he wrote that he was an 'ardent supporter of expansion of free primary education in the State'. He, however, stood against the introduction of 'any law of compulsion either universally or in selected areas'. For, he believed, 'The measure will be looked upon as a *zoolam* and will therefore be extremely unpopular, the motive will be misunderstood'.[152] His opinion seems to have prevailed and only free primary education was expanded. His proposal to have a school attached to the silk factory where education was to be imparted compulsorily to the boys working in the factory had been opposed by the British Director of Sericulture. The reasons for his opposition were that

> . . . the boys work here from six in the morning till four in the afternoon, and during these hours they could not be spared unless the silk factory was closed entirely thus depriving the State of one of its paying Department.
>
> If the boys were compelled to attend school for two hours after four O'clock, I think that they would prefer to stop away altogether and take up work at the carpet factories etc. than work here.
>
> As it is, I find it much easier to get people with an elementary education in writing, reading and arithmatic in vernacular, who consider themselves clerks than to attract men and boys to work in the filature.[153]

The Maharaja's enthusiasm did not abate and he proclaimed on 21 February 1912:

151. Ibid., Memo by Har Narain, Minister of Education, 15 January 1910.

152. Ibid., Memo on 'Free and Compulsory Primary Education' by A. Mitra, 7 June 1910.

153. Ibid., Director Sericulture to Settlement Commissioner, 16 May 1911.

> I do not agree to the postponement of compulsory Education. Trial should be given to the scheme not by introducing it in the whole State but multiplying the number of schools in the State.[154]

The intentions and efforts of Pratap Singh notwithstanding, it was his successor, Hari Singh, who had the Compulsory Primary Education Regulation adopted in 1930 and made immediately applicable in Srinagar, Jammu and other towns.[155]

Non-official Agencies at Work

Christian Missionary Society

The introduction of the new education, as has been seen, was the work of a non-official agency—the Christian Missionary Society. The Society inaugurated its activities in Kashmir in 1864. Its effective educational work, however, started from 1880.

Its activities were not limited to medical and educational work but included the preaching and propagation of Christianity as an essential component.[156] When it began its work in Kashmir, it made four converts.[157] In the schools run by it, not only was the Christian gospel taught, but certain other innovations were introduced by Biscoe such as playing football and cleaning of the city by the boys.[158] There is sufficient evidence to suggest that these were not palatable to the conservatives whether Brahmin or Muslim. Despite the fact that there was a reaction against the activities of what was popularly known as the Mission School, it continued to be run and, what is more, expand. Around 1931, the number of Muslim boys on the rolls of the Mission School was 'more than half' of its 'total' strength.[159]

154. Ibid.
155. Cf. H.L. Saxena, *The Tragedy of Kashmir* (New Delhi, 1975), p. 90.
156. See, for example, Neve (1912), pp. 262-63, 288-96; and Tyndale Biscoe, *An Autobiography* (London, 1951), p. 211.
157. Neve (1912), pp. 262, 263.
158. See Biscoe (1951), pp. 74, 76.
159. See the Log-book of the School for 1932-33 entitled *Riding the Storms in Kashmir*.

Popular Response and Agencies at Work

Muslims

As noted earlier, some boys from among the Muslims did attend the school run by the State Administration. Thus it appears that all members of this section were not reluctant to send their children for modern education in the beginning. It would have been very useful if the social origin of these students was known but, unfortunately, our sources did not provide us with such information. It was reported that one of the first boys who learnt English was a Muslim who was given the epithet 'Shahb Chire'[160]—Shahb, the Christian—implying that he had become a convert. It has already been noted that the 'natural leaders' of the Muslims campaigned against taking to new education. Under these circumstances, it is not surprising that the Muslims taken as a whole remained backward in modern education. It was only after modern education came into vogue at Srinagar during the next two decades that Muslims became alive to the need for this type of education.

In 1899, an organization called Nasrat-ul-Islam was founded at Srinagar.[161] Simultaneously, a *maktab* was established. It was this *maktab* which developed stage by stage into the Islamia High School in 1905.[162] The first batch of students from this institution appeared in the matriculation examination in 1908.[163]

The founder of the school was an elite from the dominant class of Muslims. He was known popularly as Rasul Baba and was the 'spiritual leader' of three-fourths of the population at Srinagar; he was designated as the Mirwaiz. The school started getting a grant from the State Administration from 1904-5 (Samvat 1961) after making an application for it.[164] After the

160. His name was Shahab-ud-Din.

161. Anjuman Nasrat-ul-Islam, *Sir Syed Kashmir, Hazrat Mirwaiz Maulana Rasul Shah Sahib: Bani Anjuman Nasrat-ul-Islam Srinagar ke Satavanven Yomi Visal Per Aek Mukhtsar Twaruf* (Urdu) (Srinagar, n.d.), p. 1.

162. Ibid., p. 3.

163. Master Mohammed Maqbool, *Ner-i-Azm: Sir Syed Kashmir* (Urdu) (Srinagar, n.d.), p. 20.

164. *OER*, 1903, F.N. 68-P-57, Judicial Member to Vice-President,

establishment of the institution, a few more initiatives were taken by others at Srinagar and elsewhere. From the official records available it appears that the State Administration responded favourably to the demands made for grants.[165]

Hindus

Though the *Karkun* Pandits took to the new education right from its introduction, yet there was also a reaction from them against the activities of the Mission School. A high school where the 'Hindu Religion and morality were taught as an essential part' of the education was founded in March 1901 at Srinagar by Annie Besant under the control of Central Hindu College, Benares.[166] When it opened three teachers and three hundred boys of the Mission School transferred to that institution.[167] As in the case of Mission and Islamia schools, it also received grant-in-aid from the State.[168]

The *Karkun* Pandits having forged ahead in school education, it was natural that an urge to have college education available in Kashmir should have been felt by them first. In 1906, a college, as a sister institution to that of the Hindu School, was established at Srinagar[169] and a few *Karkun* Pandits were conspicuously involved in the venture.[170] Grant-in-aid by the State was provided to it with the condition that the institution accept persons belonging to different creeds.[171]

The school and college were both taken over by the State in

---

17 August 1903 and Assistant Resident to Vice-President, 14 September 1903, JKA.

165. *OER*, 1909, F.N. 30/P-94; 1911, F.N. 48/P-116; 1914, F.N. 76/P-11; 1920, F.N. 22/XII-18.

166. See *OER*, 1904, F.N. 155/F-73, Private Secretary to Maharaja to Secretary to Chief Minister, 24 January 1906, JKA; and Biscoe (1951), p. 77.

167. Ibid., p. 77.

168. See *OER*, 1904, F.N. 155/F-73, JKA.

169. See *OER*, 1906, F.N. 82/P-60, Petition by Annie Besant and others to Maharaja, JKA.

170. They were Daya Kishen Kaul and Baldeo Kaul.

171. Ibid., Resident to Maharaja, 7 July 1906.

1911 because the authorities found it difficult to run the institution with the efficiency demanded by the University Regulations. Simultaneously, the word 'Hindu' was dropped from the name of the college. What remained has come down to us unchanged—Sri Pratap College.[172]

PROCESSES

The life-process of the people in Kashmir from 1846 up to 1889 and even thereafter was not confined to the boundaries of their socio-religious sections or sub-sections but cut across these. Nor were social classes, the dominant ones in particular, identifiable with any single socio-religious section or sub-section. The dominant social classes, for example the *Karkhanadars*, enjoyed the patronage of the State to bind their co-religionist workers to work in their *Karkhanas*. Nor did the people of Srinagar, the majority of whom were Muslims, deny themselves the benefit of foodgrains supplied by the State till the system was discontinued as a concomitant of land-settlement. It was, indeed, provided at the cost of the peasants whom the city people have a tradition of calling *Gam hakhur*. Even Wingate, who displayed a propensity to view Kashmiri society in terms of Hindu-Muslim dichotomy, records:

> The ignorant Mohammadan cultivator has not only no one he can call friend, but every one, whether Hindu or Mohammadan, of any influence is against him, for cheap bread by the sweat of the cultivator's brow is a benefit widely appreciated. The Mohammadan cultivator is compelled to grow *shali*, and in many years to part with it below the proper market rate, that the city may be content. If the harvest is too little for both, the city must be supplied and is supplied by any force that may be necessary and the cultivator and his children must go without. . . . The pundits and the city population have a right to be well fed, whether there is famine or not, at rupees two *chilki* per Kharwar. I said every body of influence was against the cultivator.[173]

172. *ARJKS, 1911-12*, p. 69.
173. Wingate (1888), p. 27.

The contradictions between the various social classes did not cease to exist after 1889. Nor did the dominant social classes cease to try and secure State patronage to defend their interests *vis-a-vis* their co-religionists. Instead, the new environment gave a fillip to competition between various classes and accelerated attempts by the dominant social classes to defend their interests in particular by using their position to influence the State.

In 1915, when the State was considering enacting the 'Tenancy Bill', the *Lambardars* (village headmen) of Kashmir submitted an application to the Maharaja: 'We have been kept quite ignorant as to what sort of modifications the Act is undergoing and whether they are beneficial to the landholders or not'.[174] They pleaded that

> . . . as your Highness has not yet accorded sanction to it and much scope is left for us to clamour for and represent our rights, we entertain a firm belief that your Highness will not approve of the modifications alluded to above as long as we are not explicitly informed as to how our rights stand in relation with those of the cultivators lest our rights be marred in some way or other. Hoping therefore that your Highness will most generously favour us with a hearing and thus will not allow our rights to be superseded.[175]

In 1915, when trade was suddenly dislocated because of the outbreak of the First World War (1914-18) and the artisans—in the absence of work from the merchants—were confronted with the imminent danger of starvation, the state undertook to open a *Karkhana* as a relief measure. The *Karkhandars* and dealers in Kashmir 'felt considerably uneasy' and sent a telegram on 29 March 1915 to the Maharaja who at that time was in Jammu:

> Your most gracious Highness mercifully ordered to establish relief works for maintaining your Highness's distressed subjects; method of its conduction is injurious and distressing

174. *OER*, 1906, F.N. 191/H-75, Application of landholders of Kashmir valley to Maharaja, JKA.

175. Ibid.

> to traders, Your Highness's most loyal and beholden subjects, and to ruin the trade. We are grateful for protection Your Highness and Your Highness's noble and gracious ancestors ever conferred on us in miserable times for which we pray day and night for your Highness's long life. Accordingly we most humbly request procrastination of relief works till the perusal of our petition follows for redress of our grievances. awaiting anxiously favourable orders through Khawaja azizdeen Kawosa.[176]

After the land settlement a class of *galadars*—grain dealers—came up at Srinagar with whom it became a practice to hoard foodgrains and sell them to the city population at high rates. The organization of the 'State Store' department in 1921-22 provided a measure of relief to the population of Srinagar and undercut the stranglehold of this class.[177]

The change in the taxation system, the fixation of land revenue for different periods of settlement, and the commercialization of agricultural produce brought their concomitant effect—the dependence of the peasants on the *waddar* who in the process made a good profit at the cost of the peasant. Since the institution of *Wad*, as has been noted earlier, did not directly levy interest it could safely be, and was, manned by Muslims also.[178]

At Srinagar, the institution of money-lending had become prominent by about 1931. A native contemporary historian has shown that the moneylenders were 'Hindus'.[179] This had the potential of turning into a source of religious animus in a place where the populace happened to be predominantly Muslim simply because such a practice is prohibited in Islam and as such did not have the legitimacy that other profit-making avenues had. However, despite the Quranic injunctions to the contrary, the Muslim merchants and traders did lend money on credit to

176. Ibid., 1915, F.N. 278/P-16, Telegram from Jubhar Khan and others to Maharaja, 29 March 1915, JKA.

177. See J.L.K. Jalali, *Economics of Food Grains in Kashmir* (Lahore 1931).

178. See Naseer-ud-Din (1971), p. 54.

179. Kaul (1967), p. 99.

visitors.[180] The artisans depended much upon the advance payments made by the merchants and traders and virtually lived at their mercy.[181]

The trade in arts and crafts of Kashmir was lucrative but the First World War and the economic depression of 1929 and thereafter evidently exposed its uncertainties also. This, as has been pointed out, may have prompted the trading classes to seek a secure alternative in land or State services. For both of these, competition had increased to a great extent by 1931.[182] Another important class which sought a respectable alternative might have been *Pirzadas*. The reasons why they were keen are firstly, the 'Wahabi' movement started at Srinagar during the last decade of the nineteenth century which set them back and affected their source of income.[183] Secondly, the introduction of compulsory education in 1930 at Srinagar and other towns must have also threatened their hold on society since it would inevitably deprive them of their clientele.

STATE ADMINISTRATION

Pre-1889

Gulab Singh's entry into Kashmir along with the army did not amount to the dethronement of any native power but was only the replacement of one alien power—the Sikh Nazim, Sheikh Imam-ud-Din, and his force—by another. Kashmir, it has been noted earlier, was a directly administered territory under the Sikhs as it had been under their predecessors—the Mughals and the Afghans. The force that Gulab planted in Kashmir comprised of two elements. One was the Dogra Mian Rajputs, who

180. See The Earl of Dunmore, *The Pamirs* (London, 1893), Vol. 1, p. 26.

181. See *OER*, 1915, F.N. 278/P-16, Revenue Minister's Memo, 25 February 1915, JKA.

182. Cf. "Persons who combine these two occupations [State service and Agriculture] are highly esteemed in the popular mind." *Census of India, 1931*, p. 223.

183. The origin and consequences of this movement are discussed in ch. 6.

followed the Brahmanical creed; the other was of Afghans who subscribed to Islam. To the former were awarded *jagirs* and to the latter revenue free lands.[184] The Dogras, as had their predecessors, maintained the policy of not enlisting Kashmiris in their force.[185] Gulab Singh even took steps to put a stop to the 'mimic warfare' that was practiced earlier at Srinagar as a game.[186] Generally, this policy did not lead to the deprivation of position or power of any class of people in Kashmir.

After Gulab Singh had taken possession of Kashmir and entrenched himself there, he and his successors moved every year during summer to Srinagar.[187] This was a significant development in itself because the ruling power was now present in Kashmir for about half the year which had not been the case during the tenure of the Mughals, the Afghans and the Sikhs. The administration of Kashmir was conducted through what was known as *Hakim-i-Ala* who, like his predecessors, was always a deputy of the ruling power and never a native of Kashmir.[188] The nature of the state structure determined the personnel who were recruited to this post—they came from a small number of appropriate families. Till the end of Ranbir Singh's rule and the beginning of modernization of the state administration the

184. See Walter R. Lawrence, op. cit., pp. 305, 309.

185. An argument ever given by any one of the Dogra rulers in support of the pursuance of such a policy was that the Kashmiris are a coward people. Cf. 'In the Army re-organisation I pleaded for the enlistment of a double company of Kashmiris, but one day H.H. [Hari Singh] told me that his grandfather, Maharaja Ranbir Singh, had raised a whole regiment and having uniformed and drilled them for six months in Srinagar, gave orders that they should march to Jammu. A deputation of their officers waited upon him with a petition, pointing out that in making arrangements for their march, no provision had been made for police for their protection. The Regiment was disbanded.' G.E.C. Wakefield, *Recollections: 50 Years in the Service of India* (Lahore, 1942), pp. 193-94.

186. 'Before the time of Maharaja Gulab Singh the different wards of Srinagar city used to turn out with slings and stones, and played a very earnest and serious game. But Gulab Singh did not approve of this fighting spirit, and put a stop to the mimic warfare.' Walter R. Lawrence, op. cit., p. 255.

187. See Hassan (1957), pp. 567ff.

188. Ibid., pp. 567ff; also see Walter R. Lawrence op. cit., p. 2.

main administrative activity continued to be that of revenue administration.[189] There is no evidence to suggest that any of the natives who had come to man the subordinate ranks of the revenue administration were dislodged or that the structure was disturbed. In fact, during Ranbir Singh's rule, when administration based on the territorial units of Wazarat and Tehsil was organized in Kashmir, the natives came to be gradually appointed to these posts. At the time when Lawrence arrived in Kashmir, these posts were manned mostly by the *Karkun* Pandits.[190] The clerical staff under these officials also consisted of the *Karkun* Pandits.[191] Apart from the administrative structure, there was a class of what can best be called feudal collaborators created by the Dogra rulers. This included the Zilladar, Mir Zilladar, Mir Chaudri and Assistant to Mir Chaudri. From the list of the *rasum* (perquisites) taken in one year from a village, considered to be a representative case by Lawrence, the existence of these positions and their significance is thrown into bold relief.[192] Nothing is known in detail about the identity of the personnel who manned these structures except that the name of one of the officials in the village is mentioned and he was a Muslim. This along with Lawrence's conspicuous silence about these structures despite the details he has provided about the 'Old Administration' in Kashmir suggests the possibility that most of them might have been Muslims.[193] However, this is a point which only more detailed research can establish.

189. Cf. Ibid., p. 399.
190. Ibid., p. 401.
191. Ibid.
192. Ibid., p. 416.
193. He does not tell us anything about these structures in his details when he is at pains to state and describe other structures. It is difficult to believe that he could have missed these in a moment of forgetfulness. To us, it seems that the withholding of the information with regard to these structures was deliberate because it would have been impossible to fit the fact of pre-ponderance of Muslims in these structures in the two-fold puerile scheme of 'Pandits' and 'Muslims' representing the rulers and the ruled with which the whole of his description about society and administration in Kashmir pre-1889 is coloured.

Post-1889

A survey of the Administrative Reports of Jammu and Kashmir State that were published for the years 1889-90 to 1931[194] indicates the development of several trends that crystallized in various aspects of the politico-administrative structure of the state. An understanding of these trends is sharpened by consulting the unpublished official records of those days.

The first and the most important change that was introduced can be said to have been a differentiation between the 'private' and 'public' aspect of the Maharaja: a differentiation between his person and the State. This was an innovation which even the Maharaja, Pratap Singh, took some time to grasp. As late as 1897, in his correspondence with the Resident, his perplexity is apparent:

> The State is my property, and belongs to it as my property and it is all my hereditary property, according to the treaty, although according to present constitution which has for a while been under existence I am obliged to pass orders in certain matters connected with the State in Council only, but in private none could interfere.[195]

In another communication to the Resident, he telegraphed:

> I was the heir-apparent of the State with none to contest my right, where and why was I to secure pattas like jagirdars? There was no distinction between public and private. I was master of all. Certainly if my father had foreseen all this disgrace, he would have guarded against the future; and I would have taken steps to safeguard my interests had I anticipated all these difficulties.[196]

During the period, when the State Council was in existence, this differentiation was all the more pronounced. The ruling

194. Reports for the years 1906-7 (Samvat 1963) to 1910-11 (Samvat 1967) were not published.

195. *FDP*, Secret Branch-E, February 1898, nos. 183-286, His Highness to Resident, 15 May 1897, NAI.

196. Ibid., His Highness to Resident, 17 May 1897.

powers were exercised both in substance and form by the State Council, appointed by the Government, under the supervision of its agent—the Resident. Another important introduction, from which there was no return even after the abolition of State Council, was the fixation of a Privy Purse for the Maharaja.[197] It was a potent symbol of the differentiation.

This was the beginning of the transition of the State from a personal to a constitutional one. The process once started could not be reversed after the elaborate modern bureaucratic structure had been developed, as was done during the period of the State Council and after that till 1921 when the Maharaja was bestowed with 'full powers'. The Maharaja realized the change that had been wrought as is evident in his address on the occasion of the bestowal of 'full powers' on him by the Viceroy. He grasped that even after the 'present constitution' was abolished and 'full powers' restored to him, something new had come into being which could not be done away with but rather continued:

> I have had enough experience during the last 34 years of my rule, to realise the truth, that the affairs of this world are in a constant course of transition and that policies of state must also be moulded according to the proper requirements of the times. . . . The trend of events in the territories under the direct control of the British Government must necessarily affect a change in the angle of vision of the peoples inhabiting the Indian States. As Ruler of the Jammu and Kashmir State, I welcome the change. I have never given my countenance to any autocratic dealings with my subjects and have always tried my best to accord constitutional consideration to all matters affecting their well being.[198]

A corollary to this change, and implicit in it, was the introduction of an element of constitutional restriction or limitation of the exercise of powers of the erstwhile State—the Maharaja,

197. See Dilip Kumar Ghose, *Kashmir in Transition, 1885-1893* (Calcutta, 1975), pp. 139, 142-43.

198. *OER*, 1920, F.N. 104, Maharaja's Address to Viceroy, JKA.

his feudal class collaborators and servants. This was reflected in the liabilities of the tax-payer being defined and the declaration of *rasum* as juridically illegal. This applied to all—from the Maharaja to the lowest ranks though the sufferers were largely the latter. That the subordinate ranks were the most affected is seen in an application to a settlement officer of the Land Settlement Department, made under the pressure of deterioration of the economic situation after the First World War:

> . . . although besides the salary there was some income through some illegal gratification (i.e.) "Nazrana" (now termed as bribe) Rashwatsatani, where as this triffling presentation in a way of half the price of milk, fruit, hens etc. was hardly amounting to few pieces only, and was considered by the Zamindars instead of mutual love and cooperation as a matter of extreme disgrace and disappointment in non acceptance of the same, but we are now besides the devotion and sacrifice expected to be as honest as Chief Minister or Judge High Court and other State high officials drawing pay in bundles of notes.[199]

There occurred simultaneously an extension in the strength and the activities of the administration and a diminution of the distance between the State and the natives of Kashmir. With the introduction of the State Council, a regular central establishment came to be formed. The members of the State Council headed the different departments which were created. In the very first Administrative Report of 1889-90, there is a mention of various departments such as Military, Foreign, Revenue, Judicial, Education, etc. To these came to be added many others by 1931. The result of this development can be said to have been the transformation of the Durbar from Maharaja and his Dewan and a small establishment to what we have these days—a secretariat linking the various activities of the administration. This along with the regular annual move of the Durbar during summer to Srinagar obviously brought it closer to the natives.

199. *OER*, 1920, F.N. 190/IX-14, Application to Settlement Officer, Kashmir South, Srinagar, JKA.

Its natural concomitant was the continued narrowing of the powers of the *Hakim-i-Alla* and diminution of the distance between the centre of the State and natives in Kashmir. To some extent the diminution had taken place with the establishment of the rule of Dogra Maharajas itself. For, unlike the Mughal, Afghan and Sikh sovereigns, the Dogra Maharajas were present in Kashmir almost every year. To put it briefly, the natives of Kashmir were now confronted with the State directly and could identify it.

An important ingredient in the modernization of the administrative structure was the process of the introduction of a change in the nature of the tenure of State servants. As against what was common practice earlier, their tenure now came to be governed by definite rules and regulations and its security was assured. In view of the widespread economic uncertainty in Kashmir State service became the most coveted profession.

The modernization of the administrative structure in Kashmir within the specific historical situation shaped the process of recruitment and the ensuing composition of the personnel in the administration up to 1931 and even thereafter. The process began by affecting adversely those who manned its ranks in two ways. Firstly, the big tax-gathering agency that was previously needed to supervise and manage the necessary operation was made redundant because of a change in the taxation system that accompanied the introduction of land settlement. Such a development was bound to affect the *Karkun* Pandits in the given circumstances which it did.[200] This was the first time after the creation of the State that any of the groups having even a semblance of belonging to the dominant classes suffered a social fall.

200. For those living at Srinagar Lawrence showed a particular concern: 'The future of the city Pandits is a matter of some anxiety. They have not the keen trading instinct of the natives of the Panjab, and may neglect the chances of commerce which easier communications with India should now offer. They are extremely conservative and short-sighted, and cannot believe that the old system, under which every adult Pandit had a finger in the collection of revenue, has passed away. They are deeply attached to their country, . . .the large number of unemployed Brahmans of Srinagar will not seek service in the Panjab while it is possible to eke out a bare subsistence in the valley.' Walter R. Lawrence, op. cit., p. 303.

Lawrence has left us evidence to show that the *Karkun* Pandits were seen to work in 1894 as labourers on the river embankments.[201] They were also employed in the silk factory where they engaged in manual labour.[202] From the evidence available about the normative behaviour of the *Karkun* Pandits during the contemporary period,[203] and as it is now, it is clear that those amongst them who took to manual work did so out of necessity and not because of any change in their attitude towards manual work. A change in their attitude could not be expected to occur suddenly nor was there a strong positive development that could have brought it about. On the contrary, there was the strong inherent cultural bias to handle the pen—*kalam.*[204] Moreover, the measures initiated and enforced during the Residency Raj and subsequently, except for the introduction of laissez faire in trade, worked only to reinforce the feudal frame of the society. Hence, it was natural that *Karkun* Pandits should be strongly motivated to re-establish themselves socially.

Secondly, the old administrative officials were rendered 'inefficient'. This was not unexpected in so far as they lacked the necessary training that could have equipped them with the skills required to perform the newly created administrative roles. We find mention of cases of removal of various officials in the Administrative Reports. Since it was a question of livelihood, undoubtedly the *Karkun* Pandits would try to regain lost ground.

The process of transformation and the speed at which it was sought to be imposed necessarily entailed an immediate requirement for a class of personnel that could give effect to it, i.e., a class of men who possessed the requisite training and skill to man the administration at various levels. It was inherent in the

201. Ibid.

202. Cf. 'The Kashmiri Pandits are gradually relinquishing their ideal of Government service and turning to trade and even manual labour in increasing numbers.' *Census, 1931*, p. 102.

203. 'He [Pandit] hankers after State employ. An apprenticeship in an office he hails as a gift of fortune. He is apathetic towards arts, crafts, industries, manual labour, business and agriculture.' Pandit Anand Koul, *The Kashmiri Pandit* (Calcutta, 1924), p. 41.

204. Walter R. Lawrence, op. cit., p. 303.

situation that the old officials who lacked the qualifications that were required of them should now be rendered 'inefficient'. This implied a two-fold action on behalf of the Residency Raj: to get new recruits to the State service, and to dispense with the old ones. This and the fact that the action had to be effected by the State Council appointed by the Government set in motion a specific trend. Given the exigency of the situation efficiency and loyalty would be the criteria demanded of new recruits. This in turn entailed recruiting men from outside the State territories and on a selective basis.

To dispense with the services of old officials meant depriving an influential class of men of their livelihood and posed a consequent threat, real or imaginary, to their dominant position in society. Such a situation could not but prove to be a fertile ground which would nurture anti-British sentiment and eventually become a deep reservoir for it.

Almost all the departments that were established came to be headed by the British and a few Eurasians.[205] While making recruitment to other ranks, where native Indians were brought in, Bengalis were carefully kept out. It is men from the Punjab who were brought in.[206] The Government was also eager to deal with the old officials in such a manner that the State Council would 'be able to effect a valuable reform without incurring needless unpopularity'.[207]

Modalities such as would permit the least scope for the development of discontent were adopted. Persian was retained

205. This feature of the State administration could be noticed even as late as 1922 and was reflected upon by C.E. Tyndale Biscoe as follows: 'There are also British advisers in the various departments of the State, such as the Army, P.W.D., Accountants, Land Settlement etc.' Biscoe (1922), p. 76.

206. Cf. Maharaja Pratap Singh complaints in 1897 that 'all official posts are held by aliens. The Jammu district is worked by Jullundar people, and the Kashmir district by Sagris, while Amar Nath has his own clique.' *FDP*, Secret Branch-E, February 1898, nos. 183-286, McMahon to Talbot, 8 July 1897, NAI. Also see *The Tribune*, 1 September 1904, Letter to Editor by Fair Play; and ibid., 29 November 1904, Letter to Editor by Dogra.

207. *Lansdowne Papers*/IB (iii), GI to SS, 21 January 1891, enclosure 6, India to Resident, 22 February 1890, as cited in Ghose (1975), p. 126.

as the court language for the administrative division of the Kashmir Province for the time being.[208] The services of some of the erstwhile personnel, as far as it was possible, were retained.[209] Besides, attempts seem to have been made to inspire hope amongst the disgruntled men by the State Council which declared that the residents of the State should have priority in appointment to State service as a matter of principle. This is visible from the rationale behind the adoption of certain rules that were to govern the appointments to State service.

The need was felt to frame a set of rules 'to ensure efficiency in the personnel of administration of the State'.[210] But when these came to be adopted on 6 February 1891 by the State Council, the purpose was said to be 'to ensure efficiency in the personnel of the administration and encourage the progress of education'.[211] Hence, it was thought desirable that:

> Not less than 2/3rd of the appointments in all departments, be filled by candidates who have qualified themselves by passing successfully the competitive examination hereinafter prescribed, the remaining 1/3rd being allotted to existing officials of approved service & good moral character.[212]

This was for those ranks termed as Upper Subordinates and Lower Subordinates. For recruitment to the rank of clerk or *moharir*, the requirement was to produce a certificate of having passed the Middle School Examination. Simultaneously, an

208. See *OER*, 1907, F.N. 27/Z-6. Urdu was introduced as the court language in the Jammu Province in 1888-89 (Samvat 10 Phagun 1945). But its introduction in Kashmir was withheld for some time. Even as late as 1907, when Urdu had practically become the court language in that province also, Persian continued to be officially the court language.

209. This is evident, for example, in the procedure adopted for the appointment of Patwaris. The result was that the new Patwaris who were appointed were all Kashmiris and many of them were sons or relatives of the old Patwaris. See, Walter R. Lawrence, op. cit., pp. 446-47.

210. *OER*, 1891, F.N. 9, Amar Singh to Bhagram, 2 February 1891, JKA.

211. Ibid., Rules sanctioned by State Council on 6 February 1891. JKA.

212. Ibid.

element of reservation was sought to be introduced by enunciating that for recruitment as clerk or *moharir* preference would be 'invariably given to bona fide local residents of the State'.[213] Once the principle of the right of the bona fide residents of the State to State service was accorded recognition, it led in turn to another issue: who were the bona fide residents of the State?

Within less than five months of the adoption of the rules, the State Council passed a resolution on 26/27 June 1891 wherein it acknowledged the 'prior claim' of the 'subjects' of the 'State' to 'all appointments'. Heads of Departments were asked to be

> good enough to note that persons not inhabitants of this State will only be appointed to such offices for which persons of education, experience and ability required to perform the duties of those offices are not forthcoming among the inhabitants of the State.[214]

They were further told that by

> appointing men of high ability it is intended to give practical training to the State Subjects so that they may gradually be qualified to assist in the administrative and other branches in the State.[215]

As regards 'Competition', it stressed that it was to be 'among the inhabitants of the State only', the education among 'every sect, religion and grade of the subjects' being in the 'same state (Kashmiri Pundits excepted who are comparatively more advanced)'.[216]

However, from the concluding part of the resolution given below and what followed later, it seems that the resolution was passed only to conciliate ruffled tempers and preempt the development of anti-British sentiment amongst the dislodged elements of the administrative structure. The resolution concluded as follows:

213. Ibid.
214. Ibid., State Council Resolution No. 9 dated 26 and 27 June 1891.
215. Ibid.
216. Ibid.

> An outsider will be appointed to such posts only in cases where the services of a candidate who has passed the Middle School Examination of the State are not procurable or another qualified inhabitant of the State is not available. As the number of the candidates who pass the middle school examination in this State is yet very very small.[217]

Subsequently, in 1895-96, the Judicial Member of the State Council with its approval issued a circular: 'Declaring the eligibility of State school boys for service in preference to outsiders.'[218]

The fate of this declaration is self-evident from the fact that the State Council had to adopt a 'few simple rules' in May 1904 that could have

> the effect of bringing to the notice of Heads of Departments the names of all such candidates as are desirous of employment in the service of the State and who because of being natives of the soil would be deserving of being given preference over others who are either outsiders or have not special claim for appointment in the service of the State.[219]

These rules were sought to be introduced because

> the existing system of recruiting for the subordinate clerical service in the State has for sometime past been the subject of anxious consideration and proposals have been made . . . from time to time as to the best means of improving it, so that young men from the State Schools who could be said to be fit for employment in the public services of the State might get fair chances of employment in the different departments of the State.[220]

The measures that were adopted were the first real effort to see that those who were educated and wanted to be employed were

217. Ibid.
218. *ARJKS, 1895-96*, p. 197.
219. *OER*, 1904, F.N. 40-S-18, Extract from Proceedings of State Council's Meeting No. 35 on 16 May 1904 regarding Judicial Member's Memo dated 16 March 1904, JKA.
220. Ibid.

absorbed in State service. And this was professedly done because it had been a matter of 'anxious consideration' for some time past—the reference here evidently being to a period only after 1899. As is obvious from a communication in this connection, the source of 'anxious consideration' was 'men of the Pundit class'.[221]

Within about one year, a memorandum was sanctioned and adopted to the effect that the candidate would be required to serve as an unpaid apprentice for six months before he could be considered for employment. The reason given was that 'in the interest of office work it is in most cases not desirable to appoint boys fresh from schools unless they have passed through a certain period of apprenticeship in an office'.[222] This was clearly a step further in the contradiction between 'efficiency' and 'prior claims'.

Subsequently, 'clerical and commercial' classes were opened in the State high schools to provide facilities to the Maharaja's 'subjects' and 'locally trained men in the service of the State'. Four students, who came out after passing the 'university examination on these subjects', in 1910, despite a circular from the Minister to the effect that the 'clerical and commercial passed youth may be given the first chance in every Department' found that 'no Head of any department paid any attention to it'.[223] So they made a protest to one Minister—a Bengali—A. Mitra, who pleaded their cause and forwarded a request to the Maharaja to pass an order to provide 'these men with suitable posts in preference to outsiders'.[224] He further remarked that a circular that had been issued before by the Maharaja in this connection was 'not usually acted upon'.[225] The Maharaja ordered in response: 'The proposal made by the P.W. Minister

221. *OER*, 1904, F.N. 122/F-66, Secretary, Games Preservation Department to Secretary, Foreign Department, 24 September 1904, JKA.

222. *OER*, 1904, F.N. 162, Judicial Member's Memo, 10 May 1905, JKA.

223. *OER*, 1909, F.N. 21/F-219, Petition to the P.W.D. Minister by Kasho Nath, Suraj Bal, Suraj Bhat and Sona Pandit, May 1910 (Samvat 8 Jeth 1967), JKA.

224. Ibid., Memo by A. Mitra, 23 May 1910.

225. Ibid.

is a commendable one: State subjects duly trained must have preference over outsiders.'[226]

A little before Mitra's intercession the State Engineer had raised the question of the definition of the term 'State Subject'.[227] Before this could be stated, the Settlement Commissioner, W. S. Talbot, passed an order to the effect that in future his subordinates seek his prior 'order before appointing (or accepting a candidate for appointment), any person who is not a State subject by *birth*'.[228] Although it said that there was 'no need to import outsiders' for appointments which were 'ordinary' and required no special qualifications exceptions were made such as for 'the son of a man who had passed all his official line doing good work for the State [and] should be more entitled to consideration than a State subject without any claims of that kind'.[229]

The deliberations which were triggered by the State Engineer finally resulted in the adoption of a definition for 'State Subjects' on 1 June 1912. It read as follows:

> 1. That the expression 'State Subjects' means all bonafide subjects of His Highness the Maharaja Sahib Bahadur.
> 2. All persons who have tendered a duly executed Rayat Nama and have acquired immovable property within the State territories.
> 3. All persons who have resided within the State territories for not less than 20 years and are subject to all the laws and regulations promulgated from time to time by His Highness the Maharaja Sahib Bahadur and have an intention to live in the said territories for an unlimited time.
> 4. The descendents of the persons mentioned in the foregoing clauses.[230]

226. Ibid., Maharaja's Order No. 227, 30 May 1910.
227. See *OER*, 1910, F.N. 63/F-101, P.W. Minister to Chief Minister, 30 May 1910, JKA.
228. Emphasis in original.
229. *OER*, 1910, F.N. 63/F-101, Order of the Settlement Commissioner, 20 December 1910, JKA.
230. Ibid., Chief Minister's Memo, 8 April 1912 and Maharaja's Order No. 413, 1 June 1912.

The definition, keeping in view the circumstances, not only spelled out who a 'State subject' was but in the process recognized his prior claim to State service. The definition *ipso facto* came to equate the claim of both bona fide subjects, to whom 'prior claim' was assured in 1891, and almost all who had come thereafter either for employment or trade. Besides, it was also stipulated that for appointments reserved for State subjects the following persons too would be considered eligible:

(i) Any State servant who though not a State subject has not less than 10 years approved service in the State.

(ii) The children of such State servants (also remoter descendants provided that the connection of the family with the State service has not been interrupted without due reason).[231]

This unleashed resentment from those who considered themselves to be bona fide State subjects.[232] At this, what seem to have been lukewarm official deliberations were started to look into the matter but nothing concrete came of it until 'full powers' were bestowed by the Viceroy upon Pratap Singh in 1921 and subsequently Hari Singh was made the Senior and Foreign Member of the newly introduced Executive Council.

Hari Singh, who as we know already, was at this time completely under the influence and patronage of the Government and their representative—the Resident—took the lead to have the State subjects associated more closely with the administration and thus gave effect to what the Viceroy had contemplated as a matter of general policy to be pursued by Pratap Singh when 'full powers' were bestowed upon him. In other words, he set out to correct a situation that had developed under the control of the Government, a situation which was clearly the result of the logic of its imperatives, but which the Viceroy now professed publicly should be remedied. In the process, Hari Singh came to be regarded as the representative and the defender of the interests of the 'State subjects'.

231. Ibid.

232. For details see the discussion on *Karkun* Pandits and their struggle for jobs in the State services at ch. 6.

Earlier, Hari Singh had acquired a reputation for being concerned about the people in general and protecting their interests. While the resentment against the definition of the State subject as adopted in 1912 was being given expression and the official deliberations were on, (Raj Kumar) Hari Singh, who was just twenty years of age and under the perfect hegemony of the Government, came to recognize and acted to secure the interests of bona fide subjects of his *jagir*, and then of those in the other territories of the State, in that order of preference, in the case of appointments to service in the administration of his own *jagir*.[233]

In 1922, after (Raja) Hari Singh had taken over as the Senior and Foreign Member of the Executive Council, he proposed and secured the order of the Maharaja to the following effect:

> In future no non-State subject shall be appointed to any position in my State without my express order passed in Council in each case, and each proposal shall be accompanied by a full statement of reasons in writing as to why it is considered necessary to appoint a non-State subject it being definitely stated whether there is no State subject qualified and available to hold the appointment proposed. In like manner no scholarship or training expenses of any kind shall be granted to any non-State subject. Any infringement of this order will be severely dealt with.[234]

233. In a letter to the Members of the Committee, that had been formed as a part of the above stated deliberations, Hari Singh wrote on 5 April 1915 that '. . . whenever in future any vacancy occurs or any new post is created in any department of my Jagir the Head of the department should endeavour to fill it in the first instance with a Jagir bonafide subject fit for the post, but if a fit person of the Jagir might not be forthcoming he should try to secure the services of a fit and able Kashmir State bonafide subject for such post or vacancy.

Failing in both the claims of other be considered and my sanction may be obtained before anyone (who is neither a Jagir subject nor a Kashmir State subject) is employed. Heads of all departments of my Jagir may kindly be informed accordingly.' *OER*, 1910, F.N. 63/F-101, JKA.

234. *OER*, 1921, F.N. 239/10, Maharaja's Order No. 225-C.S., 12 May 1922, JKA. Also see Wakefield (1942), p. 184.

By the same order, the Senior Member was asked to select and form a Committee for the purpose of 'definitely defining the term State subject'.[235] The recommendations of this committee were to be submitted to the Maharaja for further orders.

Subsequently in January 1927, after the death of Pratap Singh and Hari Singh was the Maharaja, the definition of a 'Hereditary State Subject' was fixed.[236] It was a rigorous definition and was tantamount to securing the interests of bona fide State subjects in the State services. Thus, the 'prior claim' of the State subjects to all State services that had been recognized in 1891 moved full circle.

Such a development obviously necessitated the availability of State subjects with higher qualifications. To meet this contingency a beginning had been made in 1923 with the appointment of a committee that was asked 'to consider the future requirements of the different departments in technical qualifications and experience, and make proposals for grant of scholarships for training to qualified State-Subjects'.[237] This committee was reconstituted in 1927 as the 'Scholarship Selection Board'.[238] The Board was to select persons who could be sent on scholarship for training in 'higher branches' of the State services 'such as Engineering, Forest, Medical etc.'[239] Its aim was that 'hereditary State subjects whatever their community should be trained and made efficient for the purpose of holding higher posts. The test was personal merit and not a proper division among the communities'.[240] In 1927, twelve scholarships were advertised. The persons to whom these were awarded included eleven

235. This was to consist of six official and four non-official representatives of the Provinces of Jammu and Kashmir. *OER*, 1921, F.N. 239/10, Maharaja's Order No. 225-C.S., 12 May 1922, JKA.

236. See Kaul (1967), p. 99.

237. His Highness' Government, Jammu and Kashmir, *Modern Jammu and Kashmir State, 1925-43* (Jammu, 1944), p. 2.

238. Ibid.

239. His Highness' Government, Jammu and Kashmir, *Evidence Recorded in Public by the Srinagar Riots Enquiry Committee, 1931* (Jammu, 1931), Finance and Development Minister's Statement (hereafter *Evidence SREC*).

240. Ibid.

Hindus and one Muslim. Out of eleven Hindus, seven were Kashmiri Pandits. The single Muslim candidate recommended for the award was not selected on merit but because the Board Members were 'alarmed' to see the overwhelming number of the Hindus being selected.[241]

The feeling of alarm among the Board Members had apparently as its basis the growing Muslim movement for proportional representation in the State services. Muslims as a religious segment of society in Kashmir, as has been noted earlier, took to modern education late. But they had developed an awareness of being under-represented in the State administration that found clear expression first in 1907 and increasingly so from then onwards.[242] They had expressed a desire and also placed a demand to have reservation introduced for them in the State services.[243] Not surprisingly then, bitter resentment was voiced by Muslim associations, both in Kashmir and Jammu, against the pattern of the distribution of the scholarships in 1927.[244] As a result, the Maharaja issued instructions that the scholarships be distributed equally between Hindus and Muslims.[245]

A memorial with a view to securing reservation for the Muslims in the State services was presented to the Maharaja in June 1929 by a few elite Muslims from Jammu.[246] Thereupon, according to Bazaz, a secret understanding was reached between them and the State Government to the effect that 50 per cent of the vacancies would be henceforth filled by the Muslims.[247] A State 'Civil Service Board' came to be appointed in early 1930.[248] The Board was enjoined to adjust the communal proportion in the State services through a procedure of recruitment initially laid down. One-third of the candidates were to be taken through

241. Ibid.

242. The development of the Muslim demand is traced in ch. 6.

243. Ibid.

244. *Evidence SREC*, Finance and Development Minister's Statement.

245. See and cf. G.S. Raghavan, *The Warning of Kashmir* (Allahabad, 1931), p. 65; *Evidence SREC*, Deputy Revenue Minister's Statement; and ibid., Islamia School Head Master's Statement.

246. Bazaz (1941), p. 99.

247. Ibid.

248. See *The Ranbir*, 4 March 1930 and *Evidence SREC*, Agha Syed Hussain's Statement.

competition; one-third through promotion; and another third through nomination.[249] This was an administrative solution and could hardly satisfy those who had been seeking what was essentially a political demand—the demand for proportional Muslim representation. Moreover, the episode which took place at Srinagar in the beginning of 1930, of which more later, assumed importance. It apparently displayed the State government's unwillingness to have the reservation principle introduced for the Muslims in the State services or its inability to withstand the Hindu opposition encountered in the process of implementing it. This and the establishment of the 'Civil Service Board' seems to have precipitated the situation and led to the kind of struggle that unleashed the events of 1931.

249. Raghavan (1931), pp. 65-66.

6

IDEAS AND MOVEMENTS

Towards the early nineties of the nineteenth century the people of Kashmir had come to have fairly set and stable ideas about the issues connected with their day-to-day life. 'At the present time', wrote Lawrence, 'the Kashmiri is ruled by *Rawaj* [custom] and is content to abide by the *Ain* [code of customs] of the country'.[1] This implies an acceptance by the people of the idea of the immutability of the nature of their life-process and the institutions governing it. However, the situation could hardly be expected to remain the same once changes took place in those very conditions that governed their life-process. Such changes, it has been seen, started in 1880 and became more pronounced so from 1889 onwards. Besides, we must also take into account the direct consequence of this very process—the exposure of the people to new trends in social thought and ideas prevalent in British India, particularly in the adjacent province of the Punjab. A two-fold implication of all this for the people was: (*a*) the changes taking place required new

1. Walter R. Lawrence, *The Valley of Kashmir* (Reprint, Srinagar, 1967), p. 9.

adaptations and adjustments to avoid disruption; and (*b*) things that had appeared constant and everlasting seemed now amenable to change. The latter is corroborated by what Maharaja Pratap Singh observed in reply to the suggestion made to him in 1921 by the Viceroy to associate his subjects more closely with the administration. He confessed that his experience during the 34 years of his rule brought to him the realization that 'the affairs of this world are in a constant course of transition and that policies of state must also be moulded according to the proper requirements of the times'.[2] Thus, certain important aspects in the changing pattern in culture and the consequent responses to these eventually acquired the form of the social movements.

We have already seen from the socio-religious composition of the people and their culture around 1846, that nearly the entire population of Kashmir subscribed to Islam. A great majority of them upheld the Sunni tadition and the rest the Shia. Among the non-Muslims, the majority subscribed to Brahmanical Hinduism and the rest followed the Sikh cult. Each one of the socio-religious segments, or sub-segments had its specific set of social and religious practices which have been recorded very adequately.[3] Lawrence's observations of the practices of the Sunni Muslims and the Hindus were such that he stated that 'Kashmiris are at heart Hindus'.[4] Sunni Muslims, as noted earlier also, were great believers in the efficacy of the powers of the dead saints. They displayed idolatrous tendencies and 'certain places' were held 'in reverence by Hindus and Musalmans alike'.[5] For example, the imprint of a foot in a stone was worshipped by the Muslims as the Prophet's footprint (Kadam-i-Rasul) and by the Hindus as Vishnu's foot (Vishna pad).[6] Brahmins, Lawrence wrote,

2. *Old English Records*, 1920, File No. (F.N.) 104, Maharaja's address to Viceroy, Jammu and Kashmir State Archives (Jammu) (hereafter *OER*, JKA).

3. Walter R. Lawrence, op. cit., chapters entitled 'Social Life' and 'Religions'.

4. Ibid., p. 286.

5. Ibid.

6. Ibid.

'do things which would horrify the orthodox Hindus.'[7] They would drink water brought by a Muslim; they would eat food cooked on a Muslim boat; the foster-mother of their children would be usually Muslim women; and a foster-brother often obtained 'great power in a Hindu household.'[8] At the time when Lawrence arrived in Kashmir, he found 'delightful tolerance' between the followers of the two religions.[9]

This state of affairs with regard to religion apparently persisted during the reigns of the first two Dogra rulers—Gulab Singh and Ranbir Singh. It can be attributed to their protection of the economic interests of the dominant classes, the observance of religious tolerance and a determined policy to curb the entry of unsettling influences into Kashmir. G.T. Vigne pays tribute to the political sagacity of Gulab Singh in being 'tolerant and liberal in his religious opinions'.[10] Moreover, the 'advice' given to him by Henry Lawrence to ensure 'stability' in his dominions contained a clear injunction to the effect that he ought to 'make no difference' between his subjects belonging to different religious sects and that he should allow them to follow the 'precepts' of their respective religions.[11] Gulab too assured him that he would treat all sects 'alike'.[12] During Ranbir Singh's time there was an attempt to introduce what are reported as the 'Wahhabi doctrines' into Kashmir and about 200 families in the Shupiyon tehsil accepted this faith. But the 'propagandists' were 'promptly stamped out' by him.[13] Similarly, permission to enter Kashmir was refused to the founder of the Arya Samaj Movement, Swami Dayanand

7. Ibid., p. 300.
8. Ibid.
9. Ibid.
10. G.T. Vigne, *Travels in Kashmir, Ladak, Iskardo and the Countries Adjoining the Mountain Course of the Indus, and the Himalaya North of the Panjab* (London, 1842), Vol. 1, p. 184.
11. *Foreign Department Proceedings*, Secret Branch, 26 December 1846, nos. 1243-47, Lawrence to Gulab, 6 November 1846, National Archives of India (New Delhi) (hereafter *FDP*, NAI).
12. Ibid., Gulab to Lawrence, 13 November 1846.
13. Walter R. Lawrence, op. cit., p. 285.

Saraswati.[14] An early attempt by a Christian Missionary to settle in Kashmir was discouraged by his officials. It was only in 1864 that a Christian Medical Mission came to be established at Srinagar and that too for only six months in the year. This seems to have been reluctantly permitted, because missionary sources speak about the uncompromising and thwarting attitude of his government.[15]

The situation, however, changed after the personalized State of the Maharaja was replaced in 1889 by the State Council administration. Reform movements came to operate both amongst the Sunni Muslims and the Pandits. Among the Muslims the 'Wahhabi doctrines' came to be propagated as Lawrence noted. Lawrence's observations span five years from 1889 to 1895—and he states these doctrines were preached and 'many Rishis of shrines' and others who spoke 'with authority' to him declared that 'Wahhabi ideas' were 'gaining ground'.[17] What these ideas were is not specified. Nor does he give us any information as to the agency that was responsible for preaching whatever those ideas were. However, in view of later evidence about the denomination of the different sub-segments among Muslims in 1907,[18] it appears that the reference made by Lawrence is with regard to the preaching conducted by Rasul Shah or Rasul Baba.

14. Gwasha Lal Kaul, *Kashmir Then and Now* (Srinagar, 1967), 8th edn., p. 89. Kaul says that Ranbir Singh had personally nothing against Dayanand's entry into the State territories but was persuaded by the Brahmin priests to disallow that. This argument, however, seems to be untenable in view of the fact that Ranbir was known for his activities with regard to the conservation of the Brahmanical creed.

15. See *FDP*, Pol.—A, July 1864, nos. 79-81, Robert Clarke to Cooper, 25 April 1864, NAI.

16. Walter R. Lawrence, op. cit., p. 285.

17. Ibid.

18. This is available in a letter which Maharaja Pratap Singh wrote to the Private Secretary to the Viceroy in 1907. The Maharaja wrote: 'There are, as you know, two main sections of the Mahommedan community in Kashmir; the Shiahs and the Sunnis. The Sunnis again are divided into two main factions: (1) those who follow the six *baqas* (shrines), and (2) the whabis'. *Minto Papers*, (microfilm), Pratap Singh to Private Secretary, 28 October 1907, NAI.

Rasul Shah was represented in 1904 to condemn the 'worship and deification of saints and other holy personages'.[19] This was clearly a new trend, though revivalist in nature, in the religious thought prevalent in Kashmir and as such was bound to create conflicting situations. And it is known for certain that he and his followers were engaged in some kind of religious dispute in 1899 and 1904.[20]

Rasul Shah's preaching acquired the character of a movement and his role as its leader became institutionalized as the hereditary position of Mirwaiz. This appelation was used for him as early as 1901.[21] The movement grew in scope and the institution of the Mirwaiz not only got consolidated but also the influence wielded by its successive incumbents came to be enormous. In 1901, Rasul Shah was considered to be the 'only man' who had 'large influence' over the Muslims of Srinagar with a following of about three-quarters of the people.'[22] Around the time of Rasul Shah's death, which occurred in 1909 (Hijri 1327),[23] his followers were said to be in a 'majority' at Srinagar.[24] The influence wielded by his brother and successor, Maulvi Ahmed Ullah, can be judged by the scenes at his death which occurred in April 1931 (Hijri 14 Ze Qaidh 1349). Over one lakh people are believed to have been present in his funeral procession;[25] and people, who apparently must have been his followers, are said to have even taken his *schalan wone* (Kashmiri for the sip of the water used in giving the ritual bath to a dead body).[26] He was succeeded by his nephew,

19. *The Tribune*, 29 November 1904, Dogra's letter to the Editor.
20. *OER*, 1910, F.N. 169/N-109c, Judge High Court's Memorandum, 24 November 1910, JKA.
21. See in *OER*, 1898, F.N. 52/L-II, Governor, Kashmir, to Vice-President, State Council, 11 March 1901, JKA.
22. Ibid.
23. Master Mohammed Maqbool, *Ner-i-Azm*: *Sir Syed Kashmir* (Urdu) (Srinagar, n.d.), p. 31.
24. *OER*, 1910, F.N. 169/N-109c, Judge High Court's Memorandum, 24 November 1910, JKA.
25. See Maqbool, op. cit., p, 32.
26. This was related in personal interviews with some old people in the locality.

Maulvi Mohammed Yusuf Shah,[27] who likewise wielded a lot of influence as was apparent during the agitation and upsurge in 1931 and after.[28]

Thus the movement which started with the preaching of Rasul Shah had some important social consequences in Kashmir. The first and the immediate consequence was the creation of a social cleavage and conflict between the votaries of the new trend and the upholders of the conservative tradition. The latter, calling themselves '*ahli aitqad*'—believers in 'six baqas (shrines)'—were led by the chief priest of the shrine of Khanqah-i-Moulla at Srinagar.[29] They came to be known as '*Khanqashia*' or '*Cheka*'. The followers of the Mirwaiz were known as '*Kota*'. The second consequence was the creation of a single centre of a great mass following and influence under the Mirwaiz, under-cutting the standing of many lesser Pirzadas and making them redundant. As a result the latter were faced with dire consequences to their social position and economic prosperity.[30] The third consequence was implicit in these two—to cast off the traditions that were a result of the past 'contamination' with *Kufur* or idolatory. A fourth consequence is also likely; it was the deepening of Muslim communal consciousness in the segment of the population that followed the Mirwaiz. There is evidence to suggest the prevalence of some kind of Hindu-Muslim tension at Srinagar in 1910.[31]

27. Maqbool, op. cit., pp. 32-33.

28. It continues to be a subject for debates as to whether it would have been possible 'to launch struggle for freedom in 1931 if Maulvi Yusuf Shah had withheld his support'. The Maulvi subsequently turned against Sheikh Mohammed Abdullah and became his chief political opponent and rival.

29. The six shrines referred to are probably the same places as were mentioned by Lawrence to be held in high esteem. These are: Hazrat Bal, Shah-i-Hamdan mosque, Jama Masjid, Chhrar Sharif, Ziarats of Dasgir and Makhdum Sahib. Walter R. Lawrence, op. cit., p. 292.

30. This inference is drawn on the basis of an observation made regarding the impact of the Mirwaiz's descendent preaching in different shrines on the economic position of the Pirzadas. See Pir Mohammed Afzal Maqdoomi, series of articles on 'Tahriq Huriyat Kashmir' in *Aieena*.

31. A petition was submitted by a few Hindus on 18 September 1910 to the Maharaja in which mention was made about the prevalence of 'a

Rasul Shah's reform activities were not confined to the religious sphere alone. He was also responsible, as has been indicated already, for pioneering private efforts in 1899 to spread modern education amongst Muslims.[32] It was a significant move in the sense that the Muslims who had by and large abstained from opting for modern education were provided with an opportunity of obtaining both religious and secular instruction at the same place. This educational work was carried on by Rasul Shah and his successors through the instrument of the association called the Nasrut-ul-Islam. Formed in 1899,[33] the association seems to have received help and support largely from a section of the Muslim elite—in particular from Hassan Shah Naqashbandi, Aziz-ud-Din Kawoosa and Abdul Samad Qaqru.[34]

Aside from the puritanical movement which operated through the institution of the Mirwaiz, the Ahmadiya Movement from Punjab also penetrated Kashmir. By the early twenties of the present century, the protagonists of this movement were very active in Kashmir. In 1922, members of this sect were found 'residing in the various parts of Kashmir also especially in the [rural] Districts of Shopian, Kolgam and Bandipura' and were engaged in the furtherance of their 'movement'.[35] They did not confine their activities to Muslims alone, but also worked for conversions from other religious groups.[36] Towards the

general rumour that the Mohammadans of the vally [sic] have a [sic] malicious intention of plundering Hindu people similarly as was the case of *Shia sect* in the year 1929 (A.D. 1872-73), as soon as your Highness departure to Jammu.' *OER*, 1910, F.N. 258, 'Hindu Subjects' Petition to Maharaja, 18 September 1910, JKA.

32. Discussed in Popular Response and Agencies at work in ch. 5.

33. Anjuman Nasrat-ul-Islam, *Sir Syed Kashmir, Hazrat Mirwaiz Maulana Rasul Shah Sahib: Bani Anjuman Nasrat-ul-Islam Srinagar Ke Satavanven yomi visal per Aek Mukhtsar Twaruf* (Urdu) (Srinagar, n.d.), p. 1.

34. See Maqbool, op. cit., p. 21.

35. *Political Records*, 1922, F.N. C.S./P.B. 116/Misc 29, Additional Secretary, Ahmadiya Community, to Maharaja, 3 June 1922, JKA.

36. This is apparent from the fact that in 1923 information was sought from Qadian as to whether there were 'law orders in vogue from the State Council, prohibiting the State subject to be converted from their religions'. *PR*, 1924, F.N.C.S./P.B. 7/M-102, Additional Secretary to

late twenties, a votary of this sect, Maulvi Mohammed Abdullah Vakil, was actively engaged in the preaching of this faith in the heart of Srinagar.[37] Unlike the Mirwaiz, and the rival chief of the *Khanqashis*, who both held conservative views regarding women's progress, he deprecated the use of *purdah* and stressed education for girls.[38] Though he could not create much of a following he succeeded in influencing many Muslim young men. These included Ghulam Nabi Gilkar and Sheikh Mohammed Abdullah,[39] both of whom were amongst the leaders of the agitation in 1931.[40] As a matter of fact, the Sheikh's first public appearance took place at a meeting organized by Maulvi Abdullah for the first ever public celebration in Kashmir of the Prophet's birthday—the *Id-e-Milad-un-Nabi.*[41]

Like the Sunni Muslims, the Pandits also witnessed the emergence of a reform movement in the last decade of the nineteenth century. This happened under the auspices of two associations, namely the Bishen Sabha and Dharma Sabha. The report of the Census of 1901[42] mentions the existence of both these associations but does not say exactly when they were formed. However, it is evident from another source that the Dharma Sabha existed in 1896.[43] Not much is known about the Bishen Sabha and its role in Kashmir, except that the sabha 'advocated latitude in certain social matters.'[44] The sabha was an extension of social reform activities initiated by Pandit Bhishen

---

His Holiness the Khalifa-tul Massih, to Minister, Kashmir State, 6 August 1923, JKA.

37. Prem Nath Bazaz, *Daughters of the Vitasta: A History of Kashmiri Women from Early Times to the Present Day* (New Delhi, 1959), p. 243.

38. Ibid., p. 243.

39. Ibid.

40. *Written Statements Part I, Srinagar Riots Enquiry Committee, July 1931.* (Jammu, 1931), p. 1.

41. Interview with Sheikh Abdul Samed Ahmadi, 9 December 1977 (Srinagar).

42. *Census of India, 1901*, Kashmir (Lahore, 1902), Part I, p. 24.

43. *Interview with Master Zinda Kaul by Ali Mohammed Lone on 13 April 1961* (Kashmiri). This is preserved in the Srinagar station of the All India Radio and was broadcast in the *Husn-i-Mazi* programme of the station on 1 May 1977.

44. *Census 1901*, p. 24.

Narayan Dar amongst the Kashmiri Pandits domiciled in the then North-Western Province.[45] Dar had 'very liberal views on religion and social reforms'.[46] He was a very strong propagandist for giving up the taboo against 'foreign travel';[47] his plea was that India needed 'liberal education of the modern type' for its all-round regeneration and development and this kind of education could 'best be obtained in England'.[48]

As against the Bishen Sabha, the Dharma Sabha is said to have consisted of 'Orthodox Hindus'.[49] It was this association that continued to exist and came to be fairly well-known amongst the Pandits of Kashmir. Right from its establishment, it seems to have been the handiwork of Pandit Hargopal Kaul. The Pandit was descended from a family which had migrated earlier to the Punjab and had been born and brought up there. He and his brothers returned to the home of their ancestors around 1876 and settled there.[50] In 1896, Pandit Hargopal Kau lwas the 'Secretary' of the Sabha[51] as also one of its most

45. See and cf. ibid. and Akhilesh Misra, 'Dar, Bishen Narayan: 1864-1926', in S.P. Sen, ed., *Dictionary of National Biography* (Calcutta, 1972), Vol. 1, pp. 331-32. Dar was the descendent of a family, which like many others, had migrated earlier from Kashmir and were domiciled now in other parts of the Indian sub-continent. He went to England for higher studies and returned home in 1887. On his return he was asked to undergo *prayaschit*. This he boldly refused and succeeded in association with other progressive persons of the community to break the old Dharma Sabha and establish a separate association, Bishen Sabha.

Dar was also associated with the Indian National Congress and rose to be its President in 1911. For some more information regarding his profile, see Misra in Sen (1972), pp. 331-3; and K. Iswara Dutt, *Congress Cyclopaedia: The Indian National Congress, 1885-1920* (New Delhi, nd.), Vol. 1, pp. 251-52.

46. Misra in Sen (1972), p. 332.

47. See Pundit Bishan Narayan Dar, 'Foreign Travel', in C. Yajnesvara Chintamani, ed., *Indian Social Reform* (Madras, 1901), Part I.

48. Ibid., pp. 203-4.

49. *Census of India, 1901*, p. 24.

50. See Abdul Qadir Sarwari, *Kashmir ke Do Adib—Do Bhayee: Pandit Hargopal Kaul Khasta aur Pandit Saligram Salik ke Halat aur un ke Karnamoon per Tabsurra* (Urdu) (Hyderabad, 1965), pp. 9, 13, 25.

51. AIR interview with Kaul by Lone.

influential members.[52] Even towards the end of his life, which came in January 1924,[53] he was its moving spirit.[54]

The activities of the Dharma Sabha or, to put it more appropriately, Kaul were directed towards reforms in the social practices of the Pandits and their educational advancement. In the religious sphere, he did not advocate any kind of revivalism and was a votary of the conservative religious creed—Sanatan Dharma.[55]

The social reforms which were advocated by him and were successfully introduced during his lifetime were the curtailment of expenditure incurred at the time of marriage ceremonies by eschewing the costly item of meat[56] thereby relieving the financial burden on the parents of the bride and the adandonment of the use of superfluous paraphernalia by the bridegroom on the day of the wedding.[57]

The one reform which he advocated but which was not successful during his lifetime was widow remarriage. He, incidentally, tried to initiate the process by getting his daughter remarried—she had become a widow very young. He had even arranged for a match for her but the arrangement could not come to fruition because of strong social resistance.[58] As a matter of fact, the first widow remarriage among Pandits took place only four years after his death.

Kaul was also associated with the pioneering efforts in the spread of female education. The first school started specially for the education of Hindu girls at Srinagar had his widowed daughter on its teaching staff. The credit of working as the first teacher

52. For this, see *OER*, 1898, F.N. 52/L-II, Judgement of Judicial Member in Council in a case of the alleged contempt of religion by Yahya Shah against Hargopal Kaul, JKA.

53. Interview with Shiv Narayan Fotedar, January 1976 (Jammu).

54. This was locally conveyed to us by some older persons.

55. For an account of the activities of Hargopal and his brother—Saligram, see Sarwari (1965).

56. Ballads were also composed on this and other activities and events connected with Hargopal.

57. The first person in whose marriage such paraphernalia was discarded was Raghu Nath Mattu.

58. Bazaz (1959), p. 235.

and having boldly faced taunts from the reactionaries however goes to another Pandit lady, Tekri.[59]

It seems that Kaul and his brother, Saligram, were also associated with those who made successful efforts for the establishment of a college at Srinagar.[60] This was established in 1906 as Pratap Hindu College, later known as Sri Pratap College, the first of its kind in Kashmir.

The natural concomitant of these reform activities was an emphasis upon the fraternity and solidarity of those whose professed betterment or interest the Sabha sought. This occurred quite early and left such an imprint on the receptive mind of a small school-going boy who later grew up to be a famous poet—Master Zinda Kaul—that it resulted in his first *nazam*. It was entitled '*Itifaq te Hamdardi*' which in Kashmiri means Unity and Sympathy, and was recited by him at one of the meetings of the Sabha in 1896.[61]

The tradition of reform amongst the Pandits under the leadership of Hargopal was continued after his death though in different streams. Different individuals embraced the various aspects just as if they had been waiting in the wings for the opportunity to do so. The tempo remained in full swing up to 1931, nor did it slacken after that eventful year.

In 1926, an organization known as the Women's Welfare Trust was formed with the object of 'advancing the welfare of the Kashmiri women by imparting to them knowledge, by stimulating home industry among them and by promoting their physical health and well-being.'[62] Its founders, Mrs. Margaret E. Cousins, Mrs. L.D. Van Gheel Gildemeester, Sri Kanth Tohakhani, Shridhar Kaul Dulloo and Aftab Kaul Nizamat were theosophists. The brain behind the movement was Toshkhani while Nizamat became the heart and soul' of the

59. Ibid. pp. 217-18.

60. This appears to have been the case when we view the substance of the following verse from one of the *nazams* from Saligram (Salek) in comparison with the background of the activities of the two brothers:

(College was started in Kashmir due to our efforts and graduates from this college have the cheek to argue with us.) Sarwari (1965), p. 81.

61. AIR interview with Kaul by Lone.

62. Quoted in Bazaz (1959), p. 222.

trustboth were native Pandits.[63] Toshkhani had awakened to the idea of women's uplift in particular during his stay in Agra where he did his master's course in philosophy. It was there that a book entitled *Courageous Deeds* fell into his hands and he realized how much women were being exploited.[64] His interest in women's uplift received a further impetus after he returned home and engaged himself in legal practice in the local court where he encountered cases relating to traffic among women. In 1925, he went to Madras and persuaded Mrs. Cousins and others to extend their help to improve the lot of women through imparting education to them. In 1926, with the help of Nizamat, he founded the trust. Its membership was strictly confined to those who professed to be theosophists. This rule was made, says Toshkhani, to exclude people who did not consider all religions true and thus avoid the taint of communalism.[65] This seems to be corroborated by the fact that soon after its initial success the trust also launched a school for Muslim girls in 1929.[66]

Widow remarriage, which had been taken up by Hargopal Kaul, found outspoken votaries among a few Pandits from 1924 onwards.[67] The group was led by Chandra Joo, an advocate in the High Court. Another strong supporter of the movement was Swami Hari Har Kaul. They were 'jeered at, ridiculed and pelted' but they met with success in 1928 when a widow remarriage was solemnized.[68] In 1929 and 1930, more than half a dozen such marriages were celebrated.[69]

After the initial battles had been won by them, the leaders of the movement submitted a memorial to the Maharaja in 1930 to legalize the marriage of Hindu widows in the State

63. Cf. ibid., pp. 222-23 and *Interview with Sri Kanth Toshkhani by P.N. Pushp and others* (Kashmiri). This is preserved in the Srinagar station of the All India Radio and was broadcast in the *Myon Kar Myon Zindgi* programme of the station on 27 September 1977.
64. AIR interview with Toshkhani by Pushp and others.
65. Ibid.
66. Bazaz (1959), p. 224.
67. Ibid., p. 235.
68. Ibid.
69. Ibid., p. 236.

territories as had been done earlier in British India.[70] The State Government ordered an enquiry to ascertain Hindu public opinion. With this purpose in view, a meeting of the Hindus representing various viewpoints was convened at Srinagar under the auspices of one of the district officials. The meeting was held in April 1931 and was attended by over a hundered Pandits both old and young.[71] Before any conclusion could be reached, the meeting was dispersed by the official and the decision on the issue was postponed till the verdict of the Dharma Sabha was known. This was done because of strong opposition from its President, Amar Nath Kak; the sabha had apparently passed into the hands of young but conservative elements after the death of Hargopal Kaul. In a meeting held subsequently, the Sabha opposed the move[72] and temporarily halted progress on the question. The two meetings had a special significance in that at both of them a group of organized young men made an attempt to make their presence felt and their viewpoint known. This group was an informal association formed in 1930, known by its members as the 'Fraternity'.[73] These young men[74] were imbued with zeal to reform their society and had on their agenda, besides other things, the spread of education among women and freedom for widows to remarry. The senior member of the group, Prem Nath Bazaz, joined the staff of the Women's Welfare Trust in August 1930.[75] He entered into correspondence with Mahatma Gandhi and sought his guidance on how to encourage widow remarriage[76]

70. Ibid., p. 236.
71. Ibid., pp. 236-37.
72. Ibid., p. 240.
73. Ibid., pp. 237-40.
74. It is an interesting fact that many of these young men were also successful later in their personal careers. For example, T.N. Kaul became Indian ambassador to USSR and USA, M.L. Dhar became Vice-Chancellor, Benaras Hindu University, Prem Nath Bazaz a well-known politician and author, Dwarika Nath Kachru became Private Secretary to Jawaharlal Nehru, and Saligram Kaul was the Principal, Medical College, Srinagar.
75. See Bazaz (1959), pp. 225, 233.
76. This is evident from the contents of a letter that was written by

As a result of the meeting held under the auspices of the Dharma Sabha, public reaction was aroused and antipathy towards both the reformers and the Fraternity spread.[77] However, this antipathy remained shortlived. With the developments following the Muslim agitation, the Fraternity was soon pushed to the forefront in an endeavour to defend the interests of the Pandits in general and renamed itself the Sanatan Dharm Young Men's Association.[78]

Simultaneously with the developments in the socio-religious sphere which have been surveyed, there occurred a change in the political culture of Kashmiris, or at least of the residents of Srinagar. Having lived for centuries under autocratic political regimes, they had little training in liberal democratic culture. But from 1879 several agencies had helped, directly or indirectly, to dispel the notion of the inevitability of the autocratic nature of political authority. In other words, these agencies helped to sow the seeds of what may be termed a nebulous liberal democratic political culture. Awareness as to the possibility of influencing governmental policy was sufficiently displayed by various groups even before 1931, implying thereby that the new culture was already being imbibed and internalized by some. Moreover, the governing authority too had on occasion displayed its newly acquired sensitivity towards public opinion.

The first crack in the edifice of the autocratic political structure and traditional culture was caused in 1879 when an accident occurred[79] and Hargopal Kaul questioned the Maharaja's

---

Gandhi to Bazaz. The letter, as given below, is of much interest for it contradicts the notion that Gandhi upheld the caste system:

'I have your letter. What young men can do is to make up their minds to marry only widows and if they cannot secure widows in the Pandit caste they should travel outside, if only by way of Satyagraha. But if they are desirous of restricting themselves to their caste in the first instance they should reason with the caste elders and give them notice that they would go outside the caste if they did not merely permit but encourage widows to re-marry,' *The Tribune*, 12 June 1931.

77. Bazaz (1959), p. 240.

78. Ibid., pp. 241, 249. The association was popularly know as Yuvak Sabha.

79. This happened as a result of the proceedings in a case of inquiry relating to the validation of a rumour that a boat carrying paupers was

authority to act as a judge in the case against him. He contended that the Maharaja being the prosecuter in the case against him could not sit in judgement as well.[80] Further, he entered into an argument with him on being harshly scolded by the Maharaja.[81] The Maharaja was so incensed that he drew his sword to attack Hargopal. Hargopal would have probably fallen a victim to the Maharaja's warth but for the timely intervention of the councillor, Wazir Punno, who reminded the Maharaja that the accused was a Brahmin.[82] The result was that Hargopal and his brother Saligram were imprisoned for a few years away from home at Jammu. Undoubtedly Hargopal had a hot-headed disposition for later, in 1898, Hargopal and his brother were involved in a dispute with a neighbour, Yahya Shah, who recalled in his petition to the British Resident that

---

drowned in the Wular Lake. The rumour had appeared against the background of the severe famine that ravaged Kashmir in 1877-79 and it was further alleged thereupon that the drowning was not an accidental happening but a deliberate official act to escape the onerous job of feeding poor hungry subjects.

80. Interview with Fotedar, January 1976. This is largely corroborated by a relevant piece of evidence found in contemporary British official records. Cf. 'Indeed Hargopal himself is said to have observed in the course of the trial that he was the accused and the Maharaja of Kashmir was the accuser but that he should like to know who was the judge.' *FDP*, Pol.-B, December 1880, nos. 132-6, F. Henvey, Officer on Special Duty in Kashmir to Secretary to Government, 26 September 1880, NAI.

81. Hargopal told the Maharaja:

آپ والیِ مُلک ہیں ۔ میں آپ کا رعیت ہوں ۔ اگر آپ والیِ مُلک نہ ہوتے اور میں
آپ کا رعیت نہ ہوتا تو شاید جو زبان آپ نے استعمال کی تو میرا جواب بھی
اُسی زبان میں ہوتا ۔

(You are the sovereign of this land and I am your subject. Had it not been so, I would have answered you in the same language that you have used.)

82. Interview with Fotedar, January 1976. Wazir Punno also told the Maharaja that he should feel proud that he had a subject like Hargopal who could dare say such a thing openly to his sovereign. Ibid. Cf. Sarwari (1965), p. 30.

Kaul had a history of being 'defiant towards the reigning power'.[83]

The institution in 1885 of the British Residency in the State and the perpetual struggle that ensued between the Maharaja and his opponents in the State Council contributed to the trend of taking political activities beyond the confines of the royal entourage. Individuals outside it were encouraged to write in the Punjab Native Press either for or against the two parties. For example, in 1894 Saligram published an Urdu weekly, *Shumali*, from Sialkot and wrote a critique of the Maharaja and one of the councillors, Sardar Muhammad Hayat Khan.[84] Similarly, attempts were made to articulate and use the discontent of the different segments of the population. In 1897, the Maharaja was alleged to have encouraged some people to demonstrate against the other Members of the State Council at Srinagar.[85]

The political developments in the British Indian Provinces also had reverberations in Kashmir. When the anti-British agitation broke out in Punjab in 1907, the Maharaja issued a proclamation[86]—it was circulated by the beat of the drum—

83. *OER*, 1898, F.N. 52/L.11, Yahya Shah's petition to Resident, 9 September 1898, JKA.

84. See and cf. *Selections from the Vernacular Newspapers Published in the Punjab* (S.V.N.P.), 1894, No. 49, from *Shumali* (Sialkot), 26 November 1894, NAI and Sarwari (1965), pp. 77-78. Sarwari's observation that the paper was edited on the behest of Maharaja is however wrong. The reference in the couplet quoted by him from Salek (Saligram) could be to either of the two Rajas, Ram and Amar Singh, and not to the Maharaja. For the attributive word used in the couplet is Raja Sahib:

راجہ صاحب

and not Maharaja. Further, contrary to what Sarwari says, the Maharaja never fell out with Sardar Mohammed Hayat Khan.

85. See *FDP*, Secret Branch—E, February 1898, nos. 183-286, Talbot to Cunningham, 20 July 1897, NAI.

86. 'I notice with greatest regret that some disaffected people in the Punjab and elsewhere in British India are trying to vilify the British Government by misleading and exciting the ignorant and uneducated masses to make a common cause and adopted a defiant attitude towards the Government, so much so that during the last year, and more particularly recently, most unfortunate and highly objectionable proceedings have taken the form of public demonstration.

condemning it and warned his subjects to use 'better sense and judgement' in avoiding 'any disloyal or seditious movements'.

It was intended to pre-empt any such happening in his territories. How effective the circulation of such a proclamation was is not our concern. The fact that the proclamation needed to be made betrayed the first signs of the loosening of the earlier confidence of the autocratic authority. The issuing of such a notice had the potential in itself of creating an awareness among the people that dissent was also possible. Times *had* changed and idea could not be prevented from flowing in from outside; there was now regular contact between the people of Kashmir and the outside world.

The climax of the process of this interaction was reached in 1921 when the Maharaja issued, after he had been asked by the

---

I, however, hope that the subjects of the Jammu and Kashmir State, loyal and devoted as they have always been, with their Chief, to the British Government, will look with the utmost contempt and disdain on such disloyal agitations, which instead of proving in any way beneficial to the cause of the country are likely to lead to further stringencies on the part of the Government, and to make the country unhappy as a whole. As, however, there is the possibility of the poisonous contagion spreading out to this country on account of its close proximity to a Province that has recently shown a tendency to absorb this poison, and give expression to it in the most objectionable form, I consider it necessary that the people living in the territories of the Jammu and Kashmir State should know that I strongly condemn such disloyal movements, and earnestly hope that people would use better sense and judgement to consider their own interests as well as those of the country.

With view, therefore, to safeguard against the possibility of any similar mischief working itself through the subjects of this State and thus disturbing their peace and contentment, it is hereby notified, for general information, that any person found to have any dealings, directly or indirectly, with any disloyal or seditious movements, or to have even taken interest in, or expressed sympathy with, persons connected or associated with such movement, will be subject to the severest punishment that the Durbar can, under the Political Law, inflict.

Persons making any speech, either in public or private, or even holding private meetings to cause any kind of disaffection or public demonstration of individual feelings of discontent, will be equally severely dealt with.'

FDR, Secret Branch—I, September 1907, nos. 9-39, Maharaja Kashmir's Proclamation, 11 May 1907, NAI.

Viceroy to associate his subjects closely with the State adiministration, a proclamation at Srinagar about his intentions of introducing a 'Representative Assembly'.[87] Although the intention was not translated into action immediately, the proclamation was significant in that it recognized the institution of a Representative Assembly as a legitimate goal and as such worth pursuing. The proclamation cut at the very root of the doctrine of the finality of political autocracy.

New ideas with regard to the nature of political authority had not only been diffused in Kashmir, but awareness as to the possibility of influencing governmental policy by organizing public opinion had also been shown by some. This is displayed by the sustained efforts aimed at seeking the appointment of hereditary natives to the State services in preference to outsiders and to have the reservation principle introduced for Muslims in State service. These efforts were not discreet requests made by a single individual or a small group of individuals to the political authority. On the contrary, they were demands made virtually as a matter of right and assumed the form of, as shall be seen below, two movements which spanned a long time.

The hereditary division of labour, a phenomenon which in a way characterized the recruitment to the State services also, was widely prevalent earlier. In other words, the members of different occupational groups considered particular positions or jobs to be their 'natural' calling in life. Deviations, we know, existed but they were an exception rather than the rule. By 1931 the situation changed. As indicated earlier, there developed trends of increasing competition for land and the State services. The competition for the State services in particular assumed the form of two movements: the Hereditary State Subjects movement and the movement for the proportional representation of Muslims in the State administration. The first found success in 1927 with the enactment of the Hereditary State Subjects definition and the second was the primary issue which the leaders of the agitation in 1931 wanted settled.

Competition for the State service and the forms it assumed seems to have been determined by the overall socio-economic

87. See ch. 3.

and political framework of Kashmiri society and the policies pursued by the Government of India.

Entry to the State services entailed some kind of a pre-disposition for the job and a modern literary education which had been associated with State service right from the beginning. Ultimately whether an individual went in for education depended upon personal circumstances and the level of advancement among the different segments of society. There needed to be a guardian willing to make an investment in education without any hope of an immediate return, and leisure which was possible only when the ward could be released from participation in the family occupation. Moreover, there was a lack of strong cultural bias towards education amongst the bulk of the Muslims, besides the absence of association with the clerical state service in the past, and the policy of the state in regard to the distribution of the services under it being governed by feudal considerations. This meant that the competition was mainly among those who were associated with State service in the past or among those who came from dominant social classes and had leisure even though they may not have been associated with state service in the past. The latter's entry into the new arena presupposed a change in their attitudes and aspirations, and that could only have come about as a result of some inducement. The *Karkun* Pandits, particularly those who were resident at Srinagar, had all the requisite qualifications and motivations to take to modern education in right earnest. Little wonder, then, that they were in the forefront of the competition for State service right up to 1931.

The struggle of the *Karkun* Pandits was shaped by the recognition extended by the State Council in 1891 to the inhabitants of the State as 'State subjects' and an acknowledgement of their prior right in the State services. Their clamour for the appointment of State subjects in the State services in preference to non-state subjects, first publicly heard perhaps in 1894, continued to be heard till 1927 when the State formulated a strict definition of who the 'Hereditary State Subject' was. Others too were involved in this struggle. The dominant classes amongst the Dogras launched an identical struggle through an association founded in 1903 known as 'Dogra Sabha'. The Sabha included both Hindus and Muslims and was in the forefront particularly in the struggle to have the definition of 'State subjects', as formulated first in 1912, changed to the advantage of bona fide State subjects.[88] Later on, the Sabha strove to have (Raja) Hari Singh, who had apparently identified himself with the cause of the State subjects by keeping his *Jagir* reserved for bona fide *Jagir* and State subjects, appointed as Chief Minister.[89] With the enactment of the Hereditary State Subjects definition in 1927 culminated the struggle of the Sabha but not that of the *Karkun* Pandits. Their struggle continued, only it was directed against different people and it took a different form.

Because of the position which they had occupied in the revenue administration since medieval times the *Karkun* Pandits had the potential for coming into conflict with any new ruling power. Any effort on the part of the ruling power to introduce elements from outside into the administration was likely to affect *Karkun* Pandits adversely. Equally, the top echelons of the *Karkun* Pandits could also make a bid for positions of power. The *Karkun* Pandits did, in fact, find themselves competing against the non-Kashmiri officials in Kashmir during the early phase of Dogra rule.[90] But the threat to the continuance of their position when the administrative changes came to be effected was colossal —and unprecedented in their experience. The threat was probably mitigated due to certain circumstantial factors, yet it was there. They found themselves labelled as inefficient in the new administrative set-up and were expected to acquire new skills to retain their foothold. By the time they were able to do so they had to confront a new situation. The natives of the then British India, who along with British and Eurasions had come to occupy positions of power in the State, tended to give employment in departments under their charge to their own men from outside the State territories.[91] No wonder this resulted in some kind of

88. See *Dogra Sabha Resolutions*, in *OER*, 1910, F.N. 63/F-101, JKA.

89. See *FDP*, Deposit—Int., June 1917, nos. 6-21, Telegram from 'Dogra Public', 6 April 1917, NAI.

90. See Bawa Satinder Singh, *The Jammu Fox: A Biography of Maharaja Gulab Singh of Kashmir, 1792-1857* (London, 1974), p. 171.

91. See, for example, *FDP*, Secret Branch—E, February 1898, nos. 183-286, McMahon to Talbot, 8 July 1897; *S.V.N.P.* 1897, No. 6. from *Rafiq-i-Hindustan* (Lahore), 1 February 1897, NAI; *The Tribune*,

ferment amongst the native aspirants. The British seem to have consciously and subtly intervened to give this ferment a definite form and direction. The first was the recognition of the identity of State subjects by the State Council which, as has been seen earlier, was just an instrument for the implementation of the Resident's authority. The second was the instruction issued by the Viceroy in 1899 to British and Eurasion officers to give preference to natives for employment in their departments.[92] A vivid manifestation of this policy was seen in 1910 in the orders passed in the Settlement Department—to restrict appointments in the department to those who were State subjects 'by birth'.[93] Under the circumstances this provided legitimacy to native aspirations and also channelled their antagonism towards the Indian, non-State subjects.

The first instance of the articulation by a *Karkun* Pandit of the demand for preference to State subjects *vis-a-vis* outsiders in the State services occurred in 1894. Saligram, who edited an Urdu paper *Shumali* from Sialkot, pleaded therein that the State Council should no longer overlook the claims of the subjects of the State to State service and should make amends for the mistake which, according to him, had for so long been perpetrated.[94] Subsequently, when the *Karkun* Pandits acquired a modern education and clamoured for preference in the State services, they proved to be a source of 'anxious consideration' for the State Government. When the rules referred to earlier were formulated by the State Council in 1904 to ensure the employment of the young men educated in the State schools in the State services and the Secretary of Games Preservation Department was informed of those rules, he sent a reply that presumed, *ipso facto*, that the educated men in question belonged to the 'Pundit class'.[95]

---

29 November 1904, Dogra's Letter to Editor; *The Civil and Military Gazette*, 21 March 1907, X.Y.Z.'s letter to Editor.

92. As discussed in ch. 3.

93. *OER*, 1910, F.N. 63/F-101, Settlement Commissioner, W.S. Talbot's Order, 20 December 1910, JKA.

94. *S.V.N.P.*, 1894, No. 51, from *Shumali* (Sialkot), 17 December 1894, NAI.

95. In response to the instructions sent to him, he wrote: '. . . I have

The Land Settlement Commissioner had conveyed to the Resident in 1916 that the State subjects from Kashmir, along with those from Jammu, 'feel very strongly that outsiders obtain an altogether excessive proportion of any appointments which are available'.[96] By 1921 an articulate expression of this feeling among the advanced *Karkun* Pandits was given in the form of a protest in the press outside the State territories. Shankar Lal Kaul, writing under the pseudonym of 'Kashmiricus,' gave vent to his feelings thus:

> . . . Kashmiris are treated as strangers in their own house. In their own country, their status is nil. A post of rupees forty falls vacant in some office—and ninety to ten an outsider is brought to fill it up—and the State officials who indulge in this luxury, have not good sense enough to bring at least as good a man from outside to fill up the post, as could be available in Kashmir. It would have been something to appoint an outside graduate to some post in preference to a local graduate—but what is done is that a good-for-nothing outsider almost illiterate—but whose qualification is a communal or geographical alliance with some powerful official in the State—is given a post to which a Kashmiri graduate may not aspire.[97]

---

no appointments in the department under my control except those of watchers, and I am doubtful if men of the Pundit class would be capable of doing this work.' *OER*, 1904, F.N. 122/F-66, Secretary, Games Preservation Department to Secretary, Foreign Department, 24 September 1904, JKA.

96. *OER*, 1910, F.N. 63/F-101, Talbot to Fraser, 8 February 1916, JKA.

97. *United India and Indian States*, 22 September 1921. A copy of this issue is preserved in *OER*, 1921, F.N. 73/97-C, JKA. 'Kashmiricus' also gave, what he believed to be the 'inner reasons' for such a trend: 'Kashmir is a lovely country—nature has been very lavish of her gifts there. The cost of existence in the state was only the other day cheaper than it is elsewhere. The state officials, therefore, satisfy, their sense of philanthropy by giving refuge under their patronising umbrella to as many men from outside as they conveniently can. They make so many homes happy. In reviewing their work they are able to satisfy themselves that so many people owe the good things of life to them—for it is the very acme of luxury to load one's relatives and acquaintances with

The conflict with the outsiders was not born out of an abstract ideology but was prompted by concrete interests. This is evident from what 'Kashmiricus' wrote on the same occasion:

> The state has established two colleges—one at Jammu and the other at Srinagar. Education in both is incredibly cheap—and no wonder that every year more and more students pour into them. They pass the F.A. or the B.A. examination and then they stop as all do who have learnt to labour and to wait. And what are their prospects? The answer is blank: The state has encouraged them to be ambitious, it has made them refine and multiply their wants, it has diverted them from and unfitted them for pursuing humbler occupations—in short, the end is—it has ruined them.

Kashmiricus drew a picture of the then personnel of the Civil and Military list—this included the upper ranks—and differentiated in it State subjects thus:

> The latest Civil and Military list of the State presents the miserable spectacle of five per cent Kashmiri Hindus, one per cent Kashmiri Mussalmans—and less than seven per cent of the rest of the state subjects—and by state subjects, we mean the children of the soil of Jammu and Kashmir—whatever the state authorities might mean by it.[98]

After the State Government's decision in 1922 to the effect that the State services be kept reserved for bona fide State subjects and the subsequent enactment in 1927 of the definition of Hereditary State subject, the *Karkun* Pandits found themselves

---

benefits, and to be talkedof as a highplaced Minister of the good old days, who filled every office from among his kith and kin, not forgetting his Barber's and Washerman's families. Again jobbery is a pleasant trade—it is twice blessed—it blesseth both the giver and the recipient. These are the inner reasons for the presence of so many outsiders in the various public departments of the Jammu and Kashmir State.'

98. Ibid.

in conflict with the Dogras who, though less qualified, were favoured in appointment to high positions.[99] This conflict later worked as an important factor, so it seems to us, in pushing Sheikh Mohammed Abdullah and the mass movement that erupted in 1931 towards secular politics later on.

As we have seen, the spread of education among a section of the Muslims in Kashmir proceeded apace almost right from the beginning. Who these early aspirants to education were and what social background they came from is not certain. However, the fact remains that the new education was opposed for long by the Pirzadas[100] and, until 1899, no visible effort was made by any section of the Muslim population to take to new education along with religious instruction. It was only in 1899, that the small elite among the Muslim dominant classes took the first step to impart modern education to Muslims. By then the *Karkun* Pandits already had a head start of about two decades in acquiring the new education. As a matter of fact, they were at this time struggling to be inducted into the State services in preference to the non-State subjects and the Government was taking steps that were perhaps meant to remove their discontent and dissuade them from developing anti-British tendencies—steps that would eventually legitimize their plea.

The start made in 1899 passed through an important developmental stage in 1907, the beginning of which year marks an unprecedented turning point in the life of the Muslims in Kashmir. It saw the emergence of the 'Representatives of Kashmiri Mussalmans', five in number—whom it has not been possible to identify—who became expressly alive to the fact that 'Muhammadans' were 'almost totally unrepresented in the State administration' and aware that they were 'bound to remain so as long as they are not sufficiently educated'.[101]

In the same communication the relative backwardness of 'Mussalmans' in taking to new education was attributed by the

99. See Prem Nath Bazaz, *Inside Kashmir* (Srinagar, 1941), pp. 94-96.

100. See Munshi Naseer-ud-Din, *Tarikh Jangi Azadiye Kashmir* (Urdu) (Srinagar, 1971), p. 25.

101. *FDP*, Int.—A, February 1907, nos. 163-64, Representatives of the Kashmiri Musalmans to Sir Louis Dane, Secretary to Government of India in Foreign Department, NAI.

'Representatives' to 'Hindu officers' who 'for the past 20 years' were alleged to have 'practically neglected to show any safeguard of the Muhammadan interests.' Nor is this all; they were also alleged to have 'all along tried to adopt measures which would suppress education among the Mussalmans.' They argued that a 'cursory glance at the number of Mussalman teachers and students in the State schools is sure to prove the point.' Whether this argument was tenable is doubtful. However, it is certain that the imagination of the 'Representatives' had been fired by the idea of educational backwardness among 'Mussalmans.'

The 'Representatives', as a measure of redress and remedy, asked the Secretary to the Government in the Foreign Department for the appointment of some 'Muhammadan' officer of 'high standing and learning' to succeed Rai Narayan Das,[102] a Minister who had held charge of education from February 1900 and was now to revert back to British service. The 'Representatives', however, appear to have been themselves doubtful about the possibility of a replacement by a 'Muhammadan' substitute. Therefore, an appeal for an alternative was made. They proclaimed that the 'Education Department (which is really the backbone of national prosperity)' be 'placed under a Muhammadan officer' failing which they would 'prefer this Department to be under a European officer than to see it under a Hindu of Narayan Das type who has nothing more dear to his heart than the doing of wilful injury to the Muhammadan interests.'[103]

From the timing of the appeal and the way it was made,[104] it appears that the bone of contention was Narayan Das and the rest was mere padding. There was some basis for Narayan Das to become the object of the wrath of the elite among the dominant social classes of the Muslims. The State grant for

102. Ibid.
103. Ibid.
104. 'We learn with the deepest sense of relief that you have been so just and kind as not to grant any more extension of service to R.S. Bhagat Narayan Das, the Foreign Minister, who is an avowed foe of the Muhammadans. It will take years to rectify the mischief done by him to the Mussalmans during his tenure of office in the State, but we take the first opportunity of expressing our high gratitude to you for affording this deliverance from the hands of a well known bigoted Arya. This act of pure justice on your part makes us believe that you have the welfare of poor Muhammadans at heart.' Ibid.

Islamia school was initially sanctioned for two years, and had obviously to be renewed in 1906. An extension of the grant for another year was sanctioned vide Maharaja's Order on 11 July 1906.[105] Prior to the sanction, a recommendation to this effect was made by the Inspector of schools, the Minister incharge of Education Department—Narain Das, and the Chief Minister—Amar Singh.[106] However, the order of the Maharaja conveying the extension of the State grant contained a provision to the effect that the 'school authorities may be directed to replace the existing unqualified teachers by a competent staff'.[107] The idea had first come from Narayan Das who, while making favourable recommendation, had suggested:

> The education among the Mohammedans being rather in a backward condition I am of opinion that the grant should be continued and the school authorities should be asked to replace the existing unqualified teachers within 6 months from the date of receipt of order.[108]

Amar Singh, while forwarding the case to the Maharaja, recommended the continuation of the grant 'for another year, subject however to the condition proposed by the F.mr.irr. that of substituting qualified teachers to replace the existing incompetent ones.'[109]

The Muslim elite connected with the school submitted a memorandum to Amar Singh personally and complained of the 'hardship' implied in the provision. They urged that since the

> Islamia School had not yet emerged from the state of infancy, the condition was calculated to suppress its growth & defeat the very object which the grant in aid was intended

105. *OER*, 1903, F.N. 68-P-57, Maharaja's Order, 11 July 1906, JKA.
106. See ibid., Memorandum by Foreign Minister, 30 May 1906, and Amar Singh's endorsement.
107. Ibid., Maharaja's Order, 11 July 1906.
108. Ibid., Foreign Minister's Memo, 30 May 1906.
109. Ibid., Amar Singh's endorsement.

> to aim at, in as much as it was impossible to comply with the condition at this stage with the limited funds at their disposal.[110]

They added 'that even the State cannot lay claim to have in their educational service a teaching staff duly qualified for all the similar institutions.'[111]

Amar Singh had already favourably recommended the withdrawal of the provision,[112] Narayan Das concurred,[113] and consequently submitted a memorandum to that effect on 8 January 1907 to the Chief Minister.[114] This was forwarded to the Maharaja for approval, which was accorded subsequently on 12 March 1907.[115] Meanwhile the 'Representatives of the Kashmiri Mussalmans' addressed a 'letter' (petition) to Sir Louis Dane, Secretary to the Government of India in the Foreign Department. The 'Representatives' began by expressing their 'deepest sense of relief' that no more extension had been granted to Narayan Das's service who, they alleged, was an 'avowed foe of the Muhammadans' and had done 'mischief' during his tenure which it would take 'years to

110. Ibid., Chief Minister to Foreign Minister, Confidential, 18 September 1906.

111. Ibid.

112. 'I am of opinion that the grounds put forward by the memorialists require serious consideration. It is undeniable that the Mohammadens form the majority of His Highness' subject in Kashmir. Any institution like this which has the propagation of learning among them in view, must, therefore, receive encouragement from the Darbar & anything likely to create an unfavourable impression on the public as to the attitude of the Darbar should until such time as may permit of the expansion of the institution on proper lines, be carefully avoided. While admitting the benignant intention of the Darbar in the sanction of the grant in aid, I am inclined to think that for the present the condition regarding the engagement of a qualified staff by the Islamia school might be advisably dropped.' Ibid.

113. 'The condition was imposed in the interest of the school itself. But as it appears from your letter under reference that the managers of the school consider it hardship, the condition may if approved be withdrawn.' Ibid., Foreign Minister to Chief Minister, 26 November 1906.

114. Ibid., Foreign Department Memorandum, 8 January 1907.

115. Ibid., Maharaja's Order, 12 March 1907.

rectify.' Further, they expressed their gratitude for having been afforded 'deliverance from the hands of a well known bigoted Arya.' So, they had come to believe, or at least profess that Louis Dane had the 'welfare of poor Muhammadans at heart.'[116]

The end of 1908 saw a growing concern among the Muslims for the employment of 'Mussalmans' in the State administration. This is evident from another petition forwarded by the 'Representatives of Kashmiri Mussalmans,' now thirty-seven in number, to the Private Secretary to the Viceroy.[117] The theme of the whole petition is a concern for the paucity of sufficient Muslims in the State administration and a need for their education. The petition also contained emphatic assertions the germ of which was already contained in the earlier one and which carried far-reaching implications for the future. The first and foremost was the elaboration of an ideology of 'Moslem interests' as opposed to the 'Hindu cause.' It was asserted that the 'Hindu cause' was sought to be furthered by the 'Punjabi Hindus' who were employed in the State and was the result of

> the birth in the Upper India, during the last quarter of the past century, of a federation of Nationalist Hindus under a religious garb styled as Arya Samaj, which eventually took the form of "Indian National Congress". This federation has for its object '*Hindustan for Hindus*'. Finding that Hindus far outnumbered other communities (sic) and were foremost in education, their frenzied National Spirit soon assumed a formidable form and began to assert itself dangerously in many a way in and out.[118]

'As a result of this policy,' the petitioners further claimed,

116. *FDP*, Int.—A, February 1907, nos. 163-64, Representatives of Kashmiri Musalmans to Dane, NAI.

117. *FDP*, General—B, January 1909, nos. 15-16, Representatives of Kashmiri Mussalmans' Confidential petition to Private Secretary to Viceroy, NAI.

118. Ibid.

'the Moslem interests are not only utterly ignored but their legitimate aspirations are cruelly suppressed.'

Having begun the petition with an acknowledgement of the 'support and benevolence' of the successive Residents towards 'Moslems' and by making a favourable comparison with the pre-Residency era,[119] the petitioners asserted further on:

> 'Had it not been for the protection afforded by the Kashmir Residency and other British Officers, the condition of Mussalmans would have been irreparably miserable and wretched'.[120]

Finally, the petition made a plea for the appointment of at least two Muslim ministers, one to be placed at the head of the Revenue Department; the appointment of a Muslim to one of the two posts of Governor and Chief Judge; instructions to

119. 'We shudder with feelings of horror when we think of the days when the 'Azan' (call to prayers) was prohibited; the Zamindars of the valley who were unfortunately all Moslems, were treated as laden beasts with human faces; and were left no wherewithal for their own personal consumption, merely to end their sad days by subsisting on the forest products and the bark of trees. The horrible atrocities, which reigned here before the establishment of the British Residency, are still within living memory and are too well-known to require any explanation on this occasion. No sooner the Kashmir Resudency [sic] was established here than the things took a turn for the better. Laws were enforced to protect life and property. Disorder and chaos gradually gave way to order in all the departments of the State. What has been done so far through the kind efforts of the Residency is, it may be conceded, not a little in view of the difficulties that lay in the way of reform. Much, however, remains to be accomplished, and we feel certain that the Residency is anxious soon to bring justice and safety to the Kashmir Mussalmans and relieve them of the tyranny and zulum which has with the advance of times taken a new form to express itself.

The policy of reform inaugurated on the advent of the British Residency, evidently meant equality, impartiality, fair play and no favour. For a time all seemed to go on well, and there were unmistakable manifestations that the new policy would have an easy and smooth course to run. A new factor however soon appeared on the stage, which influenced the course of events considerably.' Ibid.

120. Ibid.

be issued to all heads of departments to encourage more Muslim elements in their respective departments till a reasonable proportion of posts is conferred upon Muslims; for placement of the education department under the control of a European officer; affording of immense facilities for the spread of primary education among the 'Mussalman' subjects by liberal grant of free books and scholarships; and the placing of the police department under the control of an European officer.[121]

The justification offered for this was that Muslims formed '95% of the total population and are loyal and law abiding.' It is, thus, clear that the demand was made as a matter of right and was based on the principle of proportional representation. The constituency which the petitioners claimed to represent was that of 'Muslims' which, in their estimate, comprised of 95 per cent of the population. The existence of a 'Muslim' constituency, which was first expressed in the remark of the Secretary of State for India to the Viceroy in 1884, had later become an accepted notion with the governing authorities. This was implied in the manoeuvres of the British representative and the two factions in the State Council. Pratap Singh's alliance with the Council Member, Sardar Mohammed Hayat Khan, against the opposite faction is a case in point. However, the principle of proportional representation was something that was still to be recognized by the state authorities. The Muslim struggle towards this objective remained bound intrinsically with the spread of new education amongst them, until it reached another important stage in 1924.

The movement for imparting new education to Kashmiri Muslims after the establishment of Islamia School did not remain a concern only of its elite. The cause came to be espoused by the associations established in the then British Indian territories. The All-India Mohammedan Educational Conference gave overt expression to this cause at its annual meeting held at Rangoon in December 1909. The Conference first thanked the Maharaja for having decided about the establishment of a technical institute and then asked for a share

121. Ibid.

for Muslims on its staff. It also complained that, though the Muslims comprised 75 per cent of the population of Kashmir State, the number of Muslim teachers and students in the State schools was negligible. Therefore, it requested the Maharaja to make reasonable additions to the existing number of Muslims in the teaching and inspection staff and institute special scholarships for Muslim students so that they would be encouraged to seek education. Copies of the resolutions were despatched to the Private Secretary to the Maharaja on 24 March 1911.[122]

The Muslim Kashmiri Conference, an organization that was initially mooted in 1911 at Lahore (Punjab), also took an interest in the spread of education among the Muslims of Kashmir. The Conference, at its very first session, passed a resolution inviting the Maharaja's attention to the resolutions passed by the All India Mohammedan Educational Conference.[123] The resolution was proposed by Sheikh Abdul Samad Kukroo, a native elite Muslim of Kashmir.[124] Perhaps, as a measure of censure for this act, Kukroo was not invited by the Maharaja to attend the Coronation Durbar held that year at Delhi.[125]

At its annual session in April 1912, the Muslim Kashmiri Conference took upon itself to offer 'heartiest thanks' to the Maharaja for the 'introduction of free education in the State.' Further, it expressed the hope that the Maharaja would devise means that would enable the Muslims to benefit from such a

122. See *OER*, 1911, F.N. 70/P-37, Honorary Joint Secretary, All India Mohamadan Educational Conference to Private Secretary to Maharaja, 24 March 1911, and enclosure, JKA.

123. Ibid., Secretary, Kashmiri Conference, to Chief Secretary to Maharaja, 21 April 1911, with enclosures.

124. Ibid.

125. The Maharaja, evidently on an application from him, ordered: 'Nobody can acquire a right to be invited to public Durbars. The applicant is not more suitable than the Reises invited. He should not have bothered the authorities when his application on the subject was not granted. He should have shown himself worthy of the honour which he is applying for.' *OER*, 1911, F.N. 222, Maharaja's Order No. 1641, 15 November 1911, JKA.

reform.[126] The conference deemed it essential to 'appoint a large number of Musalman teachers in the Primary Departments of the State Schools' in order to attain the stated end. Further, it prayed for the 'employment of Musalmans from the Punjab in the State Service if competent Musalmans in the State are not available for the various departments of the State'.[127]

As noted earlier, the movement for reservation in the State services for State subjects had gained ground by this time. The reply sent to the office bearers of the Muslim Kashmiri Conference by the Chief Minister to the Maharaja[128] outlined the government's policy to reserve jobs for the State subjects reiterating the need for efficiency which had been stressed by the government since innovations were made in the administrative structure.

At its annual session in April 1913, the Muslim Kashmiri Conference expressed deep disappointment at the reply that had been sent to them and declared that it was a 'clear manifestation of the gross indifference of the Ministers of the State towards the claims of the Muslim subjects of the State.'[129] An address touching upon the 'educational needs' of the Muslims of Kashmir was presented in September 1913 at Srinagar by Aftab Ahmed of the Mohammedan Educational Conference to the Maharaja,[130] and a deputation on behalf of the Muslim Kashmiri Conference waited the Maharaja at Lahore in January 1915 in the same connection.[131] At its annual session held in April 1920, the Muslim Kashmiri Conference invited the attention of the Maharaja to these numerous deputations and regretted that the 'Durbar have so far paid

126. *OER*, 1912, F.N. 254/P-127, President, Central Standing Committee, Muslim Kashmiri Conference, to Private Secretary to Maharaja, 17 November 1912, with enclosures, JKA.

127. Ibid.

128. *OER*, 1912, F.N. 254/P-127, Chief Minister to President, Muslim Kashmiri Conference, 8 April 1913, JKA.

129. Ibid., Secretary, Conference, to Chief Minister, 3 May 1913, enclosure.

130. *OER*, 1917, F.N. 77/P-21, Letter from Aftab Ahmad, 30 January 1917, enclosure, JKA.

131. *OER*, 1915, F.N. 261, Secretary, Muslim Kashmiri Conference, to Minister of Education, 14 July 1915, JKA.

little attention to the submissions made on the above occasions.'[132] It also regretted that there was a 'paucity of Mussalmans in the Judicial, Forest and Public Works Department Services of the State' and requested the Durbar to appoint 'competent Muhammadans in these Departments' and if 'competent Muhammadans be not available in the State itself, then competent Kashmiri Muhammadans be imported from outside the State just as non-State subjects of other communities are imported for State services.' The conference also asked for the introduction of 'compulsory primary education in Jammu and Kashmir State'.[133]

In 1923, the Anjuman-i-Islamia Punjab, Lahore, requested the Maharaja 'to remove the causes that stand in the way of the Muslim subject of His Highness in acquiring Education.' And the causes, it said, were 'fully discussed in the address presented by a deputation of Mohammadans headed by Sahibzada Aftab Khan in 1913.'[134]

The same year the Muslim Kashmiri Conference resolved at its annual conference that

> a deputation of leading Mussalmans should wait upon His Highness the Maharaja Sahib Bahadur and should represent all the grievances of the Mussalmans of Kashmir as embodied in the various resolutions passed by the Conference at its various sessions and other representations sent from time to time to the Durbar.[135]

Consequently, a request was sent to the Private Secretary to the Maharaja for the reception of such a deputation. On being asked to intimate in what regard the deputation wanted an audience with the Maharaja, the Honorary General Secretary of the Conference wrote back that the deputation would submit

132. *OER*, 1920, F.N. 2/Mis.-14, Honorary Secretary, Muslim Kashmiri Conference, to Chief Minister, 11 May 1920, enclosure, JKA.

133. Ibid.

134. *OER*, 1923, F.N. 28/HE-15, Honorary General Secretary. Anjuman-i-Islamia, to Private Secretary to Maharaja, 27 October 1923, JKA.

135. Ibid., Honorary Secretary, All India Muslim Kashmiri Conference, to Private Secretary, Maharaja, 29 November 1923,

their views on 'the educational need of the Mussalmans of Kashmir, the causes of their backwardness in education and on other kindred subjects.'[136] These were, in brief, the issues which had been the chief concern of the Conference over the years.

The All India Muslim League also stepped in, at its fifteenth session at Lahore, to press for support to the cause which had hitherto been espoused by the Kashmiri Muslim Conference and other organizations. In a resolution, it deplored what according to it was

> the continued unsympathetic and indifferent attitude of the Kashmir Darbar towards the political and educational needs and aspirations of the Musalmans of Kashmir State, . . . and to give the Musalmans of Kashmir, who form 95 per cent of the population of the State [sic], their rightful place in the public services and in the administration of the State.[137]

The attitude of the State Government, as evident in a public speech by Maharaja Pratap Singh on the occasion of Jammu College Prize Distribution towards the end of April 1924, was to give posts according to merit and not population. He remarked that it was therefore the duty of the Muslims to equip themselves as others did. He contended that the Muslims were themselves to blame for the paucity of students on college rolls for he had not only provided equal opportunities for all classes of his subjects but had, contrary to his convictions, provided special facilities for Muslims. He further said that, if in spite of that they were found lagging behind in education it meant that either they were not taking full advantage of such facilities or they sincerely believed that literary education was not the *summum bonum* of life and there were other lucrative vocations they could equally well adopt without being proficient in letters and the arts. But in that case, he declared, the Muslims had no

136. Ibid., Honorary General Secretary, All India Muslim Kashmiri Conference, to Secretary to Foreign Member, 24 March 1924.

137. See A.M. Zaidi, ed., *Evolution of Muslim Political Thought in India* (New Delhi, 1975), Vol. 2, p. 278.

justification for blaming the administration if they succeeded in securing only a small number of posts in the State services.[138]

By making such a speech the Maharaja might have 'hit the nail on the head' and represented himself to be 'no worshipper at the altar of communal representation.'[139] But to the Muslim elite which had taken it upon itself to strive for the proportional representation of Muslims in the State services, and their patrons from the British Indian territories, the Maharaja's statement was an obvious setback.

Perhaps as a sequel to this open declaration of policy by the Maharaja, or possibly as a spontaneous extension of the scope of the Muslim movement, a demand for the appointment of Muslim officials in place of the Hindus came to be heard in July 1924 from the workers of the State Silk Factory at Srinagar.[140] The workers also demanded an increase in their wages.[141] They had earlier gone on strike in 1917 and 1920 to seek an increase in their wages[142] but the demand for Muslims as their officials was raised for the first time now.

Whether the Muslim elite had a direct involvement in the raising of such a demand by the workers cannot be known. However, it is certain that the demand both symbolized and reflected an extension in the scope of the movement started by them. There were educated men amongst the workers and, after the trouble was over, the British Resident desired some of these educated workers to be promoted to 'posts of responsibility.'[143] It is probable that these educated men, whose immediate interest the demand raised by the workers was expected to serve, helped in disseminating ideas of the Muslim movement regarding the representation of Muslims

138. *The Tribune*, 4 May 1924.

139. Ibid.

140. *The Ranbir*, 15 July 1924.

141. Ibid.

142. See *OER*, 1920, F.N. 26/R.S. 6, Director, Sericulture, to First Assistant to Resident, 31 March 1920, JKA.

143. *Home Department*, Political, 1924, File No. 25, Fortnightly Report for Second Half of August, Wood to Thompson, 4 August 1924, NAI.

in the State services and thereby inculcating a new consciousness amongst them.

Encouraged by the British Resident in what can fairly be said to have been only an extension of the earlier developments, the Muslim elites presented a memorial to the Viceroy, Lord Reading, at Srinagar in October 1924. It made a plea for proportional representation of Muslims in the State services.[144] The memorial was handed over by the Viceroy to the State Government. The latter appointed a Committee to look into the grievances of the memorialists which 'expressed a hope that as more Mohammedans got educated more of them would be employed in the public services.'[145] However, the Committee took exception to some charges in the memorial which it considered were an attack on the ruler and accorded punishment to three of the memorialists: Said-ud-Din Shawl was externed, Hassan Shah Naqashbandi's *jagir* was confiscated and Noor Shah Naqashbandi, a *tehsildar*, was dismissed from State service.[146]

The Kashmir Muslim Conference resented the attitude of the State government and took up the cause of the Muslims.[147] Not long after Hari Singh's accession to the *gaddi* the Kashmiri Muslim Conference asked for an audience with the Maharaja to present a schedule of grievances. They were informed that the Maharaja could not receive any address from a body of non-State Muslims regarding the grievances of his subjects who themselves had the liberty to present their grievances to him at any time.[148]

The enactment of the definition of a Hereditary State Subject in January 1927, which excluded all Kashmiris domiciled in the Punjab, was also disliked by the Muslims. They felt that non-state subject Muslims would sympathize with their aspirations more than would State subject Hindus.[149]

When only one Muslim was selected after the formation of the

144. *Evidence SREC*, Finance and Development Minister's statement.
145. Ibid.
146. G.S. Raghavan, *The Warning of Kashmir* (Allahabad, 1931), p. 61.
147. *Evidence SREC*, Finance and Development Minister's statement.
148. Ibid.
149. Ibid.

Scholarship Selection Board in 1927 it was bitterly resented by Muslim associations both in Kashmir and Jammu. As a result, more scholarships were awarded to Muslim candidates in 1928 and 1929. The scholarships were now distributed equally between Hindu and Muslim candidates.[150]

The distribution of scholarships between Hindus and Muslims on an equal basis was clearly a retreat from the earlier position that merit was to be the sole criterion for appointments in the State services. It also marked, howsoever nebulously, an advantage gained by the Muslim point of view which now carried some weight and achieved a modicum of recognition. In fact, as Bazaz says, the memorialists from Jammu in 1929 were told secretly that henceforth 50 per cent of the vacancies would be filled by the Muslims.[151] Whether such a policy was followed or not, as asserted by Bazaz,[152] is difficult to verify. However, a shift in the recruitment policy of the State Government was manifested in 1930. This became visible when certain posts were advertised specifically for Muslim candidates. Further, it is said that the Civil Service Board, instituted in early 1930, was enjoined to take into consideration communal proportion in the State services.[153]

In early 1930, the President of the Srinagar Municipality issued a notice while calling for applications to fill certain posts under him that only Muslims need apply.[154] The notice was withdrawn when there was strong reaction from the Hindus who termed it as 'communalism'.[155] Nonetheless, the fact remains that public recognition was now extended to the Muslim demand for reservation in the State services. A Muslim student from Srinagar interpreted the notice as the recognition of, what he called, the 'Muslim backward majority'.[156]

The episode regarding the issue and withdrawal of the

150. Ibid.

151. Bazaz (1941), pp. 99-100; Prem Nath Bazaz, *The History of Struggle for Freedom in Kashmir* (New Delhi, 1954), p. 148.

152. Ibid.

153. Raghavan (1931), pp. 65-66.

154. *The Ranbir*, 17 February 1930.

155. See *The Ranbir*, 17, 24 February, and 18, 25 March 1930.

156. *The Ranbir*, 11 March, Ghulam Nabi's letter to Editor.

notice by the President of the Srinagar Municipality, who incidentally happened to be a Kashmiri Pandit,[157] was a decisive stage in the Muslim movement which marked the lines along which the subsequent political battle in the beginning of 1931 would take place. It was no longer an issue to be settled between the Muslim elite and the State Government—they also had to be contended with opposition from the Hindus.

It is only reasonable to assume that there was a lot of unrest, at least at Srinagar, in the beginning of 1930. It is against this immediate backdrop that in the spring of 1930 a batch of about a dozen young educated Muslims returned after having completed their courses in various British Indian Universities. They found the Civil Service Recruitment Rules a hurdle in the attainment of their natural aspirations.[158] The rules encompassed a competitive examination and an age limit. The young men, concerned as they obviously must have been about their careers, arranged for a place where they could meet and discuss their 'mutual problems and those affecting their community.'[159] Thus, was established what was called the 'Reading Room' for which permission was sought from the District Magistrate. The members of the Reading Room elected one amongst them, Mubarak Shah Naqashbandi, as Secretary and asked the Head Master of Islamia High School, Pirzada Ghulam Rasool Shah, to be their Chairman.[160]

On 11 September 1930, a memorial, to which two members of the Reading Room—Abdul Aziz Fazili and Sheikh Mohammed Abdullah—were signatories, was sent to the 'Cabinet'[161] which had been formed by the Maharaja when he left to attend the First Round Table Conference at London. The memorialists were granted an interview by the Cabinet which sought to impress upon them that the rules had been framed with the specific purpose of securing their interests and a written reply was despatched by

157. *Evidence SREC*, Head Master Islamia High School, Pirzada Ghulam Rasul's Statement.

158. Ibid., Retired Minister of State, Agha Syed Hussain's Statement.

159. Note by Mubarak Shah Naqashbandi received on 18 May 1978 (Srinagar).

160. Ibid.

161. Bazaz (1941), p. 101,

the Cabinet on 28 January 1931.[162] It is reported to have stated that Muslims were not totally unrepresented in the State services and gave an account of the Muslims in employment in the State services. This left the men concerned not merely dissatisfied but positively enraged.[163]

From the time that the Cabinet despatched its reply until the receipt of the news that an heir-apparent had been born to the Maharaja on 9 March 1931 at Cannes in France, where both the Maharaja and the Maharani had moved after the former's participation in the Round Table Conference, no overt reaction was visible.[164] Meanwhile some of those who had arrived in the spring of 1930 had been profitably employed in State service. However, it seems that around this time the Ahmadiyas were active in Kashmir and were working towards starting mass agitational politics in Kashmir.[165] Towards this end they were preparing one of the less fortunate of the Reading Room members, Sheikh Mohammed Abdullah, to come on to the public stage as the 'leader'. Nevertheless, nothing could be done until Muslim dominant classes extended their support to the initiative of the would be leader. This was soon forthcoming.

After the news of the arrival of the heir-apparent, Yuvraj Karan Singh, was received at Srinagar, a public meeting was called by the aristocratic elites of Kashmir.[166] It was resolved there that apart from holding a reception after his arrival home,

162. Ibid., p. 103.

163. Interview with Mufti Jalal-ud-Din, December 1977 (Srinagar).

164. It is common for 'knowledgeable people' to trace the activities with regard to the beginning of the 'freedom struggle in 1931' to the t me when the news of the arrival of a heir-apparent to Maharaja Hari Singh was received at Srinagar.

165. This inference has been drawn on the basis of information obtained from various sources with regard to the antecedents of Sheikh Mohammed Abdullah. However, the exact nature of the link that obtained between him and the Ahmadiyas during the earliest phase of his political career is difficult to know. For Ahmadiya involvement in Kashmir politics in 1931, see Spencer Lavan, *The Ahmadiyah Movement: A History and Perspective* (New Delhi, 1974), Chapter entitled 'The Ahmadiyah in the Kashmir Crisis; 1931-1934'.

166. Interview with Fotedar.

a golden cradle would be presented to the Maharaja.[167] However, the Muslim aristocratic elite had second thoughts and a meeting with other important Muslims was called where it was decided to accord a separate reception to the Maharaja on behalf of the Muslims. The meeting was called by Mir Mohammed Maqbool Gilani but was in reality the work of Noor Shah Naqashbandi.[168] It was this separate gathering of Muslims that set the trend for what eventually happened.[169] Naqashbandi was at the helm and Sheikh Mohammed Abdullah was one of the Muslims present. A deputation, comprised of Noor Shah Naqashbandi, Pir (Mir) Mohammed Maqbool Gilani and Ghulam Ahmed (Lalimatu), was sent to Bombay to welcome the royal family on its arrival and convey the Muslim decision to the Maharaja and request him to accept a separate reception on behalf of the Muslims.[170] They intended to present a memorandum of Muslim demands to the Maharaja on this occasion. The eventuality for this did not arise because the Maharaja refused to accept a separate reception on behalf of any one community. The Maharaja arrived home in early May 1931—to witness the unfolding of the first stirring of trouble which came to a head in the events of 13 July: the first ever open public challenge to his government.

167. Ibid.

168. Interview with Master Ghulam Ahmed Zohra, December 1977 (Srinagar). See also Pir Mohammed Afzal Maqdoomi, 'Tahriq Huriyat Kashmir,' in *Aieena* 7 September 1971.

169. Cf. Maulana Mohammed Sayed Masoodi, 'Mir Mohammed Maqbool Gilani: Tahriq Huriyat', in *Aieena*, 3 November 1977.

170. Interview with Ghulam Mohammed (Lalimatu) 3 January 1978 (Srinagar).

7

CONCLUSION

The primary aim of this study has been to delineate the forces that led to the upsurge in Kashmir in 1931 which, as we have seen, did mark the emergence of mass political awakening. On an investigation of various sources, it is found that, contrary to popular belief and the assertions of various authors, the upsurge was not a result of any single cause, immediate or of a long duration, but was an outcome of the interaction of various historical forces over a period of time. The development of those forces has been traced and the principal results of the study may now be summarized.

Kashmir, situated as it is in the northern extremity of India, came within the purview of British imperial expansion late in 1846, though repercussions from the expanding British administrative frontier had been felt there earlier. The State of Jammu and Kashmir was created by the British Indian Government to meet its immediate imperial requirement of weakening the Sikh Power by driving a wedge between its two main factions, the Sikhs and the Dogras. This was accomplished by making Raja Gulab Singh, the chief feudatory of the Sikh Power, a Maharaja and entering into a treaty with him. With this was foisted a political structure in Kashmir which lasted until 1931 and beyond. Simultaneously, not only Kashmir but all other territories put under the State were brought within the orbit of British paramountcy.

The Government saw to it, by advising Gulab Singh to enforce certain measures, that his authority was established and also made viable. Simultaneously, a process of indirect exploitation of the territories and the people within the State was also set in motion by making Gulab take other measures, some of which were purported to be in the name of the people. Neither Gulab Singh, nor his successor Ranbir, was eager to comply with the Government's demands, but both father and son were only too conscious of the strength of the British. Even before Gulab Singh had consolidated his territories, the Government demonstrated the demoniac weapon of posting a British Resident in his territories in the eventuality of his failure to meet its 'just' demands. Gulab Singh and Ranbir passively resisted the demands but when the Government was stubborn, yielded. This is what happened uptil 1885 when the Government took the unilateral decision to appoint a Resident.

The decision of the Government to appoint a Resident, which came under the guise of a plea seeking to reshape the whole economic, administrative and military structure of the State, was dictated by a desire to reorient the State in order to meet the new needs of the Paramount Power in the frontiers. The restructuring of the economic structure also envisaged, as was later unfolded, an extension of the market for British machine goods and of opening the much coveted 'happy valley' to the investment of British expertise and capital.

The appointment of the Resident, and the circumstances in which this act was enforced, amounted undoubtedly to interference in the internal affairs of the State. This was a contingency that the State Power had been keen to forestall all along, and the Government too had, time and again, proffered assurances that it would not resort to such interference. However, once such a course of action was decided upon, there was an obvious need to have some kind of leverage to use against the Maharaja. Guidelines for such an instrument had been laid down by the Secretary of State for India and obviously included extension of recognition to, and politicization of, the fact of the different religions to which the Maharaja and the majority of his subjects belonged.

From 1885 to 1931 there ensued a struggle between the successive representatives of the Paramount Power (the Residents) and the two Maharajas—Pratap Singh (1885-1925) and Hari Singh (1925-1931)—for the quantum of power to be exercised by each. This struggle assumed two major forms, firstly to coax the Muslim majority into their hegemony and, secondly, to exercise hegemony over administration. This had obviously to be done by the British within the limitations set by the parameters, both objective and subjective, within and outside the State. The Government could not ignore the policy that it had adopted since 1858 of sustaining and conciliating the Native Indian Princes. They had also to contend with the increasing importance of Indian public opinion after the emergence of the Indian National Congress in 1885. And each of the Maharajas had the twin constraint of being both a feudal prince and carrying the burden of religious diversity with a substantial majority of his subjects who belonged to another faith. The interaction between the all-pervading compulsions of British imperialism, the forces it generated and the changes it wrought in Kashmir seems to have resulted in the upsurge of 1931.

Kashmir, with nearly the whole of its population comprising of Muslims, was placed under the dynastic rule of a Dogra Hindu Rajput. Within the native population, the caste-class of *Karkun* Pandits was bound naturally with the administration as a result of socio-historical reasons. Thus, it was inherent in the situation that the proportion of Muslims in the State administration should be very small. The Government, after the establishment of Residency Raj, did nothing to change the situation materially except to notice what they termed as Muslim interests and extend recognition to them.

The Muslim elite which had embraced the idea of communal representation in the State administration and obviously thought it possible to effect such a policy, petitioned the Private Secretary to the Viceroy in 1908. The Government did not intervene then.[1] But, as is clear from the official noting in the Foreign Department of the Government, it very carefully reserved for itself an option for the future.[2] The Muslim elite were obviously conscious of the real fulcrum of power—the Government. Hence any kind of action on their part was ruled out unless a strong largely independent class could develop which would be able to forge ahead. This was not on the cards in 1931. However, it is possible that the Government or its agencies abetted the intentions of the Muslim elite in, or around, 1931. Nonetheless, the circumstantial evidence relating to the involvement of the Naqashband family that had long-standing direct connections with the Government agencies, and the departure of the British Minister of the State, G.E. Wakefield, under mysterious circumstances during the upsurge both point to this possibility. Moreover, the confession of Munshi Naseer-ud-Din that the agents of the British Government supported those who launched the struggle for freedom, before it started and while it lasted, goes to support such a contention.

Once the leading agitators, with the connivance and active backing of the dominant classes had given the call to secure both the religious and the secular interests of Muslims—this would obviously encompass nearly the whole population—it was natural that a sizeable section of the population should have believed that their interests were at stake and rallied to the cause.

We have also seen that the primary task of the leaders of the 1931 agitation, including Sheikh Mohammed Abdullah, was to seek the acceptance of the long-standing Muslim demand of

1. See in *Foreign Department Proceedings*, Gen.—B, January 1909, nos. 15-16, National Archives of India (New Delhi) (NAI).

2. Cf. Assistant Secretary in the Foreign Department in a note suggested that the petitioners be informed that in 'a matter affecting the internal administration of Kashmir state, the government of India are unable to interfere on their behalf in the manner indicated.' It was not approved by the Deputy Secretary. He preferred to give no reasons. The rationale, which he put forth for such a course, was: 'In view of past practices and our special position in Kashmir we must be careful now we play the non-interference card.' Ibid.

proportional representation in the State services. This was a communal demand and had thus to be necessarily sought from a sectional platform. The demand was informed clearly by the communal ideology. The nature of the demand and the ideology in which it was clothed leads to the conclusion that the agitation launched in 1931 was communal in character. Since it was the communal forces that mobilized the masses and invoked their support against the Maharaja's government, the mass political awakening came to be enveloped by a communal ideology and was inevitably accompanied by communal discord.

SELECT BIBLIOGRAHPY

PRIMARY SOURCES

Unpublished

(a) *Government Records*

Government of India, *Foreign Department Proceedings* [Available in National Archives of India, New Delhi (NAI)].

——, *Home Political Files* (Fortnightly Reports) [NAI].

——, *Selections from the Vernacular Newspapers Published in the Punjab* [NAI].

His Highness' Government, Jammu and Kashmir, *Old English Records* [Available in Jammu and Kashmir State Archives, Jammu (JKA)].

——, *Political Records* [JKA].

(b) *Private Papers*

Halifax Collection, Private Papers of Lord Irwin (microfilm) [Available in Nehru Memorial Museum and Library, New Delhi (NMML)].

Minto Papers, Private Papers of Lord Minto (microfilm) [NAI].

His Highness' Private Records (Maharaja Pratap Singh's Personal Records) [JKA].

(c) *Manuscripts*

Report on Revenue Arrangements Under Indian Rulers, C. 1788,

Ms. 6586 [British Museum].
Shah, Ghulam Nabi, *Wajiz-ul-Tawarikh* (Persian). [Available in Research Library, University of Kashmir, Srinagar (RL)].

(d) *Oral Records*

Kaul, Master Zinda by Lone, Ali Mohammed (Kashmiri), 13 April 1961. [Available at Srinagar Station of the All India Radio].
Toshkhani, Sri Kanth by Pushp, P.N. and Others (Kashmiri). [Available at Srinagar Station of the All India Radio].

(e) *Personal Interviews*

Abdullah, Sheikh Mohammed, 1973-74 (New Delhi).
Ahmadi, Sheikh Abdul Samad, 9 December 1977 (Srinagar).
Ahmed, Pirzada Ghulam (Shounth), 1984 (Srinagar).
Bazaz, Prem Nath, 1975 (New Delhi).
Bhat, Damoodhar, 22 November 1977 (Srinagar).
Fazili, Abdul Aziz, 1984 (Srinagar).
Fotedar, Shiv Narayan, January 1976 (Jammu).
Jalal-ud-Din, Mufti, December 1977 (Srinagar).
Lalimatu, Ghulam Mohammed, 3 January 1978 (Srinagar).
Naqashbandi, Mubarak Shah (Written Note), received on 18 May 1978 (Srinagar).
Zohra, Master Ghulam Ahmad, December 1977 (Srinagar) and Others.

Published

(a) *Government Publications*

Aitchison, C.U., ed., *A Collection of Treaties, Engagements and Sanads: Relating to India and Neighbouring Countries* (Neudelin: 1973), rep., Vols 1 & 12 [Craus Reprint].
Punjab Government Records, Political Diaries (Lahore, 1915), Vol. 6 [NMML].
Administration Reports, Jammu and Kashmir State (1891-1934). [JKA (Reports for the years 1906-7 to 1910-11 were not published)].

Wingate, A., *Preliminary Report of Settlement Operations in Kashmir and Jammu* (Lahore, 1888) [NMML].

Census Reports, Government of India, Jammu and Kashmir State, 1891, 1901, 1911, 1921, 1931.

Bates, Charles Ellison, *A Gazetteer of Kashmir and the Adjacent Districts of Kishtwar, Badarawar, Jamu, Naoshera, Punch and the Valley of the Kishen Ganga* (Calcutta, 1873) [NAI].

Gazetteer of Kashmir and Ladak (Delhi: Vivek, 1974), rep. [first published in 1890].

The Imperial Gazetteer (Faridabad: Today and Tomorrow's, n. d.), rep. [first published in 1908].

His Highness' Government, Jammu and Kashmir, *Written Statements Part* 1, *Srinagar Riots Enquiry Committee, July 1931* (Jammu, 1931), [JKA].

——, *Evidence Recorded in Public by the Srinagar Riots Enquiry Committee, 1931* (Jammu, 1931) [JKA].

——, *Modern Jammu and Kashmir State, 1925-43* (Jammu, 1944) [JKA].

Government of Jammu and Kashmir, Ministry of Revenue, *On the Way to Golden Harvests: Agricultural Reforms in Kashmir* (Jammu, 1951).

——, *Jagirs, Muafis and Mukarraris* (Srinagar: 1956).

(b) *Memoirs, Travel Accounts, etc.*

Aynsley, Mrs. J.C. Murray, *Our Visit to Hindostan, Kashmir and Ladakh* (London, 1879) [Available in Research Library, Srinagar, Kashmir (RL)].

Baden-Powell, B.H., *The Land-Systems of British India* (Delhi: Oriental, 1974), rep., Vols 1 & 3.

Baird, J.G.A., ed., *Private Letters of the Marquess of Dalhousie* (Shannon: Irish University Press, 1972), rep.

Bazaz, Prem Nath, *Daughters of the Vitasta: A History of Kashmiri Women from Early Times to the Present Day* (New Delhi: Pamposh, 1959).

——, *The History of Struggle for Freedom in Kashmir, Cultural and Political: From the Earliest Times to the Present Day* (New Delhi: Kashmir, 1954).

——, *Inside Kashmir* (Srinagar: 1941) [NMML, RL, Sapru House Library, New Delhi].

Bellew, H.W., *Kashmir and Kashgar: A Narrative of the Journey of the Embassy to Kashgar in 1873-74* (London, 1875) [RL].

Biscoe, Tyndale, *An Autobiography* (London, 1951) [B.M.S.L.].

——, *Kashmir in Sunlight and Shade* (London, 1922) [NMML, RL].

——, *Men in the Making in Kashmir* (Oxford, 1914) [Available in Tyndale Biscoe School Library, Srinagar, Kashmir (T.B.S.L.)].

Bose, Jogendra Chandra, *Cashmere and its Prince: An Authentic Exposition of the Recent Imbroligo in Cashmere* (Calcutta, 1889) [NMML].

Brinckman, Arthur, 'The Wrongs of Cashmere,' in Gadru, S.N., ed., *Kashmir Papers* (Srinagar: Free-thought Literature Company, 1973).

Cunningham, Alexander, *Ladak: Physical, Historical and Statistical* (London, 1854) [RL].

Cunningham, Joseph Davey, *A History of the Sikhs: From the Origin of the Nation to the Battles of the Sutlej*, Garrett, H.L.O., ed. (Delhi: Chand & Co., 1966), rep.

Dar, Bishan Narayan, 'Foreign Travel,' in Chintamani, C. Yajnesvara, ed., *Indian Social Reform* (Madras, 1901), Part 1 [NMML].

Digby, William, 'Condemned Unheard,' in Gadru, S.N., ed., *Kashmir Papers* (Srinagar: Free-thought Literature Company, 1973).

Drew, Sir Frederic, *The Jammu and Kashmir Territories: A Geographical Account* (London, 1875) [RL].

Dugsal, *Letters from India and Kashmir, Written 1870* (London, 1874) [RL].

Dunmore, The Earl of *The Pamirs* (London, 1893) [RL].

Dutt, Parmananda, *Memoirs of Motilal Ghose* (Calcutta, 1935) [NMML].

Eckenstein, Oscar, *The Karakorams and Kashmir* (London, 1896) [RL].

Forster, George, *A Journey from Bengal to England, through the Northern Part of India, Kashmire, Afghanistan, and Persia* (London, 1808), Vol. 2 [RL].

Hardinge, Charles Viscount, *Viscount Hardinge* (Oxford, 1891)

[Available at Jawaharlal Nehru University Library, New Delhi].

Hassan, *Tarikh Kashmir* (Political Section), Maulvi Mohammed Ibrahim, trans. (Urdu) (Srinagar, 1957) [Available with Ghulam Mohammed Noor Mohammed Publishers, Srinagar].

Hasrat, Bikramjit, ed., *The Punjab Papers: Selections from Private Papers of Lord Auckland, Lord Ellenborough, Viscount Hardinge, and the Marquis of Dalhousie, 1836-1849 on the Sikhs* (Hoshiarpur, 1970) [Published by the Author].

Honigberger, John Martin, *Thirty-Five Years in the East* (Calcutta, 1905) [RL].

Hugel, Baron Charles, *Travels in Kashmir and the Panjab*, Major, T.B., Jervis, trans. and ed. (Delhi: Light & Life, 1972) rep.

Jalali, J.L.K., *Economics of Food-Grains in Kashmir* (Lahore, 1931) [RL].

Kaul, Gwash Lal, *Kashmir Then and Now* (Srinagar: Chronicle, 1967), 8th edn.

Knight, E.F., *Where Three Empires Meet* (London, 1905) [RL].

Koul, Pandit Anand, *The Kashmiri Pandit* (Calcutta, 1924) [RL].

Lawrence, Walter R., *The Valley of Kashmir* (Srinagar, Kesar, 1967), rep.

Markham, Clements R., *Narratives of the Mission of George Bogle to Tibet and of the Journey of Thomas Manning to Lhasa* (London, 1876) [Ranbir Library, Jammu].

Markham, Colonel Fred., *Shooting in the Himalyas* (London, 1854) [RL].

Morison, Margaret Cotter, *A Lonely Summer in Kashmir* (London, 1904) [RL].

Naseer-ud-Din, Munshi, *Tarikh Jang Azadiye Kashmir* (Urdu) (Srinagar, Kashmir Book Depot, 1971).

Nasrat-ul-Islam, Anjuman, *Sir Syed Kashmir, Hazrat Mirwaiz Maulana Rasul Shah Sahib: Bani Anjuman Nasrat-ul-Islam Srinagar Ke Satavanven Yomi Visal per Aek Mukhtsar Twaruf* (Urdu) (Srinagar: n.d.) [Available in Islamia High School Library, Srinagar].

Neve, Arthur, *Thirty Years in Kashmir* (London, 1913) [RL].

Neve, Ernest F., *Beyond the Pir Panjal: Life Among the Mountains and Valleys of Kashmir* (London, 1912) [RL].

Plamenatz, John, 'Public Opinion and Political Consciousness', in Ridley, F.F., *Studies in Politics* (Oxford, 1975).

Raghavan, G.S., *The Warning of Kashmir* (Allahabad, 1931) [RL].

Ram, Diwan Kirpa, *Gulabnama*, Charak, Sukhdev Singh, trans. (New Delhi: Light & Life, 1977).

Riding the Storms in Kashmir 1932-33 [T.B.S.L.].

Suri, Lala Sohan Lal, *Umdat-ul-Twarikh*, Suri, V.S., trans. (Chandigarh: Punjab Itihas Prakashan, 1972), Daftar 4, pts. 1-3.

Temple, Sir Richard, *Journals Kept in Hyderabad, Kashmir, Sikkim, and Nepal* (London, 1887) [RL].

Thorp, Robert, 'Kashmir Misgovernment' (1870), in Gadru, S.N., ed., *Kashmir Papers* (Srinagar: Free-thought Literature Company, 1973).

Torrens, Lt. Colonel, *Travels in Ladak, Tartary, and Kashmir* (London, 1862) [RL].

Vigne, G.T., *Travels in Kashmir, Ladak, Iskardo, and the Countries Adjoining the Mountain Course of the Indus and the Himalaya North of the Panjab* (London, 1842) [RL].

Wakefield, G.E.C., *Recollections: 50 Years in the Service of India* (Lahore, 1942) [RL].

Wakefield, W., *The Happy Valley* (London: 1879) [RL].

Wilson, Horace Hayman, ed., *Travels in the Himalayan Provinces of Hindustan and the Panjab, in Ladakh and Kashmir, in Peshawar, Kabul, Kundurz, and Bokhara by Mr. William Moorcroft and Mr. George Trebeck, from 1819 to 1825* (New Delhi: Sagar, 1971), Vols. 1 & 2, rep.

Younghusband, Sir Francis, *Kashmir* (New Delhi: Sagar, 1970), rep. [first published in 1908].

Zaidi, A.M., ed., *Evolution of Muslim Political Thought in India* (New Delhi: Michiko & Panjathan, 1975).

Zuhara, G.A. Hamadani, *A Brief History Shah-Hamdan-Mosque, Known as Khanquah-i-Moulla, Srinagar-Kashmir and Mir Sayyid Ali Hamdani* (Srinagar: The Young Attendants of Khanquah-i-Moualla, n.d.).

(c) *Newspapers*

Aieena (Srinagar).

Civil and Military Gazette, (Lahore) [Microfilm, NMML].

The Bengalee (Calcutta) [Microfilm, NMML].

The Hindoo Patriot (Calcutta) [Microfilm, NMML].

The Indian Mirror (Calcutta) [Microfilm, NMML].

The Pioneer (Allahabad) [Microfilm, NMML].

The Ranbir (Jammu) [Microfilm, NMML].

The Statesman and Friend of India (Calcutta) [Microfilm, NMML].

The Tribune (Lahore) [Microfilm, NMML].

United India and Indian States (Issue dated 22 September 1921) [Available in *Old English Records*, 1921, F.N. 73/97-C, JKA].

SECONDARY SOURCES

Ahmad, Imtiaz, ed., *Ritual and Religion Among Muslims in India* (Delhi: Manohar, 1980).

Alder, G.J., *British India's Northern Frontier, 1865-95: A Study in Imperial Policy* (London: Longman, 1963).

Bajpai, S.C., *The Northern Frontier of India: Central and Western Sector* (Calcutta: Allied, 1970).

Bal, Sarjit Singh, *British Policy Towards the Punjab* (Calcutta: New Age, 1971).

Bamzai, Prithivi Nath Kaul, *A History of Kashmir, Political, Social, Cultural: From the Earliest Times to the Present Day* (New Delhi: Metropolitan Book Co., 1973), revd. edn.

Bazaz, Prem Nath, *Kashmir in Crucible* (New Delhi: Pamposh, 1967).

——, *Democracy Through Intimidation and Terror: The Untold Story of Kashmir Politics* (New Delhi: Heritage, 1978)

Bilgrami, Asghar H., *Afghanistan and British India, 1793-1907: A Study in Foreign Relations* (New Delhi: Sterling, 1972).

Birdwood, Lord, *Two Nations and Kashmir* (London: Robert Hale Limited, 1956).

Chakravarty, Suhash, *From Khyber to Oxus: A Study in Imperial Expansion* (New Delhi: Orient Longman, 1976).

Das Gupta, Jyoti Bhusan, *Jammu and Kashmir* (The Hague: Martinus Nijhoff, 1968).

Dutt, K. Iswara, *Congress Cyclopaedia: The Indian National Congress, 1885-1920* (New Delhi: n.d.), Vol. I. [Published by the Author].

Dutt, Romesh, *The Economic History of India* (New Delhi: Govt. of India, Ministry of Information and Broadcasting, 1970), 2nd rep., Vols. 1 & 2.

Fauq, Mohammed-ud-Din, *Mukamal Tarikh Kashmir* (Urdu) (Lahore: 1912), Vol. 3. [Available at Jawaharlal Nehru University Library, New Delhi].

Gadru, S.N., *Kashmir Papers* (Srinagar: Free-thought Literature Company, 1973).

Ghose, Dilip Kumar, *Kashmir in Transition, 1885-1893* (Calcutta: The World Press Private Ltd., 1975).

Gopal S., *British Policy in India, 1858-1905* (Madras- Cambridge University Press, 1975).

Habib, Irfan, *The Agrarian System of Mughal India, 1556-1707* (Bombay: Asia, 1963).

Hasrat, Bikrama Jit, *Anglo-Sikh Relations, 1799-1849—A Reappraisal of the Rise and Fall of the Sikhs* (Hoshiarpur: 1968) [Published by the Author].

Hassnain, F.M., *British Policy Towards Kashmir, 1846-1921: Kashmir in Anglo-Russian Politics* (New Delhi: Sterling, 1974).

Kapur, M.L., *Kashmir Sold and Snatched* (Jammu: 1968) [Published by the Author].

Kaushik, Devendra, *Central Asia in Modern Times: A History from the Early 19th Century*, N. Khalfin, ed. (Moscow: Progress, 1970).

Khan, Mohammed shaq, *History of Srinagar, 1846-1947: A Study in Socio-Cultural Change* (Srinagar: Aamir, 1978).

Khan, Sardar M. Ibrahim, *The Kashmir Saga* (Lahore: Ripon Printing Press Ltd., 1965).

Khilnani, N.M., *British Power in the Punjab, 1839-1858* (Bombay: Asia, 1972).

Korbel, Josef, *Danger in Kashmir* (Princeton: Princeton University Press, 1954).

Kumar, Virendra, *India Under Lord Hardinge* (New Delhi: Rajesh, 1978).

Lamb, Alastair, *Britain and Chinese Central Asia: The Road to Lhasa, 1767 to 1905* (London: Routledge and Kegan Paul, 1960).

Lavan, Spencer, *The Ahmadiyah Movement: A History and Perspective* (New Delhi: Manohar, 1974).

Lce-Warner, William, *The Life of Marquis of Dalhousie* (London: 1904), Vol. 2 [NMML].

Lelyveld, David, *Aligarh's First Generation: Muslim Solidarity in British India* (Princeton: Princeton University Press, 1978).

Mahajan, Jagmohan, *Circumstances Leading to the Annexation of the Punjab, 1846-49: A Historical Revision* (Allahabad: Kitabistan, 1949).

Majumdar, R.C. ed., *The History and Culture of the Indian People: British Paramountcy and Indian Renaissance* (Bombay: Bharatiya Vidya Bhavan, 1963).

Maqbool, Master Mohammed, *Ner-i-Azm: Sir Syed Kashmir* (Urdu) (Srinagar: Nasrat-ul-Islam, n.d).

Morison, J.L., *Lawrence of Lucknow, 1806-1857: Being the Life of Sir Henry Lawrence Retold from His Private and Public Papers* (London: 1934) [NMML].

Panikkar, *The Founding of the Kashmir State: A Biography of Maharaja Gulab Singh, 1792-1858* (London: George Allen & Unwin, 1953).

Parimu, R.K., *A History of Muslim Rule in Kashmir, 1320-1819* (Delhi: People's 1969).

Prasad, Sri Nandan, *Paramountcy Under Dalhousie*, (Delhi: Ranjit Printers, 1964).

Ramusack, Barbara N., *The Princes of India in the Twilight of Empire: Dissolution of A Patron-Client System, 1914-1939* (Columbus: Ohio State University Press, 1978).

Saraf, Muhammad Yusuf, *Kashmiri Fights for Freedom* (Lahore: Ferozsons, 1977), Vol. 1.

Sarwari, Abdul Qadir, *Kashmir Ko Do Adib—Do Bhayee: Pandit Hargopal Kaul Khasta aur Pandit Saligram Salik ke Halat aur un ke Karnamoon per Tabsurra* (Urdu) (Hyderabad: Majlis-E-Tahqiqat-E-Urdu, 1965).

Saxena, Dr. H.L., *The Tragedy of Kashmir* (New Delhi: Nationalist, 1975).

Sen, S.P., ed., *Dictionary of National Biography* (Calculta: Published by Editor, 1972), Vol. 1.

Singh, Bawa Satinder, *The Jammu Fox: A Biography of Maharaja Gulab Singh of Kashmir, 1792-1857* (London: Southern Illinois University Press, 1974).

Singh, Khushwant, *A History of the Sikhs* (Princeton: Princeton University Press, 1966), 2 Vols.

Singh, Lt. Col. Bhagwan, *Political Conspiracies of Kashmir* (Rohtak: Light & Life, 1973).

Sufi, G.M.D., *Kashir: Being a History of Kashmir, from the Earliest Times to Our Own* (New Delhi: Light & Life, 1974), 2 Vols.

Taseer, Rasheed, *Tahrik Huriyat Kashmir: 1931 to 1939* (Urdu) (Srinagar: Mhafiz, 1968).

Teng, Mohan Krishan and Others, *Kashmir Constitutional History and Documents* (New Delhi: Light & Life, 1977).

INDEX